Métis Politics and Governance in Canada

Kelly Saunders and Janique Dubois

Métis Politics and Governance in Canada

UBCPress · Vancouver · Toronto

28 27 26 25 24 23 22 21 20 5 4 3

Printed in Canada on FSC-certified ancient-forest-free paper (100% post-consumer recycled) that is processed chlorine- and acid-free.

Cataloguing data is available from Library and Archives Canada.

978-0-7748-6075-8 (hardcover)
978-0-7748-6076-5 (softcover)
978-0-7748-6077-2 (pdf)
978-0-7748-6078-9 (epub)
978-0-7748-6079-6 (Kindle)

Canadä

UBC Press gratefully acknowledges the financial support for our publishing program of the Government of Canada (through the Canada Book Fund), the Canada Council for the Arts, and the British Columbia Arts Council.

This book has been published with the help of a grant from the Canadian Federation for the Humanities and Social Sciences, through the Awards to Scholarly Publications Program, using funds provided by the Social Sciences and Humanities Research Council of Canada.

Printed and bound in Canada by Friesens
Set in Garamond and Meta by Sharlene Eugenio
Copy editor: Joanne Richardson
Proofreader: Caela Moffet
Indexer: Cheryl Lemmens

UBC Press
The University of British Columbia
2029 West Mall
Vancouver, BC V6T 1Z2
www.ubcpress.ca

Contents

Foreword

By Clément Chartier

MÉTIS POLITICS AND GOVERNANCE IN CANADA by Kelly Saunders and Janique Dubois is a welcome addition to books written about the Métis Nation. On the pages that follow, the authors masterfully capture the distinctness of the Métis Nation and make a valuable contribution to the understanding of both the historical political development of the Métis Nation as well as its current contemporary governance and aspirations.

For the people of the Métis Nation whose homeland exists in western Canada, progress towards the recognition of Métis rights has been a testament to the inner strength of the many Métis women and men who, over the past century and more and in the face of insurmountable odds, have kept the flame of Métis nationalism alive. From the dispossession of their lands and resources through various and nefarious federal government means, to decades of being ignored, oppressed, persecuted, and excluded from federal government services provided to other Indigenous peoples, the Métis Nation has stood steadfast with heads held high.

This historical struggle is skillfully woven into the authors' discussion of the modern Métis nationalist movement. They provide a useful analysis of how Métis organizations, originally incorporated as non-profit corporations, subsequently evolved into representative and democratically elected governments.

The role of women in the Métis political movement and governance is also deftly explored in this book. In chronicling the role and prominence of women in contemporary Métis Nation governance, the authors clearly show that this engagement is grounded in the central place historically occupied by Métis women.

The authors' use of Michif, the official language of the Métis Nation, is compelling and helps explain some of the concepts involved in Métis politics and governance as well as social familial relationships. It is also a welcome and much appreciated tribute to Métis Nation citizens that their language appears so prominently in a narrative describing their existence as a people.

Overall, *Métis Politics and Governance in Canada* provides a balanced approach, which helps the reader understand the governance space occupied by the Métis Nation today and the continuing evolution of the recognition and implementation of Métis rights, including the right of self-government. From the historic struggles for the recognition of Métis rights after the dispossession of their lands and resources in the nineteenth century to the re-emergence of the Métis nationalist movement and the entrenchment of Métis rights in the Constitution Act, 1982, the authors bring us to the current efforts of reconciliation fostered by the Trudeau government.

This new nation-to-nation, government-to-government relationship, described in the book, has manifested itself under the auspices of reconciliation between Canada and the Métis Nation. A central feature of this approach is the co-development of policies and programs under the Canada-Métis Nation Accord signed by the prime minister and Métis Nation leadership in 2017 and the establishment of section 35 rights reconciliation tables that have enabled the Métis National Council's Governing Members to negotiate self-government agreements with Canada.

As the authors explain, the future well-being of the Métis Nation and its citizens is intertwined with the outcomes of these processes and the depth of knowledge and experience of Métis Nation leaders and governments. By taking us through the emergence and long evolution of the Métis Nation, the authors provide a sound background, analysis, and rationale for how the Métis Nation got to where it is today and for why it is finally getting the recognition and attention that it so richly deserves.

Clément Chartier was first elected president of the Métis National Council in 2003 and is currently serving his fifth term. A lawyer, scholar, lecturer, and activist, President Chartier is best known for his work on Métis and Indigenous rights, both nationally and internationally. A founding figure in the Métis nationalist movement in Canada and recipient of a Queen's Counsel distinction for his work in law, President Chartier continues to provide counsel in ongoing Métis-specific cases.

Foreword

By Jason Madden

> *When the Government of Canada presented itself at our doors it found us at peace. It found that the Métis people of the North-West could not only live well without it ... but that it had a government of its own, free, peaceful, well-functioning, contributing to the work of civilization in a way that the Company from England could never have done without thousands of soldiers. It was a government with an organized constitution whose jurisdiction was more legitimate and worthy of respect, because it was exercised over a country that belonged to it.*
>
> – LOUIS RIEL, 1885

This powerful and enduring statement by Louis Riel was written before he was executed by the Canadian state on November 16, 1885, for being one of the leaders involved in the establishment of the second provisional government of the Métis people of the Northwest. Riel's hanging came after the Canadian state orchestrated an illegitimate, unjust, and corrupt trial, and it remains a stain on Canada's "justice" system today.

As a citizen of the Métis Nation and a lawyer who has been counsel in many trials and appeals dealing with Métis rights and claims over the last fifteen years, I have always been struck by Riel's consistency and clarity of purpose throughout his short and inspiring life, namely, his goal to protect the lands, rights, and freedoms of *his* people – the Métis Nation – through their "more legitimate" self-government structures.

While different groups and populations in Canada confuse, misuse, and appropriate Riel for their own purposes today – whether that be in the name of western alienation, French language rights, Canadian multiculturalism, or self-indigenizing groups in eastern Canada with no connection to the Métis Nation – what lives on is *his* aspiration for *his* peoples' "more legitimate" self-government structures being recognized and respected by the Canadian state.

In the same way as it was during Riel's time, contemporary Métis Nation governments continue to struggle to have their "more legitimate" structures recognized by the Canadian state after generations of denial, disrespect, and disruption by settler governments. Instead of sending colonial armed forces westward to thwart Métis self-government, Canadian and provincial governments have used different tactics in modern times.

Whether it be the complete denial of the existence of the Métis Nation's inherent right of self-government and self-determination as a distinct Indigenous people, never-ending attempts to explain or understand Riel's people through mere biological mixing or derivative rights approaches, or the undermining of modern day Métis Nation governments by referring to them as nothing more than corporate bodies or associations, the colonial strategy has been largely the same. Namely, deny, disrespect, and disrupt Métis Nation self-government.

The unity, determination, and perseverance of Riel's people in organizing and keeping Métis self-government alive at the local, regional, and provincial levels across the Homeland, combined with successful legal and political strategies in recent decades, appear to have slowly chipped away this colonial legacy of denial, disrespect, and disruption.

Most notably, in a series of landmark cases over the last fifteen years, the Supreme Court of Canada has recognized collectively held Métis land rights (*R. v. Powley*, 2003), outstanding Métis claims against the Crown (*Manitoba Metis Federation v. Canada*, 2013), and Canada's constitutional responsibility to deal with the Métis (*Daniels v. Canada*, 2016). In 2015, the federal election of the second prime minister Trudeau brought about new political commitments to the Métis Nation, including the following direction in the mandate letter to the Minister of Indigenous and Northern Affairs: "Work, on a nation-to-nation basis, with the Métis Nation to advance reconciliation and renew the relationship, based on cooperation, respect for rights, our international obligations, and a commitment to end the status quo."

The confluence of these legal and political events has led to the signing of a series of framework agreements between Canada and some of the Métis Nation's governments in 2016 and 2017.[1] These framework agreements – contrary to previous federal policies that have been in place for generations – establish the first formal negotiation processes with Métis south of the 60th parallel to address Métis rights, lands, self-government, and outstanding claims against the Crown.

Only time will tell if these newly created negotiation processes actually accomplish Riel's aspiration of seeing the Métis Nation achieve "its own, free, peaceful, well-functioning" governments yet again. Canada's colonial legacy – and systemic biases towards Indigenous peoples generally and the Métis Nation specifically – run deep. Overcoming more than one hundred and fifty years of denial, disrespect, and disruption will not be easy.

While the Métis Nation will need to remain vigilant and protect against the new obstacles that will undoubtedly be put in their way during these negotiations, this process will also require Métis citizens from across the Homeland to engage and take up Riel's vision from over one hundred and fifty years ago. As reflected in Riel's writings, the legitimacy of the Métis Nation's self-government comes from its citizens, not recognition from any settler government.

The ongoing evolution of Métis "political organizations" with "memberships" and "bylaws" to "governments" with "citizenship," "constitutions," and "laws" has been well under way for decades; however, the final metamorphosis of being recognized as Indigenous public governments through negotiated modern day self-government agreements or treaties will be monumental. These new governments will need to be built on the Métis Nation's strong self-government foundations and traditions, while also ensuring that they are authentic, relevant, and durable governments for generations to come.

This is one of the reasons why *Métis Politics and Governance in Canada* is such an important contribution to Métis scholarship at this moment in time. While there has been increasingly more research and writing on Métis history, Métis identity issues, and Métis legal developments in recent years, there remains limited in-depth research and writing on contemporary Métis self-government. This book begins to fill this significant gap in the literature.

The authors also helpfully connect Métis history, laws, and politics to the modern day manifestations of the Métis Nation self-government, which are currently in negotiations. Unlike other academic works that simply look at the Métis Nation's self-government as frozen in time and tied to 1869/70 or 1885, this book compellingly tells the "rest of the story" up to the present day. Uniquely, it also looks to the Métis Nation's own language – Michif – to identify and understand key principles of Métis governance that continue to today. This book is essential reading for those who want to better understand the current state of Métis Nation self-government in Canada.

Achieving ultimate success in the Métis Nation's renewed negotiations with other governments requires that future Métis-made constitutions, laws, and policies be familiar to its citizens and a natural fit. In all Indigenous self-government negotiations, getting back to a people's authentic laws, traditions, and relationships is often challenging. While "muscle memory" may still be there, it is often blurred, confused, or affected by colonization. *Métis Politics and Governance in Canada* will be an invaluable resource to those assisting the Métis Nation in this next stage of its self-government journey as well as to those interested in Riel's people today.

Jason Madden is a citizen of the Métis Nation and descendant of the Halfbreeds of Rainy Lake and River who collectively adhered to Treaty #3 in northwestern Ontario in 1875. He is co-managing partner of the law firm Pape Salter Teillet LLP. Jason has been legal counsel in a majority of the cases establishing Métis rights from Ontario westward and has appeared before the Supreme Court of Canada in all of the cases dealing with Métis rights and claims over the last fifteen years.

Acknowledgments

WHO KNEW THAT A CONVERSATION after a panel on Indigenous women in politics at the Canadian Political Science Association conference almost a decade ago would lead to this book? Over the years, we have debated the ideas that shape this book and have benefitted from the wisdom of many people to whom we extend our sincere thanks.

Foremost among them are the elders and leaders who have taken the time to share their knowledge with us as part of this project. We acknowledge David Chartrand, Clément Chartier, Verna DeMontigny, George Fleury, Norman Fleury, Margaret Froh, Gerald Morin, John Morrisseau, Melanie Omeniho, Audrey Poitras, and Jean Teillet – *maarci kishkayhtanihk aen confidence.* We owe a special thanks to Al Benoit, John Weinstein, Jason Madden, and Murray Trachtenberg for their valuable insights and good humour in answering our endless questions. To the women of the Métis Nation, who continue to inspire us with their perseverance, strength, and wisdom, *maarci.* This book would not have been possible without the participation of citizens from across the Métis Nation who repeatedly welcomed us to their gatherings and into their homes with open hearts.

We also thank colleagues who, through conversations over the years, have directly and indirectly helped shape the ideas in this book. A special thanks to Joe Sawchuk, Peter Russell, Martin Papillon, and Sébastien Grammond.

This project was made possible with the support of the Social Science and Humanities Research Council of Canada. We are also indebted to Brandon University, the University of Ottawa, and Brock University for providing institutional support to enable community-driven research. Some of the ideas in this book have been presented at conferences and workshops, including the Canadian Political Science Association conference, the Native American and Indigenous Studies Association conference, and the Prairie Political Science Association conference.

We thank our editor, Darcy Cullen, for patiently guiding us through the publication process and acknowledge the research assistants who have worked on various aspects of this project: Xavier Bériault, Benjamin Emerson Martin, Adam Leo Paul, and Julia Riddle.

Janique and Kelly would like to thank their respective families.

Janique: Thanks to my late father, Gustave, whose library collection is featured in this book and who sowed the seeds for the ideas in this book long ago. Un merci sincère à ma mère, Roberta, whose company on road trips across the prairies made fieldwork fun and to Justin and Danielle, mes lecteurs les plus critiques. I am grateful to Kevin for asking difficult questions and to Edgar for reminding me that the answers matter.

Kelly: Thanks to my parents Ken and Elsie and my brothers Kevin and Kirby, who taught me the importance of belonging and remembering where you came from, and to Will Goodon, my first and finest teacher of what it means to be Métis. Thank you for allowing me to be a part of this journey and for your steady encouragement as I came to embrace Riel's people through your eyes. Last, but certainly not least, to my children, Hunter and Taylor. You are my heart and my soul and I love you more than words can ever say. I dedicate this book to you.

Abbreviations

MMF	Manitoba Métis Federation
MNA	Métis Nation of Alberta
MNBC	Métis Nation British Columbia
MNC	Métis National Council
MNO	Métis Nation of Ontario
MN-S	Métis Nation-Saskatchewan

Michif Vocabulary

aen ishi mamoonakatwayhtamaahk
how we think together/our collective frame of mind

aen ishi wiichayaamitooyahk
how we live together/how we were related all in one

ka ishi pimaatishiyaahk
our way of life

ka niikaaniichik
those who lead us

ka tipaymishooyahk
we who own ourselves

ka tipaymishoshik
the free people

kiihtwaam ooshtaahk lii goovarnimaan di Michif
rebuilding Métis governments

ki tipemishoonaan
we are all free

la noovel Naasyoon
the new nation

la Viktwayr daan la Plenn di Goornouyayr
the Victory at Frog Plain/Seven Oaks

li shmayn ishi tipaymishoohk
the road to freedom

lii drway di Naasyoon di Michif ka paashpiiwahk
the rights of the Métis Nation will survive

lii faam di Naasyoon di Michif
mothers of the Métis Nation

lii gens libres
the free people

lii goovarnimaan di Michif
Métis governments

lii lway di Michif
Métis laws

lii valeur di goovarnimaan di Michif
principles of Métis governance

miyeu waahkootoowin
being related in a good way

nootr goovarnimaan
our government

Métis Politics and Governance in Canada

Introduction

IN A BANQUET ROOM not far from what was once the headquarters of Louis Riel's provisional government, the newly elected representatives of the Manitoba Métis Federation gathered to take their oaths of office. One by one, as they made their way to stand in unity beside a blue flag with a white infinity symbol, each elected official solemnly pledged to be loyal and faithful to the Métis people and to bring honour to the Métis Nation. They further promised to dedicate their office to the fair and just treatment of all Métis and to serve their people to the best of their ability "in the spirit of Louis Riel."[1] Almost 150 years have passed since Riel founded his government on the banks of the Red and Assiniboine Rivers in 1869. Yet, on that warm July evening, as the newest representatives of Manitoba's Métis government pledged their allegiance to the legacy bestowed upon them by their forebears, it was clear that the past was very much present in the hearts and minds of all those gathered. As the president of the Manitoba Métis Federation, David Chartrand, noted, "we are walking the same path as other Métis leaders before us."[2]

Contemporary Métis leaders, like those that preceded them, remain committed to fulfilling Riel's vision of a self-governing Métis Nation within Canada. For the Métis, self-government involves exercising their right to live according to what they refer to as *ka ishi pimaatishiyaahk* (our way of life).[3] In their own Michif language, Métis elders speak of the achievements of *ka niikaaniichik* (those who lead us) and affirm the enduring commitment of the Métis to *nootr goovarnimaan di Michif* (our Métis government). Through their leaders and their governments, the Métis have engaged in an ongoing struggle to protect their right to govern their lands and their people. Described in Michif as *ka tipaymishooyahk* (we who own ourselves), the Métis view themselves as a free, self-governing, and distinct Indigenous nation. Then, as now, the vision of *ka tipaymishooyahk* remains the lifeblood of the Métis. This vision stands in sharp contrast to the historic position of the Métis in the national political landscape as "Canada's forgotten people" (Sealy and Lussier 1975; Daniels 1979).

When asked about the Métis, most Canadians would likely reference iconic figures like Louis Riel and Gabriel Dumont, or seminal events in Métis history such as the Red River Resistance and the Battle of Batoche. Others might point to the role of the Métis in the Northwest fur trade or to traditional symbols like the fiddle and the sash. That our knowledge of the Métis tends towards historical figures, events, and symbols is understandable given that the literature related to the Métis has traditionally focused on the past.[4] In recent decades, a resurgence of interest has led to a growth of scholarship in the fields of Métis law, identity, culture, and history, with edited volumes touching on a number of these themes.[5] Despite this sizeable and growing body of literature, there are few published works that examine the Métis as contemporary political actors engaged in an ongoing quest for self-determination.[6] In the words of one Métis leader: "We need to start taking that story and changing it, so people can say, when they see the Métis Nation, 'We know who they are, we respect who they are, we understand why they're fighting for what they're fighting for.'"[7]

It is surprising that little attention has been directed to Métis politics, governing practices, and institutions or to the interactions between Métis and other governments given that, at their core, the Métis have always been a political people. Indeed, it was through political organization, beginning with the buffalo hunts and continuing through such events as *la Viktwayr daan la Plenn di Goornouyayr* (the Victory at Frog Plain) in the early 1800s that a conspicuous Métis identity was fully realized.[8] For the Métis, political action has long been essential to their survival as a distinct Indigenous people.[9] Committed to remaining *ka tipaymishooyahk* (we who own ourselves), self-determination and its more practical application, self-government, is at the heart of Métis aspirations: it represents the legacy of Louis Riel and the unique people who emerged in the Historic Northwest. The Métis' ongoing struggle to control their own destiny is captured in a study prepared for the Royal Commission on Aboriginal Peoples (RCAP) by the Métis Society of Saskatchewan:

> At the outset, it is important to note that our self-determination objectives, through self-government, are not new. Métis history bears witness to a lengthy legacy of struggles aimed at asserting our fundamental right to control our own destiny. In what is now the province of Saskatchewan, for example, ever escalating political, economic, social and cultural disputes between the Métis and the European settlers culminated in the well-known Métis resistance to Ottawa in 1885. Other sites in nineteenth century Western Canada were also scenes of conflict over many of the same issues. As might be expected, while the military conflicts that sometimes erupted were relatively short-lived, the political struggle to protect Métis economic, social and cultural values and goals has persisted.
>
> This enduring theme in our Métis history – that we as a people have struggled against often overwhelming odds to reclaim our traditional Homeland and assert our sense of nationhood – lies behind much of the current drive towards self-government. (RCAP 1996a, 101)

In the present, as in the past, the Métis have remained committed to the fulfillment of their rights to land and to self-government within Canada.

For the Métis, self-government and self-determination are inherently linked; Métis leaders view self-government as the means by which they can remain *ka tipemishoshik* (the free people) and assert their independence as a unique Indigenous nation in Canada.[10] This goal has propelled the Métis forward since *la Viktwayr daan la Plenn di Goornouyayr* (the

Victory at Frog Plain); indeed, when contemporary Métis leaders speak of self-government, they often refer to historical struggles for self-determination and to Louis Riel's vision for the Métis Nation within an expanded Canadian state. In a speech at the special assembly of the Métis National Council in March 2017, Métis Nation president Clément Chartier reminded Métis leaders of the continued resonance of Riel's vision of a self-determining Métis Nation. For Chartier, like for Riel, self-determination involves the ability of the Métis to live prosperous and free lives and to determine for themselves their place within Canada. In practical terms, this involves building mutually respectful government-to-government relationships with the provinces and with Canada while also strengthening and building capacity within the Métis Nation.

As the practical application of self-determination, self-government is often used to refer to external relationships with state actors; however, as Métis leader Margaret Froh reminds us, it is a multifaceted concept that ultimately involves "taking care of our families."[11] For Métis elder George Fleury, self-government means "to be accepted for who I am, Métis; to be independent; to have our own government, to be able to govern our own affairs through the efforts of our ancestors."[12] Jason Madden, legal counsel to Métis governments, describes self-government as the goal that has sustained the Métis through long and difficult times. He sees the desire for self-government as grounded in nationhood: "It's in our political action, it's in our collective hearts, it's a part of who we are as a people."[13]

The Métis have made significant strides towards self-government in the past quarter century. Due to the persistence of Métis leaders who mobilized at the national level in the 1970s to push Ottawa for acknowledgment of their rights to land and to self-government, Canada recognized the Métis as a rights-bearing Aboriginal people alongside First Nations and Inuit in the Constitution Act, 1982. Despite this monumental achievement, however, it would take a decades-long court battle to clarify the constitutional position of the Métis vis-à-vis the state. This would come in the Supreme Court of Canada's 2016 ruling in *Daniels v. Canada,* which concluded that the Métis are "Indians" for the purposes of section 91(24) and therefore fall within the jurisdictional responsibility of the federal government. By extension, it is within the federal government's jurisdictional responsibility to enact legislation that recognizes existing Métis governments and to enable a policy environment that provides the Métis with access to programs and services that meet their specific needs.

The *Daniels* case comes on the heels of other critical Supreme Court of Canada rulings. Most notably, *Manitoba Métis Federation Inc. v. Canada* acknowledged the federal government's failure to uphold historical promises with respect to land for the Métis, and *R. v. Powley* recognized Métis harvesting rights. Through this and related jurisprudence, Canadian courts have sent a clear message that Métis rights can no longer be ignored. In response to these legal developments, Canada's prime minister, Justin Trudeau, has committed to complete the "unfinished work of Confederation" and respect Métis rights through the development of a renewed nation-to-nation relationship with the Métis.[14]

As national Métis leader Clément Chartier wrote in a message to Métis citizens, "We, as a people, are at an important time and place within our existence as a distinct rights-bearing Indigenous people in our historic homeland."[15] In spite of the increasing recognition of the Métis as significant players in the Canadian federation, little is known in academic and political circles about their systems of government or their political institutions. What are the principles and practices that underlie Métis politics and governance? How has Métis governance changed since the days of the buffalo hunts and Riel's provisional governments? What kinds of structures and processes have the Métis developed to bring their inherent right to self-government to life? How do the Métis select their political leaders, make collective decisions, and engage with their communities and other levels of government? What accounts for the ongoing prominence of women in Métis politics and governance? And what challenges do the Métis face as they continue to pursue their self-government agenda?

We explore these questions through a series of thematic chapters that offer unique insights into contemporary Métis politics and governance. As the Métis become increasingly visible actors on the Canadian political scene, we offer a novel, timely, and practical guide for students, academics, and practitioners to enable them to better understand how

Métis politics and governance have evolved within the country's federal landscape. Our aim is to contribute to a better understanding of who the Métis are and what they are fighting for. We also hope that this book will serve as an opportunity for all Canadians, and in particular citizens and leaders of the Métis Nation, to reflect on the achievements that have been made as well as on the barriers that still remain in fulfilling Riel's vision of *ka tipaymishooyahk* (we who own ourselves) within the contemporary context of the Canadian state.

Riel's People

We situate the Métis as a unique Indigenous nation, whose consciousness as a distinct people emerged most fully in the Northwest through events such as the 1816 *Viktwayr daan la Plenn di Goornouyayr* (Victory at Frog Plain) and the Resistance at Red River in 1869 and at Batoche in 1885. It was these people, whom Paul Chartrand (2017) describes as "Riel's people," who organized a civil government, defended their lands from Canada's intrusion, treated with the Crown through the Manitoba Act, 1870, forged alliances with other Indigenous peoples, and were dominant figures in the economic life of the Historic Northwest.[16] As Paul Chartrand and John Giokas (2002, 287) argue, while the Métis possessed the symbols of nationhood (including a distinctive flag, a national anthem, a unique language, music, and art), it was their collective political will to resist Canada's unilateral annexation of their lands and usurpation of their rights, coupled with the power to do so, that fuelled their emergence as a distinct people.

Our emphasis on the Métis as a distinct nation that emerged through political action stands in contrast to historical accounts that situate their origin in terms of race and hybridity and, more narrowly, in relation to their role as economic actors in the fur trade. For example, historians like G.F.G Stanley and Marcel Giraud attribute the development of a national consciousness among the Métis to the North West Company and the support it provided for Métis mobilization as a means of bolstering its own power relative to that of the Hudson's Bay Company (Stanley 1960; Giraud 1984; Morton 1978; Morton 1967). Stanley (1960, 10) goes so far as to argue that it is within the context of power struggles between trading companies that the Métis developed a distinct identity "as a separate racial and national unit, which found expression in their name, 'The New Nation.'"

Historical accounts that portray the Métis as a racial or economic by-product of these power struggles have been challenged by more recent scholarship on Métis ethnogenesis. Scholars like Jacqueline Peterson and Jennifer Brown (1985), Nicole St-Onge (2004), Brenda Macdougall (2010), and Carolyn Podruchny (2006) have shown how the social and political cohesion as well as the organizational capacity of the Métis grew through expanding kinship networks. Their research demonstrates that the Métis were not brought together by external forces but were instead united as a distinct Indigenous people through kinship bonds that traversed time and space. The ties that would bind what Chris Andersen (2014, 124) describes as "Métis nation-ness," and which occurred most strongly in Red River, were embedded in social relationships that were fundamentally distinct from those of Europeans.

Following this more recent trend in Métis studies, we take Métis ethnogenesis as rooted in political action and agency (see also Andersen 2014, 24; Gaudry 2016a, 2016b), and trace the continuities between historic and contemporary Métis political organization. In so doing, we do not suggest that the various external and internal forces that have helped shape Métis political consciousness are mutually exclusive. As we note in later chapters, the Métis have regularly adapted their governance structures to changing political, social, and economic circumstances in order to more successfully pursue their objectives. We argue that, in the years that follow Canadian Confederation, the Métis have navigated their own traditions in a political context that they no longer fully control. They have maintained some structures and practices while strategically adopting others to advance their collective objectives as Riel's people.[17] This continuity and change is at the heart of Métis politics and governance.

One of the key findings of our research is the deft ability of the Métis to adjust their tactics and practices to the challenges at hand. Foremost among these challenges has been the federal government's historic denial of Métis rights and nationhood, and Canada's long-standing refusal to recognize the Métis in state policy and law. The evidence we have gathered reveals the Métis as an Indigenous nation with unique governance practices and traditions. Compelled to work within the constraints imposed by the Canadian state and the accompanying processes of colonization, domination, and assimilation, the Métis Nation has remained an active agent of resistance and change.

We use the term "Métis" to refer to the people who developed a unique culture, identity, and political consciousness as a new Indigenous nation in the Historic Northwest. It also encompasses what scholars like John Foster (1985, 87) and Heather Devine (2001, 132; 2004, 107) have described as "proto-Métis," those individuals who contributed to the emergence of a distinct community before the Métis were constituted as a people and before the adoption of the term "Métis." Rooted in Red River, the Métis were connected to communities across the Northwest through kinship relations. Our use of the capital "M" in the term "Métis" does not imply a singular political homogeneity historically or today. The internal diversity of the Métis was historically captured by terms that emphasize their dual heritage – such as *Bois-Brûlés* in French, *wissakodewinmi* in Ojibwe, and *apitahwikosisan* in Cree – as well as by distinctions between Scottish Protestants (half-breeds) and French Catholics (Métis) (Dickason 1985; Pannekoek 1991; Spry 1985; Chartrand 2004; Foster 2007; Peterson and Brown 1985). While there was and continues to be diversity within this community, as indeed there is within any community, we follow Irene Spry (1985, 108) in arguing that it was through their mobilization and political struggles against colonial rule that the Métis became a united people.

We support Darren O'Toole's (2013, 151, emphasis in original) argument that "a nation implies not only self-ascription, but a *political* consciousness that is shaped by a dialectical movement where political action is both motivated by a strong desire and capacity to maintain the objective and subjective aspects that distinguish it from other groups and shapes the very subjectivity and agency that nourishes that desire." We use "nation" and "people" interchangeably to refer to the expressly *political* community that arose in the Historic Northwest. This language reflects that of Métis leaders who, when asked about the difference between "nation" and "people," repeatedly told us there was no real difference (for a nuanced academic discussion of these concepts, see Andersen 2014). For them, the Métis Nation is the political community that was constituted through the struggles of the nineteenth century and that persists to this day as Riel's people. Connected through kinship ties rooted in the Historic Northwest, the Métis form a single people – the Métis Nation.

As within all collectivities, identity within the Métis Nation is contested. In Métis politics, identity is entangled with questions of membership and boundaries, yet it remains deeply personal. As Adam Gaudry and Chris Andersen (2016) note, Indigenous communities are best placed to define themselves. Our goal is not to resolve debates about Métis identity but, instead, to consider how Métis politics and governance can contribute to our understanding of the evolution of Métis identity within the context of the colonial Canadian state.

Contemporary Métis Governments

Throughout the book, we focus on the contemporary governing bodies that have taken up Riel's vision of *ka tipaymishooyahk* (we who own ourselves) in the colonial context of the Canadian state. Specifically, we examine the five Métis governments that make up the Métis National Council, the national spokesbody of the Métis Nation. These are the Métis Nation British Columbia (MNBC), the Métis Nation of Alberta (MNA), the Métis Nation-Saskatchewan (MN-S), the Manitoba Métis Federation (MMF), and the Métis Nation of Ontario (MNO).[18] Collectively, these Métis governments form what is referred to as *nootr goovarnimaan di Michif* (our Métis government).

We have chosen to centre our analysis on these Métis governments, also referred to as the Governing Members of the Métis National Council, as they constitute the democratic governing bodies mandated by Métis citizens to serve as the elected representatives of the Métis Nation in Canada. They are recognized by the courts and the minister's special representative on reconciliation with Métis to represent section 35 Métis rights-holders, and engage with provincial and federal governments for the purposes of consultation and negotiation.[19] The 2017 Canada-Métis Nation Accord, signed by the prime minister of Canada and the president of the Métis National Council, recognizes that the Governing Members that comprise the Métis National Council are "mandated and authorized to represent the citizens who comprise the Métis Nation, including dealing with collectively held Métis rights, interests and outstanding claims against the Crown."[20]

Our use of the term "government" to describe these entities is intentional. It is the language used by Métis citizens and their leaders. Like other governments, Métis governments engage in program and service delivery, pass legislation, and advance the interests of their citizens. While these non-land-based governments may be "different," as noted by the ministerial special representative on reconciliation with Métis, this does not mean that "they are illegitimate or that they can or should be ignored."[21]

Métis interests have historically been represented by various groups, often in conjunction with non-status Indians. Many of these organizations emerged against a backdrop of exclusion, which has been largely maintained at the federal and, to a lesser degree, provincial levels. This history of exclusion, along with Canada's colonial past, has contributed to the emergence of a complex network of organizations that purport to promote Métis interests in various forms. These include the Congress of Aboriginal Peoples (formerly the Native Council of Canada), the Métis Federation of Canada, and the Canadian Métis Council-Intertribal. While these organizations may eventually come to play a role in the contemporary landscape of Indigenous governance, we focus our analysis on the Métis governments that evolved from the early forms of political organization in the Historic Northwest to form *nootr goovarnimaan di Michif* and that collectively negotiate the Métis Nation's place within the federation. It is these Métis governments that are legally recognized to represent the interests of the Métis Nation.

Our Research Approach

Our research and analysis have been guided by our familial and community connections to the Métis Nation in Canada. Our understanding of the Métis has been enriched not only by the time we have spent with Métis citizens across the Homeland but also by our direct observation of Métis politics and practices. For more than a decade, we have participated in numerous general assemblies, conferences, and other political events and have met with leaders, elders, and citizens from across the Métis Nation. Our objective was not only to uncover the ways in which Métis political bodies function as representative governments but also to understand how they evolved, the strategies they employ, the values they share, and the challenges they face in the pursuit of self-determination.

We have deepened our understanding of Métis governance through semi-structured interviews with elected Métis representatives at the local, provincial, and national levels, as well as with other advisors and officials who interact with the Métis. These interviews helped to clarify how Métis governments pursue their mandate as representatives of Métis citizens. In addition, informal conversations with an array of individuals at community events, celebrations, and cultural festivities allowed us to gain a broader and more contextualized understanding of how the Métis think and act politically.

We are indebted to all those who took the time to share their perspectives, stories, and insights with us and remain committed to sharing this knowledge in a spirit of humility and responsibility. This includes protecting the anonymity of those who requested it and paying respect to the Michif language, the language of the Métis Nation. Although we have a deep connection to the Métis, we are non-Indigenous scholars. We take seriously the challenge posed to us by one elder to engage with the Michif language and to "think from a Métis perspective." Our interactions with elders, leaders, and community members have encouraged us to reconsider Eurocentric assumptions about politics and governance and to embrace Métis ways of knowing. This is consistent with principles of ethical Métis research, which include building reciprocal relations, respecting the individual and the collective, as well as knowing Métis history, values, and knowledge.[22] While we have endeavoured to engage earnestly and honestly with Métis perspectives, we also acknowledge the limits we face as non-Métis academic observers. This book is our attempt to share what we have learned and to pay homage to the citizens and leaders of the Métis Nation who remain committed to what has been described to us time and time again as "the vision of Riel's people" – *ka tipaymishooyahk*.

Overview of the Book

We begin by situating contemporary Métis governance and politics in historical context. In Chapter 1, "*La Noovel Naasyoon* | Métis Political Organization in Historical Perspective," we argue that the Métis have long defined themselves as a sovereign people with an inherent right to self-government. Beginning with the buffalo hunts in the late 1700s and continuing through to the provisional governments that dotted the Historic Northwest, we show that the Métis developed their own rules, processes, and structures to manage their political, economic, and social affairs. We examine how, throughout the twentieth century, these practices evolved with the political organization of the Métis, from the creation in 1887 of the Union nationale métisse Saint-Joseph du Manitoba to the establishment of Métis associations in Alberta and Saskatchewan in the 1920s and 1930s and the creation of the Métis National Council in 1983. We argue that the evolution of Métis political organization occurred in response to the particularities of the context in which the Métis found themselves. These organizations were a means through which to assert themselves as *la noovel Naasyoon* (the new nation).

Chapter 2, "*Lii Valeur di Goovarnimaan di Michif* | Principles of Métis Governance," explores the principles that underpinned political activities in the early years of Métis mobilization and that continue to resonate today. Using Michif concepts, we highlight five principles that characterize Métis governance: freedom, kinship, democracy, the rule of law, and provisionality. We trace these principles to the various governance structures created by the Métis since the days of the buffalo hunt and consider how they have evolved over time. Although some of these principles are shared by other Indigenous and non-Indigenous communities, they interact with one another to give life to a distinct way of governing that continues to inform Métis politics.

In Chapter 3, "*Lii Goovarnimaan di Michif* | Métis Governments," we examine the characteristics of contemporary Métis governments and discuss how they operate within the Canadian federal system. We focus on the Métis Nation British Columbia, the Métis Nation of Alberta, the Métis Nation-Saskatchewan, the Manitoba Métis Federation, and the Métis Nation of Ontario, which, taken together, make up the Métis

National Council and are collectively seen as the Métis Nation's government in Canada. While the Métis increasingly govern themselves through community-level associations, regional councils, and provincial and national governments, their aspirations to self-government continue to be limited by the ambiguous position they occupy within Canada's political and legislative framework. Acknowledging the constraints imposed by the colonial state context, we critically assess some of the challenges the Métis face as they continue to work towards establishing their governing structures as legitimate and effective vehicles of self-government.

In Chapter 4, "*Kiihtwaam Ooshtaahk lii Goovarnimaan di Michif* | (Re)building a Métis Civil Service," we provide an inside look at the development of a Métis public service and assess some of the challenges presented therein through a case study of the Manitoba Métis Federation (MMF). Created in 1967 as a not-for-profit corporation with a five-member board of directors and seven staff members, the MMF has evolved into a government of seven hundred employees representing over fifty thousand registered citizens. In order to contend with this rapid growth, the MMF has sought to develop its own approach to governance – one that reconciles Canadian-style organizational practices with Métis ways of knowing. Despite its successes to date, the MMF still faces obstacles in terms of fiscal arrangements, human resource development, and capacity building. The need to address these concerns is all the more pressing in light of the Supreme Court of Canada's decision in *Manitoba Métis Federation Inc. v. Canada,* which has positioned the MMF to negotiate with state governments on land rights on behalf of the Métis in Manitoba. This chapter offers an overview of the key issues at stake as the MMF and Canada work towards reconciliation and the fulfillment of Métis rights in Manitoba through a recently signed Framework Agreement.

In Chapter 5, "*Lii Faam di Naasyoon di Michif* | Mothers of the Métis Nation," we examine how Métis women have become active decision makers within their governments. While we note this trend throughout the book, we devote a chapter to highlight the prominence of women in historical and contemporary Métis governance. While the processes of colonization and assimilation have led to the general disempowerment of the Métis within Canada – and of women in particular – Métis women have managed to retain their voice as important political actors within the Métis Nation. To help us understand the success of Métis women in contemporary politics, we rely on the experience and perspectives of female leaders who have occupied prominent positions as political representatives, community organizers, and elders. Their stories not only reveal a continuity in the historic and contemporary prominence of Métis women but also speak to how Métis women contribute to the goals of the Métis Nation as a whole.

The Métis Nation is entering a new political era. No longer relegated to the sidelines, Métis leaders have been invited to sit at the table with their federal counterparts in a nation-to-nation relationship based on rights, respect, cooperation, and partnership. This historic development was achieved with the signing of the Canada-Métis Nation Accord by the Métis Nation president and the prime minister in 2017. The accord represents the culmination of the collective efforts by the Métis over the past century and a half to bring to life their inherent right to self-government and to force Canada's hand in acknowledging and implementing this right. In Chapter 6, "*Li Shmayn ishi Tipaymishoohk* | The Road to Métis Self-Government," we discuss the significance of the Canada-Métis Nation Accord and the potential it holds for the advancement of Métis self-government in Canada. We also discuss some of the challenges that lie ahead on the road towards Métis self-government as provincial, federal, and Métis leaders are called upon to chart a path that is sensitive to Métis culture and aspirations as well as to the complex historical, legal, political, and social consequences of colonialism.

In the concluding chapter, "*Lii Drway di Michif Ka Paashpiiwahk* | The Ongoing Struggle for Métis Rights," we reflect on the Métis Nation's long-standing struggle for self-determination. This struggle, which began in the context of the fur trade and continues to live on in the actions of contemporary Métis leaders, has been key to uniting the Métis as a distinct Indigenous nation. We argue that, through political action, the Métis have become empowered in their struggle for self-determination. Using the tools available to them, they have sought to develop democratic governments to meet the needs of their people and to engage with state and non-state actors in the advancement of their collective goals. While the Métis have made progress in their ongoing efforts to remain *ka tipaymishooyahk* (we who own ourselves), Canada has yet to implement Métis rights to land and to self-government. Meaningful progress towards this goal remains contingent on good faith negotiations between state and Métis governments. As we wait for these negotiations to take shape, the Métis are continuing their efforts to build self-government from the bottom up.

This book critically examines contemporary developments alongside historical realities to better understand Métis politics and governance. As Métis elder John Morrisseau notes, "our [the Métis Nation's] strength comes from looking back at where we came from."[23] We begin by looking back to the first forms of political organization through which the Métis pursued their way of life as Riel's people.

1

La Noovel Naasyoon

Métis Political Organization in Historical Perspective

IN HIS FINAL MEMOIRS,[1] Louis Riel recounts the life of an independent, self-determining people prior to Confederation. "When the Authorities arrived in the North-West in 1870, they found a people which, if left to itself, would have been at ease, not only then, but for many years to come. They found the Métis, who, in their own home and having their land to themselves, had like any other people, a great future ahead of them" (Riel 1982, 202). Under his leadership, these independent people organized politically as *la noovel Naasyoon* (the new nation) and established a provisional government to negotiate the terms of their relationship with Canada. Riel explains: "when the Government of Canada presented itself at our doors, it found … that the Métis people of the North-West could not only live well without it … but that it had a government of its own, free, peaceful, well-functioning." He adds that "it was a government with an organized constitution, whose jurisdiction was all the more legitimate and worthy of respect, because it was exercised over a country that belonged to it" (Riel 1982, 204–5). Led by Riel, this provisional government negotiated the protection of land and rights in exchange for the peaceful entry of a new province, Manitoba, into Confederation. However, as Riel recalls, "the Ottawa Government had made with me, in 1870, an agreement not a single clause of which it ever honoured" (208). Instead, Canada imposed its authority over Riel's people and took control of their territory through military force. Despite the persecution and marginalization that ensued, the Métis remained determined to protect their freedom and way of life.

Since Canada's military takeover of the Northwest, the Métis have continued to define themselves as a sovereign people with an inherent right to self-government. The practice of developing their own rules, processes, and structures to manage their political, economic, and social affairs was not abandoned. From the founding of Métis organizations across the Canadian Prairies in the 1920s and 1930s to the emergence of the Métis National Council in 1983, the Métis remained committed to fulfilling Riel's vision of a self-governing Métis Nation through political action. As noted by Jim Brady, a leading figure in the organization of the Métis in Saskatchewan and Alberta for over three decades, "the Métis have no other weapon except organization."[2] How have the Métis used this weapon? Why has political organization been so central to Métis political life and what forms has it taken? How have Métis political structures adapted to changing circumstances and the constraints imposed by the state? We provide answers to these questions by looking back to the governing structures and processes that emerged during the first wave of mobilization with the establishment of buffalo hunt governments and provisional governments in Red River and St. Laurent. We then explore the ways in which the practices that emerged in these early years of Métis political mobilization evolved in the century that followed Canada's military takeover of the Northwest.

The Buffalo Hunt

The first forms of Métis political organization can be traced to the buffalo hunts that began in the late 1700s. As the backbone of the economy during the fur trade era, hunting was integral to the sustenance of Métis families. The buffalo hunt involved the mobilization of great numbers of Métis – often close to two thousand people at a time (Sawchuk 1981, 12). More than just a means of gathering food for consumption and economic trade, the biannual buffalo hunts were grand rallying events in the lives of the Métis, providing opportunities for families throughout the plains to come together in an expression of cultural and national pride (Goulet and Goulet 2006; Saunders 2011; Pelletier 1977). The Métis commitment to protect the social, economic, and political processes that surrounded the hunt contributed to their emergence as *la noovel Naasyoon* (Stanley 1972, 10; see also Morton 1978; Dickason 1985).

Métis oral histories and accounts captured in historical writings like the 1856 journal of Scottish fur trader Alexander Ross offer a colourful portrait of the highly structured governance systems and practices that emerged around the buffalo hunts. Métis families were generally organized according to extended family units; during the hunts, these would be transformed into hunting brigades led by the heads of each family unit (Troupe 2009, 45; Macdougall and St-Onge 2013). Hunts would occur in the fall and spring, with the commencement date and meeting place announced in parishes and missions across the region. Métis elder Auguste Vermette described how residents of Prairie-du-Cheval-Blanc would announce that the hunt would begin on a given day, at a given place, by a particular river (in Ferland 2006, 109). Family-based brigades would travel by cart to the designated location on the appointed date and set up camp. On the eve of the commencement of the hunt, heads of families would gather in an assembly to elect a chief and council and to decide upon the laws that would govern the hunt.

The laws agreed to by the assembly sought to ensure the success of the expedition as well as the protection of all those involved. Laws were adopted for the "general good" of the community and typically forbade activities such as the running of the buffalo before the general order had been given, hunting on the Sabbath, and lagging behind the hunting brigades without the express permission of those in charge (Riel 1982, 204; Ferland 2006, 119; Ross 1957, 249). Individuals found in violation of the laws were subject to punishments that varied according to the nature of the offence. Penalties for a first offence included the removal and cutting up of a saddle and bridle to the cutting up of a coat and flogging for second and third offences (Anderson 2006, 209; Charette 1980, 38; Ferland 2006, 119).

In addition to enforcing these laws, the chief and council were responsible for protecting the camp and its members from external attack, dividing and distributing the spoils of the hunt among the people (particularly the aged and the sick), and laying down plans for each day's march. As Norbert Welsh, a Métis buffalo hunter who was born in Red River in 1845, recounts in his memoirs, "we fur traders had a law of our own in the North-West" (in Weekes 1939, 51).

The hunt was run with strict military precision. Each captain elected to the council was in command of ten soldiers, or *dizaines,* who acted as a police force, along with ten guides appointed each day to help manoeuvre the caravan through the prairies.[3] Soldiers and guides were assigned to duty on a rotational basis, assisted by an alternating group of scouts. With the raising of the camp flag each morning, families were given half an hour to prepare for the day's march, which could average over twenty kilometres.[4] The chief and the guide of the day would then take their place at the head of the caravan and lead the queue of hunters, women, children, cows, and carts towards the buffalo herds. As Ross (1957, 249) explains: "While [the flag] is up, the guide is chief of the expedition. Captains are subject to him and the soldiers of the day are his messengers; he commands all. The moment the flag is lowered, his functions cease." With the lowering of the flag, leadership was passed from the guide to the chief. At the end of each day's hunt, captains and soldiers were tasked with directing the carts to form a protective circle, setting up camp, and posting sentries to guard against enemies.[5]

Together, the chief and council formed a type of mobile government, or what Riel (1982, 203) described as "a temporary provisional government" (see also Chodan and Asfar 2003). As Karen Drake (2013, 170) argues, Métis communities formulated and enforced an extensive set of laws to govern themselves. They did not exercise jurisdiction over a single, static area; instead, "the entire community went where the buffalo went, and they took their jurisdiction with them." Once the hunt was over, the leaders' authority ceased and the council and brigades disbanded (Shore and Barkwell 1997, 221). The principles that governed the hunt, however, did not disappear. Métis families that returned to settlements and wintering camps carried with them what Riel called *les lois de la prairie* (the Laws of the Prairie) (Riel 1982, 204). The Laws of the Prairie recognized the importance of organization as a way of protecting Métis interests: the centrality of family and the well-being of the community, the democratic selection of leaders, and the enforcement of agreed-upon rules. The spirit of these laws – embedded in such deeply held concepts as freedom, kinship, democracy, the rule of law, and provisionality – would continue to permeate Métis political, economic, and social life for years to come.

Provisional Government in Manitoba

The principles and practices that surrounded the biannual buffalo hunts served as an inspiration for the governing councils and provisional governments subsequently established in Métis communities throughout the Historic Northwest (L. Chartrand 2008, 152; Goulet and Goulet 2006; Shore and Barkwell 1997). This was perhaps most evident in the Red River settlement. Chris Andersen (2014, 129) describes Red River as a place where "the collective aspirations of the Métis sought – and for a brief moment attained – their fullest expression." As the Métis settled along the banks of the Assiniboine and Red Rivers, some supported themselves and their families as independent fur traders while others sought employment with one of the two main fur-trading companies at the time: the North West Company (NWC) and the Hudson's Bay Company (HBC).

Tensions in Red River would soon erupt with the arrival of Lord Selkirk's settlers in 1811. While the Métis constituted the largest community at Red River, their claim to the land was contested. The HBC, which had been granted a Royal Charter in 1670 by King Charles II, purported to "own" the land, and it essentially viewed the settlement as a fur trade company town.[6] Wanting to establish a more permanent agricultural base in the Red River valley to supply its fur trade posts, the HBC's then governor, the Earl of Selkirk, secured a grant of 116,000 square miles of land and established the colony of Assiniboia within which the Red River settlement was subsumed (Stanley 1960, 10). The arrival of the first group of Scottish settlers in Assiniboia, led by Miles Macdonnell, would not only set the stage for conflict between the two rival trading companies for control over the fur trade but would also serve as the impetus for political action by the Métis.

The Métis were angered by the settlers' encroachment on their lands and took exception to what they saw as incursions into their ability to hunt and trade freely throughout the region. Particularly troublesome were two proclamations that Macdonnell issued as the newly appointed governor of Assiniboia. The proclamations forbade the running of the buffalo and the export of pemmican – both of which were integral to the cultural and economic existence of the Métis (Anderson 2006, 208; Bumsted 2003, 13; Morton 1967, 41–52). To abate escalating confrontations between the settlers and the Métis, representatives of the HBC reluctantly agreed to sign a treaty with the Métis that demanded, among other things, the removal of the settlers from Red River (Sealy and Lussier 1975, 39; Gaudry 2016a).

The ensuing peace would prove to be fleeting with conflict soon erupting between the NWC and their Métis allies on the one hand and the HBC on the other. The power struggle for control of the fur trade led to *la Viktwayr daan la Plenn di Goornouyayr* (the Victory at Frog Plain), in which the Métis, led by Cuthbert Grant, defeated a contingent of HBC men and Red River settlers.[7] The Pemmican Wars that marked this period and that continued in some fashion until the amalgamation of the NWC and the HBC in 1821 are remembered as important events in contemporary Métis national consciousness.[8] Fred Shore (2001, 80) asserts that, "during these pivotal years, the need to wage war, to defend their homes and to organize politically to protect their investment in the fur trade radically increased the rate of Métis nation-building" (see also O'Toole 2013; Friesen 1984, 80). It was also in this context that the Métis sought to play a more significant role in governance affairs in Red River.

The colonial government in Red River consisted of a governor and council that largely represented British interests and, in particular, those of the HBC. Described by W.L. Morton (1937, 95–96) as "mild, often benevolent," the council did not serve as a useful mechanism to smooth over the social and economic tensions among the population. Attempts to mollify discontent by expanding the council to include more Métis representation did little to alter the perception that it was a tool of the HBC rather than a body representative of the people. Petitions were regularly issued by the Métis to demand, among other things, free trade, representative government, and a governor independent of the HBC.

The ongoing conflicts reached new heights in 1869 when Canada purportedly purchased Rupert's Land and the North-Western Territory from the HBC. Darren O'Toole (2010, 145) notes that, while section 146 of the British North America Act, 1867, required the legislative approval of the colonies of Prince Edward Island, Newfoundland, and British Columbia in advance of their transfer to the Dominion of Canada, no similar provisions were included for the people of the Northwest prior to the incorporation of Rupert's Land and the North-Western Territory into the Dominion. Hence, as preparations began for the transfer, "at no time from 1857 to 1869, despite some warnings by their own servants, did the Canadian ministers ever consider the matter as one requiring consultation with or assurances addressed to the people of the Northwest" (Morton 1967, 117). Much of the difficulty that would ensue was aggravated by Canada's clumsy disregard for local sensibilities. As J.M. Bumsted (1995, 23) maintains, Canada intended to govern its newly acquired lands, including Red River, as a "colonial satrapy," with a Canadian-appointed lieutenant-governor, an appointed council, and no apparent plan for local representation or responsible government.

This would prove to be a fatal mistake. Teams of surveyors sent from Ottawa to Red River were met by Métis who were adamant that Canada had no right to make surveys and enter the settlement without the express permission of its residents (Sprague 1988, 39). The Métis feared that a foreign administration would not give the people of Red River a say in how their settlement would be run. In particular, they worried that their land holdings and religious rights would not be respected and that they would not be valued as citizens.[9] The question confronting the Métis, then, was what kind of mechanism could be created to garner the will of the people in the face of Canada's westward expansion. With no existing representative body through which their views could be democratically expressed, the Métis turned to their own history for inspiration; they looked to what Morton (1967, 121) describes as "the ancestral organization of their people, the council of the buffalo hunt."

In October 1869, a group of Métis from predominantly French-speaking parishes gathered in assembly to elect a council, the Comité national des Métis (Stanley 1963, 61). With John Bruce elected as president and Louis Riel as secretary, the Comité erected a barricade to prevent the entry of the new governor of the colony, William McDougall, into the settlement. When queried about their intentions, the spokesperson of the assembled group – alleged to be Riel – responded, "We want to govern ourselves. We will accept no concessions" (in Bumsted 2001, 27). Successful in turning back the new governor, Riel informed the HBC that representatives of the Crown would not be allowed in Red River in the absence of prior negotiations with the settlement's residents. Demonstrating the seriousness of their intent and seeking to solidify the power of the Comité, a group of armed Métis seized Fort Garry, the strategic centre of the settlement and the principal trading post in the region, on November 2, 1869 (Stanley 1960, 70–71). In his account of an assembly that took place prior to this, Métis elder Auguste Vermette remembers Monseigneur Ritchot instructing the Comité to defend the fort to ensure the intruders did not take control of it. He believed the fort would give them better ground to have their rights recognized (in Ferland 2006, 159).

The Métis were steadfast in their refusal to let their lands be subsumed by Canada as a federally administered territory; instead, they intended to govern themselves through a provisional government that would "give way when satisfactory terms of the transfer were negotiated" (Bumsted 2003, 205). Recognizing the need to present a united front and build alliances with English half-breeds and settlers, the Comité invited the residents of other parishes to elect twelve representatives to join an equal number of deputies elected from the Catholic districts (Stanley 1963, 66). On November 16, 1869, the Convention of Twenty-Four was convened with participants from both the French- and English-speaking parishes in the settlement. These discussions would eventually lead to a List of Rights that was distributed throughout Red River and forwarded to Canadian representatives (Morton 1967, 126–28; Stanley 1960, 71–85). This List of Rights proclaimed the right of the people to elect their own legislature, the recognition of both English and French in the legislature and the courts, as well as fair and full representation in the Canadian Parliament.[10] According to Vermette, the List of Rights was meant to "prepare their life, their government" (in Ferland 2006, 170, our translation).

The Comité also published the Declaration of the People of Rupert's Land and the North-West, which explicitly rejected the authority of the Canadian government over the territory and asserted the right of the "people of the North-West" to "establish any form of government it may consider suitable to its wants."[11] Adam Gaudry's (2014, 221–47) analysis of the Declaration reveals a political plan that had been discussed during public assemblies held months earlier. This is further confirmed by O'Toole's (2010, 155–58) rendition of events, which saw the Métis mobilize popular support to protect their lands through negotiations with Canada. Confirming widespread support among Red River residents, over a thousand people attended a public assembly at which a larger representative body was created, the Convention of Forty. This body was entrusted to draft an amended List of Rights and to select representatives to negotiate with Canada (Stanley 1963, 93–94). While undergoing several revisions, the List of Rights outlined a plan for the continued protection of rights to land, representation, language, and religion (Begg 1956, 69).

The Convention of Forty would evolve into a more "fixed" representative entity: the Provisional Government of Assiniboia (Stanley 1963, 97–98; Bumsted 1996, 144). Comprised of fourteen representatives from each of the English- and French-speaking parishes in the settlement, respectively, and presided over by Riel,[12] the Legislative Assembly of Assiniboia would exercise a two-thirds majority over the veto of its president, who was not allowed to participate as a voting member. This composition ensured the democratic adoption of laws and motions. During the first two sessions of the assembly, which extended from March to May 1870, a series of bills were passed to address such issues as land ownership, justice reforms, the establishment of a military force, and remuneration for legislative representatives.

As evidenced by the mobilization of families during this first wave, the Métis valued political organization as a primary means to advance and protect their interests. The establishment of the Provisional Government reflected a commitment to the utility of political action, albeit in a manner that reflected the exigencies of the time. Riel recognized that in order for the Métis to be taken more seriously there was a need to create a political vehicle that would be legible to the state; as a result, the workings of the Provisional Government "reveals among Métis members of the community [an] awareness of, and sophisticated – even cosmopolitan – familiarity with forms of governance that go well beyond a reliance on traditional ways of organizing for buffalo hunts."[13] At the same time, while the Provisional Government was designed to achieve a particular purpose – notably, to represent the Métis in negotiations with Canada – it was also grounded in democracy and the rule of law, principles first laid down by the Métis during the buffalo hunts. As Gaudry (2014, 254) argues, the declarations, body of laws, and meeting minutes of the Provisional Government established a legitimate foundation for governance in the region and outlined a diplomatic strategy for treating with Canada.

The Canadian government, seeking to remove the biggest obstacle to its westward expansion, agreed to many of the Provisional Government's demands in the Manitoba Act, 1870. This act, which created the Province of Manitoba, was ratified by the Legislative Assembly of Assiniboia at its third session. In addition to protecting linguistic and religious rights, section 31 of the act promised 1.4 million acres of land to Métis children and the control of land already occupied by the Red River Métis in exchange for the province's peaceful entry into Confederation.[14] The act ensured that residents of Manitoba would retain their independence and constitute their own government, which, it was assumed, would continue to be responsive to Métis concerns as they made up the largest proportion of the local population. However, as the Supreme Court of Canada confirmed in 2013, Canada failed to live up to the promises enshrined in the Manitoba Act.[15]

Le petit provisoire | The "Little" Provisional Government

Canada's recognition of Métis rights in the Manitoba Act, 1870, was short lived. As Riel (1982, 209) explains: "when the Authorities inaugurated the Constitution of the Province of Manitoba, instead of granting freedom to all, especially to those with whom it had made agreements, it issued writs of arrest against them, circulated false reports, ill-treated the very people to whom it had pledged peace." D.N. Sprague (1988, 60–68) describes how the Canadian government unilaterally modified the terms that were agreed to in the act and ordered troops to displace Riel and his sympathizers from positions of power. Initially perceived as a "peace-keeping" force, it soon became apparent that Canadian troops intended to kill Riel. Outrage over the execution of Thomas Scott, an Orangeman who had been tried and executed by the Provisional Government, had made Riel and members of the Provisional Government a military target.

As twelve hundred Canadian troops arrived in Red River in 1870, many Métis, including Riel, were forced to flee for their lives. Colonel Wolseley, commander of the Canadian troops, makes clear in his memoirs that he had hoped that Riel would engage in military battle. Wolseley writes that Riel's choice not to fight "was a sad disappointment to all ranks." He also expresses relief that Riel did not surrender himself at the time "for I could not then have hanged him as I might have done had I taken him prisoner when in arms against his sovereign" (Wolseley 1903, 2:217–220). The years that followed the military takeover of Red River were marked by widespread persecution of the Métis (Giraud 1986, 375). By 1885, the once dominant Métis represented only 7 percent of Manitoba's population, outnumbered by Ontario-born residents by a ratio of five to one.[16]

Many Métis families sought refuge in former wintering camps and settlements along the South Saskatchewan River. Those who settled in the Qu'Appelle district and St. Albert in present-day Saskatchewan and Alberta, respectively, mobilized to develop governance structures and constitutions (Bumsted 2003; L. Chartrand 2008). In 1871, Métis gathered in the old wintering camp of St. Laurent de Grandin located in central Saskatchewan to elect a chief and council to govern on their behalf. The Council of St. Laurent was comprised of eight elected councillors and presided over by a renowned chief of the hunt, Gabriel Dumont. Described anecdotally in Métis oral history as a "natural progression from the hunting councils of earlier times," the Council of St. Laurent served a dual role as the administrative, judicial, and military body for the annual buffalo hunts as well as the governance structure of the colony during periods of residence (McLean 1987, 91; Woodcock 2003, 110–13).

In addition to updating and codifying the Laws of the Hunt, from 1873 to 1875 the Council of St. Laurent ratified nearly thirty laws covering all aspects of community life. These laws regulated the conduct of the buffalo hunts and addressed issues that included the responsibilities of councillors, the collection of taxes, the organization and construction of schools, employee-employer contracts, and social mores.[17] Penalties were established for those found in violation of the laws, which were enforced by captains and soldiers selected by the community in the custom of the buffalo hunt. A commission was also set up to settle boundary disputes and disagreements over ownership of land among community members (Woodcock 2003, 96–100).

Although Stanley (1960, 181) describes this experiment in self-government as "a complete success," it would not endure. Diane Payment (2009, 125) explains that "the distrust of the North West Mounted Police and the territorial administrators for a form of Métis government reminiscent of the Provisional Government of Red River soon erupted into conflict." As Canadian surveyors appeared in the region to mark off land as they had previously done in Red River, the Métis once again petitioned the Canadian government to recognize their land rights. These petitions – eighty-four of which were sent between 1878 and 1884 alone – were repeatedly ignored (de Trémaudan 1982, 116). By the spring of 1885, the Métis abandoned hope that their petitions would be answered and sent for Riel to help them in their fight against the Canadian state. A few weeks later, a provisional government – *le petit provisoire* – was proclaimed at Batoche (Woodcock 2003, 175).

Consistent with the demands advanced some fifteen years earlier by the Provisional Government at Red River, *le petit provisoire* pressed Canada for a democratically elected responsible government, representation in the national Parliament and in cabinet, as well as local control of public lands (Bumsted 2001, 253). Resistant to such demands, the federal government again responded with military force. Confrontations erupted at *lac aux Canards* (Duck Lake) in March 1885 and culminated with the defeat of the Métis by Canadian troops in Batoche two months later. Riel was arrested, tried, and hanged for treason on November 16, 1885. For Stanley (1972, 26; 1963, 10), "Riel's execution in 1885 marked the death of the 'New Nation.'" The Northwest Resistance was effectively over. Forced to flee or face persecution, the Métis became the target of assimilation policies that denied their rights to land and to self-government. In the eyes of the state, they would soon become what Sealy and Lussier (1975) describe as "Canada's forgotten people."

The Second Wave: Métis Mobilization on the Prairies

The years following the last stand at Batoche and the branding of Riel as a traitor led to a climate of fear, disgrace, and racism with regard to the Métis. John Morrisseau, a Métis elder and former president of the Manitoba Métis Federation, describes the various reactions of the Métis towards this oppression. He recounts that, while some Métis sought to deny their heritage and "go underground," others adopted a strategy of silent resistance.[18] The decades that followed the hanging of Louis Riel were described in French as *le grand silence*, the Great Silence.[19]

Despite this persecution, the Métis continued to organize politically. In 1887, a mere two years following the Battle of Batoche, a group of former supporters and allies of Riel formed the Union nationale métisse Saint-Joseph du Manitoba. With the stated aim of preserving and protecting Métis culture and traditions, members of the Union nationale erected a monument on Riel's tomb in the Saint-Boniface cathedral cemetery (Weinstein 2007, 24). Beginning in 1909, the organization also collected documents and first-hand accounts of the events of 1869–70 and 1885 in order to recast the story of the resistance movements at Red River and Batoche from a Métis perspective. These efforts resulted in the 1935 publication of *Histoire de la nation métisse dans l'Ouest canadien (History of the Métis Nation in Western Canada)*, by Auguste-Henri de Trémaudan (see discussion in Ens and Sawchuk 2016, 113–29).

Along with the formation of the Union nationale, the second wave of Métis political mobilization across western Canada was sparked by the pending transfer in 1930 of responsibility for natural resources from the federal government to the Prairie provinces. Dispossessed of their lands and homes as a result of settlement and the failures of the scrip land distribution process, many Métis had been reduced to taking up shelter along road allowances and in temporary shanty communities (Campbell 2012, xiv; Hatt 1983). The transfer threatened to strip Métis families of even these precarious lands at a time when they were already facing crushing poverty and social marginalization.[20] As conditions worsened for these "Road Allowance People," a group of Métis in the Cold Lake area of eastern Alberta petitioned the provincial government for land to be set aside for agriculture, hunting, trapping, and fishing as a way of reducing their dependence on provincial relief (O'Byrne 2013; Sawchuk 1981).

Initially organizing into community councils (referred to as "locals" and modelled on labour organizations), it had become clear to Métis leaders that their demands would only be taken seriously by the state if they were expressed through formal bodies with constitutions and bylaws (Dubois 2013, 438). Under the skilful leadership of individuals like Jim Brady and Malcolm Norris, Métis in Alberta regrouped into a more formal organization, the Association des Métis d'Alberta et des Territoires du Nord-Ouest in 1932 – soon known as the Métis Association of Alberta and eventually changing its name to the Métis Nation of Alberta (Dobbin 1981). In 1933, in the face of intense lobbying by Métis leaders, the provincial government passed a resolution calling for an investigation into the condition of the Métis population in Alberta (Martin 1989; Hatt 1979; Sawchuk 1998). A year later, the Ewing Commission was tasked with preparing a report on the health, education, housing, and territorial conditions of Alberta Métis. Most notably, the commission argued for the establishment of Métis colonies, a recommendation that was subsequently implemented by the Alberta government in the Métis Betterment Act, 1938. As a result of this legislation, Alberta remains the only jurisdiction in the country with a recognized Métis land base that is home to eight settlements in northern Alberta (Pocklington 1991; Bell 1994; O'Byrne 2013).

The success of the Métis Association of Alberta encouraged similar political movements among the Métis in Saskatchewan. In 1937, the Saskatchewan Métis Society was established with the goal of improving the lives of Métis in the province and "correcting the history" of the Métis.[21]

Primarily centred in the southern region of the province, the society also sought the assistance of the Government of Saskatchewan in directing its constitutional claims against Canada, which it held responsible for the historical dispossession of the Métis (Weinstein 2007, 26). Echoing and, in some respects, rivalling these efforts, the Saskatchewan Métis Association was created in 1943 to represent Métis in northern Saskatchewan (Dubois 2013, 438; Pulla 2013). In 1967, the two organizations amalgamated under the banner of the Métis Society of Saskatchewan, eventually adopting the name Métis Nation of Saskatchewan in 1993 and, in 2000, rechristened as Métis Nation-Saskatchewan.

In Manitoba, Métis were also beginning to organize in the 1930s to press their claims against Ottawa on unextinguished title to land. The first of these associations, the Northern Halfbreed Association, was a small regional organization in the northern part of the province that represented Métis and non-status Indians.[22] Throughout the 1950s and 1960s, political activity primarily occurred through the annual Indian and Métis conferences that were sponsored by the Community Welfare Planning Council of Winnipeg (Sawchuk 1978; Harrison 1985). The purposes of these conferences, which had begun in 1954, were twofold: to focus attention on the needs of Indigenous people in the city and to provide them with a platform to try to overcome their social and economic challenges (Sealy and Lussier 1975, 164). Métis attending these conferences, however, routinely complained that the proceedings focused too much on First Nations needs to the exclusion of those of the Métis (Pulla 2013, 411–13). At a workshop held in October 1967, First Nations and Métis delegates discussed the reorganization of the Manitoba Indian Brotherhood, an organization that had been in existence in various forms since the 1930s. In particular, the debate focused on whether the Métis would be adequately represented – or indeed, even invited to join – a revamped Indian Brotherhood association, or whether they would be better off establishing their own Métis-specific body. For the Métis who were present, it was clear from the tenor of the discussion that the time had come to found their own political organization, which would come in the form of the Manitoba Métis Federation (Ens and Sawchuk 2016, 373).

The Third Wave: Red Power and the Rise of Métis Nationalism

A third wave of Métis political activity emerged during the "Red Power" era of the 1960s. Not only did Métis political mobilization continue at the provincial level during this era, but it also came to play a bigger role on the national scene. The events and circumstances of this period were particularly influential in reviving Indigenous consciousness generally and Métis nationalism in particular. The civil rights movement, Quebec's Quiet Revolution, and the occasion of Canada's centennial led to the reorganization of existing Métis associations and the formation of new ones (Weinstein 2007; Brown 2002; Reid 2008). It was in this context that Métis in Ontario and British Columbia began to formally organize. In 1965, two organizations emerged in Ontario: the Ontario Métis and Non-Status Indian Association, and the Lake Nipigon Métis Association.[23] Three years later, the British Columbia Association of Non-Status Indians was established to represent the interests of Métis and non-status Indians in the province.[24] These provincial organizations would continue to evolve into the Métis Nation of Ontario in 1993 and the Métis Provincial Council of British Columbia in 1996, known today as the Métis Nation British Columbia.

While Métis-specific organizations flourished during this period, in some cases Métis also joined forces with non-status Indians to advance their political agenda. As Indigenous groups turned to the courts to seek redress for historical injustices and to improve the conditions of Indigenous peoples living both on and off reserve, Métis and non-status Indians found themselves in a similar legal position. Excluded from the definition of status Indian under the Indian Act and essentially invisible in the eyes of the state, Métis and non-status Indians formed a residual category of Indigenous peoples in Canada (Sawchuk 1992, 72). Tracing the history of Métis mobilization in Saskatchewan, Ens and Sawchuk (2016, 367–70) examine the "marriage of convenience" that emerged between non-status Indians and Métis in that province. They note that, in 1975, the Métis organization in Saskatchewan changed its name to the Association of Métis and non-status Indians of Saskatchewan as a "public recognition of the fact that not only did non-status Indians face many of the same political and social problems as the Métis ... but that many non-status or non-treaty Indians were already members." After a provincewide referendum in 1988, the decision was made to split the association and create a Métis-specific organization that eventually evolved into the Métis Nation-Saskatchewan (Dubois 2013).

At the national level, the federal government's offer to provide core funding for three national Indigenous entities led the Métis organizations from the Prairie provinces, which included non-status Indians, to form the Native Council of Canada (NCC) in 1971. The recollections of Tony Belcourt, a principal organizer who would go on to become the first president of the NCC, affirms the "marriage of convenience" argument advanced by Ens and Sawchuk. Belcourt (2013, 129) maintains that the decision to build a national organization that included both Métis and non-status Indians was deliberate for two reasons: "first, because it reflected the reality of the membership of all of our organizations at the time; and, second, because we shared the same goals and were in basically the same position – landless and without federal recognition" (see also Teillet 2012, 335). While tensions within the organization were inherent from the start, the NCC – under the formidable leadership of Harry Daniels – played a pivotal role in ensuring the constitutional recognition of the Métis in 1982 (Belcourt 2013, 131; see also RCAP 1996b, 214; Chartrand 2004; Chartrand and Giokas 2002; P. Chartrand 2008; and Grammond 2009). The inclusion of Métis as one of three Aboriginal peoples in Canada under section 35(2) of the Constitution Act, 1982, was a particularly resounding victory for the Métis. As John Weinstein (2007, 45) writes, "what may have appeared to be a simple statement of fact represented a monumental triumph for the Métis people."

The adoption of the Constitution Act, 1982, was to be followed by a series of four First Ministers Conferences, the purpose of which was to define the nature and scope of these constitutionally enshrined Aboriginal and treaty rights. Emboldened by their constitutional recognition and concerned by the fact that neither the president nor the vice-president of the Native Council of Canada at the time was Métis (a problem given that the organization was allotted two seats at the conference table), Métis leaders from the Prairies began to question whether the interests of the

Métis Nation would be fairly represented in these conferences. Deciding that the time had come for the Métis to strike out on their own, one week before the first conference was set to begin, the three Prairie Métis organizations pulled out of the NCC to form a new national Métis organization. On March 8, 1983, the Métis National Council was born.[25]

The Métis National Council evolved from the early forms of political organization. Since the era of the buffalo hunt, Métis leaders have mobilized politically to develop governance structures through which to pursue their collective goals. In so doing, they have had to contend with political realities that include the loss of land, economic hardship, and government denial of Métis rights and identity. As Métis leaders navigated changing political, economic, and social conditions, their governance structures evolved. While remaining true to the underlying beliefs and traditions that have shaped Métis political action since the days of the buffalo hunt, the institutions, practices, and processes of the contemporary Métis governments that comprise the Métis National Council are a product of the ongoing evolution of Métis political organization. It is through the process of change and continuity that the Métis Nation has asserted itself throughout history as *la noovel Naasyoon*, the new nation.

Conclusion

The Métis have long viewed political organization as a way to protect their interests and identity as well as a means to exercise their rights and freedoms. Reminiscing about how far the Métis Nation has come, Métis elder George Fleury recounts: "Everybody dreamed of a better life but didn't know how to change it. Political organization was the only way."[26] Beginning with the organization of the buffalo hunts and continuing through to the provisional governments that dotted the Northwest in the 1800s, the Métis have continuously organized to collectively govern their political, economic, and social activities. As Métis nationalism developed, so too did the institutions that supported it (L. Chartrand 2008, 150). As their petitions, protests, and resistance movements demonstrate, *la noovel Naasyoon* was not averse to taking steps against colonial powers in the face of threats to their way of life. In the wake of repeated efforts by the Hudson's Bay Company and the Canadian state to undermine their way of life, the Métis have continued to flourish as a distinct Indigenous people through political action. The commitment to political mobilization in defence of Métis rights continues to the present day.

While our research reveals continuities between early and later forms of Métis political organization, Sawchuk (1998, 51–52) takes a seemingly opposite view, asserting that "there is little similarity between the structure of the local government at St. Laurent [a provisional government struck in 1871] and the organization of the buffalo hunt." In support of this argument, he points to the sharing of leadership duties on a daily basis between captains and guides in the buffalo hunt, in contrast to the government of St. Laurent, which involved such "typically White" concepts as a formally designated council consisting of a president and seven councillors elected for one year. We assert that the two positions are not mutually exclusive when one considers the willingness of the Métis to strategically adapt their political tactics depending on the specific goal at hand.

In fact, the early forms of political organization that emerged during the buffalo hunts and the provisional governments represent distinct organizational responses on the part of the Métis to the particularities of the moment. What mattered for Métis leaders was not the specific structures that were adopted but, rather, the underlying objectives that sparked their creation. The buffalo hunts and the provisional governments illustrate the value of political action in the promotion of Métis collective goals and reflect a shared commitment to such principles as democracy and the rule of law. In the next chapter, we more closely examine the principles that underlie Métis governance from the early days of the buffalo hunt to the present day.

2

Lii Valeur di Goovarnimaan di Michif
Principles of Métis Governance

MÉTIS LEADERS SOUGHT TO FIND new ways to protect what they refer to in Michif as *ka ishi pimaatishiyaahk* (our way of life) after the military takeover of their lands by Canadian troops in the second half of the 1800s. "Political organization," according to Métis elder George Fleury, "is what saved the Métis."[1] For the Métis, political organization and the mechanisms of governance that accompany it are not ends but, rather, means through which the more fundamental goal of self-determination can be achieved. The structures born from Métis political organization fulfill distinct purposes that result from the political and legal contexts with which the Métis have had to contend.

The Métis have continuously adapted their governance structures while remaining committed to five principles: freedom, kinship, democracy, the rule of law, and provisionality. Using Michif phrases that capture *lii valeur di goovarnimaan di Michif* (principles of Métis governance), we argue that freedom, kinship, democracy, the rule of law, and provisionality interact with one another to give life to a particular Métis way of governing.[2]

From the buffalo hunt councils and the provisional governments established in the 1800s to the contemporary governments that comprise the Métis National Council, the Métis have developed their own approach to governance. Métis elder Maria Campbell captures this continuity in the memories of her childhood in the mid-1900s:

> As my brother and I talked that day, I was struck with the realization that the annual summer and autumn excursions to pick roots, berries, and nuts, and to preserve fish and meat, were a re-enactment of the old buffalo hunts of our ancestors. Of course! Why didn't I see that before – Uncle Pah cha neese was the grand chief, Dad was the captain, my uncles the guides and scouts. Instead of buffalo, it was roots, berries, nuts, moose meat, and fish that we harvested. And with each group that joined us, there was an old respected uncle serving as grand chief, a captain, and scouts. (Campbell 2012, xxi)

Campbell's memories are a reminder of the ways in which the Métis have adapted to the circumstances at hand. Through adaptation and change, the Métis have remained committed to protecting their way of life.

Métis scholars have recently examined the historical, social, and political organization of the Métis. Most notably, Brenda Macdougall (2010) describes the centrality of kinship relations and uncovers the centrifugal role of women in the evolution of community life among the Métis. These kinship relations, according to Adam Gaudry (2014), were weighed alongside the desire for freedom and self-government in the early years of Métis political organization. It is through social and political organizations that the Métis came to relate with one another as what Zoe Todd (2016) refers to as "more-than-human-beings." In this chapter, we rely on recent scholarship, biographical and historical accounts, as well as discussions with Métis leaders and elders to identify the key principles that underpin Métis governance. Although some of these governance principles are shared by other Indigenous and non-Indigenous communities, we argue that, taken together, they reflect the unique governance practices of the Métis as a distinct Indigenous nation. Métis governance is rooted in principles that aim to achieve self-determination by protecting what the Métis describe as *ka ishi pimaatishiyaahk* (our way of life).

Freedom: *Ki tipemishoonaan* | We Are Free

Leaders from Cuthbert Grant and Louis Riel in the nineteenth century to Jim Sinclair and Clément Chartier in the twenty-first century speak of the Métis as a free, autonomous, and self-governing people. In reflecting on the life of the Métis during the buffalo hunt, Métis elder Auguste Vermette recalls, "they were free in the Prairie" (in Ferland 2006, 116, our translation). As one of Canada's first historians, Alexander Ross (1957, 252), noted in 1856, "[the Métis] cherish freedom as they cherish life." To understand the Métis commitment to freedom, it is useful to situate it in relation to what is referred to in Michif as *ka ishi pimaatishiyaahk* (our way of life).

For the Métis, freedom has both an individual and a collective dimension that are interconnected.[3] Historical accounts like those reflected in the words of a voyageur in 1825 often associate freedom with individual happiness and a sense of pride: "there is no life as happy as a voyageur's life; none so independent; no place where a man enjoys so much variety and freedom as in the Indian country" (in Foster 1994, 9). While freedom can be experienced on an individual basis, it also has an implicit collective dimension insofar as the ethos of independence associated with the fur trade is rooted in kinship. A man's place within the fur trade economy not only depended on his individual abilities as a tripman, buffalo hunter, or horseman but was also intrinsically linked to wider trade networks built through kinship relations. Specifically, it was tied to Indian and Métis women who not only provided access to valuable kin-based trade networks but who were also valued for their skills, a point we explore more fully in Chapter 5 (Pannekoek 1991, 62; Sleeper-Smith 2001, 19–20). In this way, individual freedom was rooted in the larger collective: the ability of an individual voyageur to "live the good life" hinged on his connection to and the success of his kin community.

The desire to protect freedom from both an individual and collective perspective – and thereby to safeguard *ka ishi pimaatishiyaahk* – was historically achieved through political action. Scholars have traced this objective to the power struggles between the two trading giants, the North West Company and the Hudson's Bay Company, which occurred between

1814 and 1816. Gaudry (2016b) argues that the Métis' conviction of their right to trade freely and their rejection of the HBC's authority to impose sanctions on this right contributed to the emergence of a distinct political consciousness among the Métis, a position also shared by O'Toole (2013). Underlying the political awakening of the Métis was the rejection of the authority of fur trade companies, and the HBC in particular, to unilaterally impose restrictions on their activities (Ens 1996, 33).

In an 1845 letter addressed to the governor of the Red River settlement, Métis representatives asserted: "we, as natives of this country, and as half-breeds, have the right to hunt furs in the Hudson's Bay Company territories whenever we think proper, and again sell those furs to the highest bidder" (in Begg 1894, 261). Matching words with actions, more than three hundred armed men assembled in protest when Métis trader Pierre Guillaume Sayer was tried for trafficking furs with the HBC's competitor in 1849. The Métis contested the legitimacy of the HBC's Royal Charter, which was used to validate this charge. When Sayer was released without punishment despite being found guilty of having violated the Charter, it was apparent that the HBC did not have sufficient legitimacy to enforce its rules on the Métis. Reiterating the Métis commitment to freedom, the crowd gathered at Sayer's release fired gunshots and erupted in joyous chanting: "*Le commerce est libre! Vive la liberté!*" (Ross 1957, 376; Stanley 1963, 13).

For the Métis, political action was viewed not as an end in itself but, rather, as a means to secure their freedom to live and trade as they pleased. Hence, while the Sayer trial led to important economic rights for the Métis, along with some limited political reforms within Red River, the Métis remained fearful that increased settlement would threaten their way of life. These fears sparked further action on the part of the Métis in the form of new political structures such as the Comité national des Métis and the Provisional Government of Assiniboia. In a meeting leading up to the creation of the Provisional Government, Riel declared: "We are faithful to our native land. We shall protect it against the dangers which menace it. We wish that the people of Red River be a *free* People" (in Bumsted 1996, 76, emphasis added). Sealy and Lussier (1957, 80) remark that "it was natural for a freedom loving people, so threatened, to resist what they believed to be external domination." For Riel and his followers, the creation of formal political entities was a means to secure *ka ishi pimaatishiyaahk*.

This was also the case in the south Saskatchewan settlements, where the Métis mobilized politically to safeguard their freedom. Gabriel Dumont, one of the key leaders in these settlements, recounts in his memoirs: "we [the Métis] left Manitoba because we were not free, and we came here, to a country that was still wild, to be *free*" (in Combet 2006, 47, emphasis added). To that end, the Métis prepared numerous petitions demanding Ottawa recognize their right to land and to self-government. In 1884, Riel compiled these demands in a comprehensive statement of grievances that included, among other things, the right to territorial self-government, land rights similar to those promised in the Manitoba Act, the establishment of a 2-million-acre trust to provide capital to the Métis in the long-term, redress for the maladministration of the Manitoba Act, and sixty-four thousand acres of land to be distributed to future generations of Métis families (Sprague 1988, 169).

While the federal government admitted in 1882 that the land situation in the Saskatchewan settlements warranted further investigation, it repeatedly delayed addressing these concerns. George Woodcock (2003, 143) concludes that the Canadian government simply waited too long to act. As they had previously done in Manitoba, the Métis took matters into their own hands and created a provisional government to defend their rights to land and self-government. Committed to protect *ka ishi pimaatishiyaahk*, they formed *le petit provisoire* (the little provisional government), based on what Riel described as "true conceptions of public freedom and equality" (Riel 1982, 204).

Freedom continues to hold significance as a fundamental principle in present-day Métis governance. This is clearly evidenced in the constitutions of contemporary Métis governments. For example, the Constitution of the Métis Nation British Columbia states: "The Métis Nation has the right of self-determination. By virtue of that right we, the citizens of the Métis Nation, will *freely* determine our political status and *freely* pursue our economic, social and cultural development."[4] In a similar vein, the preamble of the Métis Nation-Saskatchewan Constitution stipulates: "The inherent dignity to equality and rights which can never be taken away from Métis people is the foundation of Freedom, Justice and Peace in the Métis Nation."[5] Far from being vestiges of the past, the commitment to freedom is embedded in the principles that underlie Métis approaches to politics and governance in the modern era.

Kinship: *Miyeu Waahkootoowin* | Being Related in a Good Way

For the Métis, the collective experience of freedom is informed by the meaningful relationships in which individuals are engaged through kinship connections. Recent scholarship has demonstrated that the system of social obligation that binds the Métis together is not spatial in nature but, rather, is grounded in kinship (Wolfart 2012; Macdougall 2010; St-Onge and Podruchny 2012). The family unit is at the heart of kinship relations. Family is defined through relatedness with all beings and finds expression through reciprocal relations that developed across the Northwest (Payment 2009, 42). For the Métis, being related in the right way (*miyeu waahkootoowin*) is part of *ka ishi pimaatishiyaahk* (our way of life).

Family relationships came to affect nearly every aspect of life as the Métis became increasingly linked – sometimes peripherally – through the fur trade. In the words of Heather Devine (2004, 198), kinship was the "glue" that tied together fur trade professionals, importer-exporters, outfitters and shopkeepers. In his memoirs, Métis scout, interpreter, and storyteller Louis Goulet describes the ways in which the idea of family was understood by the Métis, capturing the simultaneous immediacy and elusiveness of kinship relations.[6] He remembers: "Back then, family ties among the Métis could stretch to infinity, so to speak. If two grandfathers traded dogs one day, that was enough for their grandchildren to call themselves relatives. Children of cousins two or three times removed turned into uncles and aunts" (Charette 1980, 43). Goulet's words are a reminder that kinship relations among the Métis reached across time and space, linking people and communities throughout what would become known as the Historic Métis Nation Homeland. Extended families and relatives would (re)connect with each other as they came together to participate in buffalo hunts and other activities related to the fur trade, and would nurture these relationships upon their return to their home communities and settlements. Like a spider's web, these kinship connections "were woven in surprising and complex patterns and multiple dimensions, could be hard to see, could be easily broken and re-spun, and yet were strong and durable" (St. Onge and Podruchny 2012, 62).

To make sense of the complex relationships that inform Métis communities, Brenda Macdougall (2010, 3–8) evokes the concept of *wahkootowin*, a Cree term that captures the relatedness of land, human, and non-human beings (living, ancestral, and those to come) and the spirit world. In her study of Métis communities in northwestern Saskatchewan, Macdougall shows how values of mutual respect, reciprocity, decency, and order are manifested through behaviours that can be mapped genealogically. In so doing, she identifies matrilocal residence patterns – whereby women, with their husband and children, remained in their mother's household after marriage – as one of the behaviours that set the Métis apart from their Indian relatives (Macdougall 2010, 57–71; see also Brown 1983). Susan Sleeper-Smith (2001) adds that kin networks did not develop by chance but were instead informed by strategic considerations that linked families and communities through matrilineality.

The centrality of kinship networks to the Métis way of life is also captured in the ancient protocols that incorporate ongoing relations between living and non-living beings as well as ancestors and future generations.[7] Kinship aims to foster good relations in the pursuit of common goals. The notion of being related in the right way, *miyeu waahkootoowin*, extends beyond the family unit to other Indigenous and non-Indigenous groups. For example, Robert Innes (2013) describes how the Métis formed the *Nehiyaw Pwat,* or Iron Alliance, through kinship ties with the Plains Cree, Saulteaux, and Assiniboine, which gave these groups political, military, and economic power that complemented their respective political objectives (see also Vrooman 2012, 28–29). In his memoirs, Métis buffalo hunter Norbert Welsh describes the treaty signed between the Sioux and the "half-breeds" in order to bring to an end the conflict between the two groups as well as the numerous other alliances and friendships forged between the Métis and other Indian leaders, including Starblanket and One Arrow (in Weekes 1939, 273, 192, 140).

Today, *miyeu waahkootoowin* continues to be invoked at the beginning and end of ceremonies, assemblies, and other gatherings, and it is fostered through the role of community-based locals, women, and elders in governance activities. This idea also finds expression in Métis laws and practices – specifically, in the focus on conservation and sustainability in harvesting laws.

For the Métis, *miyeu waahkootoowin* has historically been central to their pursuit of collective freedom. As Métis elder Verna DeMontigny explains, "it is not just about the relationship between people and their government – everything comes together in a good way."[8] In his research on historical Métis political practices, Gaudry (2014) uses the concept of *ka tipaymishooyahk*, which means "we who own ourselves," alongside *wahkootowin* to explain how the Métis weighted collective obligations to relatives alongside the goal of freedom.[9] He explains that "it was in this spirit that Métis repeatedly joined together, year after year, for common purpose – to live, hunt, trade, and celebrate together, but also regularly dissolved into their extended families to live independently" (79). Kinship relations, which were developed and nurtured through the buffalo hunt, provided the Métis with a common experience, or what Gaudry describes as a "shared language," that they later applied to different contexts to protect their common interests (77). The pursuit of freedom was intrinsically tied to maintaining kinship relations – to fostering *miyeu waahkootoowin*.

The continued commitment to freedom and kinship and to maintaining *ka ishi pimaatishiyaahk* (our way of life), is evidenced in the language used by contemporary Métis leaders. At the Manitoba Métis Federation's 2015 General Assembly, speaking to the centrality of Métis unity to the advancement of both individual and collective freedom, President David Chartrand declared: "Strengthen the individual, you strengthen the family. Strengthen the family, you strengthen the community. Strengthen the community, you strengthen the nation."[10] President Chartrand's words remind us of the ways in which kinship relations remain at the heart of Métis social, economic, and political life (see also Macdougall 2010, 8). Through *miyeu waahkootoowin,* the Métis have maintained a distinct way of life as a unique Indigenous people.

Democracy: *Ka Niikaaniichik* | Those Who Lead Us

One of the key ways in which the Métis foster *miyeu waahkootoowin* (good relations) and achieve freedom is through the democratic selection of their leaders. In our examination of the councils of the buffalo hunts and the governance structures that followed, we identify three types of democratic processes used by the Métis to choose their political leadership – deliberative, direct, and representative. The historical use of these processes and the continued commitment to them in contemporary practice speaks to the centrality of democracy as a key principle of Métis governance.

Deliberative Democracy: Assemblies

In his first-hand account of an assembly in 1870, Peter Erasmus paints a vivid picture of the public assemblies that were held on the eve of the commencement of each buffalo hunt. He describes how families would deliberate and position themselves in favour of a particular candidate as contenders for chief made their way around the camp to gather support (Erasmus 1976, 201). Informal discussions throughout the camp not only served to foster agreement in advance of assemblies but also sought to minimize conflict and wounded pride during and after these public events.

Beyond their deliberative character, assemblies were also a vehicle for collective decision making and action. The act of decision making through the assembly process ensured the legitimization of decisions by kinship groups that were subsequently bound by them. In the case of buffalo hunts, the principal task of the assembly was to decide upon the rules that were to be followed during the hunt under the leadership of the elected chief and council. As Fred Shore and Lawrence Barkwell (1997, 213) explain, "everyone had a part in making the laws and leaders were commissioned to carry out only the agreed-upon laws and nothing more." During the hunt, leaders would assemble daily (except on Sundays) to discuss the occurrences of the day and prepare the line of march for the morning. Other items on the agenda included the determination of punishments for those who transgressed the laws (Charette 1980, 21–22). In his 1856 journal, Alexander Ross (1957, 252), having himself participated in such meetings, describes discussions as "free, practical, and interesting."

Given the importance placed upon them, assemblies were integrated into various aspects of governance in the settlements. Larry Chartrand (2008, 152) describes how assemblies became tools for collective decision making in St. Laurent, whereby each year residents would ratify all laws and decisions made by their elected council. In Red River, assemblies were important mechanisms for giving legitimacy to the Provisional Government and were further used to mobilize residents against the newly confederated Canadian state's incursion on their lands. This also occurred in the south Saskatchewan settlements, where residents decided upon a common strategy of resistance through the assembly process. Denis Combet (2006, 50–56) recounts how assemblies were held in Batoche, St. Laurent, and as far as Prince Albert in 1882 and 1883 to gather support for Métis rights and to prepare petitions in support of these rights. By 1884, assemblies had become an almost daily occurrence as the Métis mounted their resistance strategy in the face of oncoming military troops that were threatening to enter their communities.

Today, assemblies continue to be important events in Métis politics. The governments that make up the Métis National Council each hold an annual general assembly during which Métis citizens come together, express their views, and propose ideas. Beyond providing a forum for deliberation, these annual assemblies facilitate collective decision making insofar as Métis citizens approve all bylaw and constitutional amendments, financial and accounting statements, and significant policy proposals (Saunders 2013, 361; Dubois 2015, 194). During assemblies, members and elected officials also have the opportunity to submit motions that are subsequently voted on by the general membership.

In addition to offering a forum for deliberation and discussion, assemblies provide an opportunity to nurture and renew relationships. They often take place in the context of larger community gatherings that bring together families, elders, women, youth, executive leaders, and artists. For example, the Métis Nation of Ontario's 2014 annual general assembly was a two-day event hosted by the Métis community in Thunder Bay, and it involved workshops, an information fair, music, and a canoe expedition. Similarly, approximately three thousand delegates attend the Manitoba Métis Federation's annual assemblies, which are typically three-day events, capped off with an evening banquet showcasing Métis arts and culture. Described by Métis elder George Fleury as a time to "see the Métis family,"[11] assemblies continue to foster *miyeu waahkootoowin* and to play a socializing role similar to that played by the buffalo hunts.

Direct Democracy: Elections

Beyond the face-to-face engagement that occurs in assemblies, the Métis are directly involved in deciding upon the rules and procedures of governance and in electing their political leaders. The historic provisional governments of the Métis were set up in such a way as to ensure that leaders would be chosen by those bound by their authority (see also Gaudry 2014, 100–6). According to Peter Erasmus's (1976, 202) first-hand account of the 1870 hunt, heads of households cast their votes with wooden sticks that were then counted by a democratically agreed-upon representative. The idea that leaders should be chosen by those affected by their decisions extended beyond the election of the chief and council. For example, each *dizaine* of ten soldiers that carried out the orders of the chief during the hunt was responsible for selecting a captain from within its ranks.

Through regular and direct elections, the Métis ensured that authority would not be undemocratically imposed on individuals or groups (Payment 2009, 123). Consistent with the conduct of assemblies, the Métis remained committed to the moral equality and free will of all beings in the governance of the settlements. As Norma Hall et al. explain: "French delegates at the Convention of Forty had agreed that their councillors would be selected from amongst themselves – their parishes having already gone through the process of electing representatives on numerous occasions since the previous autumn, including settling contested seats for the convention."[12] Today, elections are regularly held to select leaders at the local, regional, and provincial levels (Saunders 2013). Although the number of representatives elected varies in each province (see Table 2.1), Métis citizens directly elect their provincial leaders through a ballot-box election typically held every four years.[13] While the direct election of the executive leadership by Métis citizens is a characteristic that is unique to Métis governments, it is important to note that participation in elections is limited to those citizens who are members of each Métis government and who are therefore on the voter list. This remains a point of contention among critics of the Métis National Council and its Governing Members since there is a significant gap between those who self-identity as Métis and those who choose to participate in the activities of Métis governments – an issue we discuss below.

TABLE 2.1 Number of elected executive positions in Métis governments

Métis government	Number of elected positions
Métis Nation British Columbia	11
Métis Nation of Alberta	14
Métis Nation-Saskatchewan	16
Manitoba Métis Federation	23
Métis Nation of Ontario	19

Representative Democracy

While the Métis have a history of participating directly in governance through assemblies and elections, some decisions are delegated to representatives. During the buffalo hunt, the council – which was selected through the consent of the members of the hunting brigade – was assigned responsibility for the management of daily affairs. As Riel (1982, 204) explained, "in ordinary matters the council acted according to the authority entrusted to it." Every decision – military, civil, or recreational – necessitated the conveyance of the council and was accompanied by ceremony, speeches, and opportunities for assent or dissent. Louis Goulet recalls that the choice of chief and council was made with such care that their decisions carried legitimacy: "I don't remember ever having first-hand knowledge of, or even hearing about, a case where the authority or decision of a council was ever even discussed, let alone challenged" (in Charette 1980, 21).

Historically, representation served the key purpose of uniting diverse interests. During the buffalo hunts, the chief routinely appointed representatives from every major household to ensure the unity of the camp. As parishes replaced households as the unit of collective decision making in the Red River settlement, they also took on the role of representation within the settlement's governance structure. Recall, for example, the discussion in Chapter 1 of the composition of the 1869 Legislative Assembly of the Provisional Government of Assiniboia, which included fourteen representatives from each of the English and French parishes.

Representation was also a means to showcase success or to apply particular knowledge. This is evident in the creation of committees entrusted to represent differing viewpoints or groups in the provisional government at Red River. Members of committees could be chosen because of their expertise or knowledge on a given matter, their leadership qualities, or their status – factors that were always weighed alongside the representation of French and English parishes. For instance, the Special Committee on Two-Mile Hay Privilege struck by the provisional Legislative Assembly of Assiniboia included farmers like Thomas Bunn and Jean-Baptiste Tourond, representing English and French parishes, respectively, as well as prominent figures in the settlement, notably John Bruce.[14] These individuals carried out the duties that were assigned to them as representatives.

Representation carried with it an obligation of accountability. This is evident in St. Laurent, where Gabriel Dumont explicitly stated that he would only take on the role of president if the members of the assembly swore to support him and his colleagues in word and deed in the enforcement of laws. Demonstrating their faith in their elected representatives, the assembly authorized Dumont and his council to make supplementary laws or regulations that they deemed necessary for the well-being of the community (Woodcock 2003, 112–13). The chief and council in St. Laurent also surrendered their power in the General Assembly after a year in office. As Woodcock writes, "with a due sense of the drama of the occasion, they begged the people to choose others in their places" (115); however, most of them were re-elected for a second term. The obligation of accountability among elected representatives remains present in contemporary Métis governance. As we note in the opening pages, the oath of office for the Manitoba Métis Federation requires executive members to swear their loyalty and faithfulness to the Métis people, to promise to uphold and defend the Constitution of the Federation, and to bring honour to the Métis Nation "in the spirit of Louis Riel."[15]

Contemporary Métis citizens continue to be represented in the governance affairs of the nation through their elected representatives. Representation in Métis governments begins at the community level, with the election of presidents, vice-presidents, treasurers, and secretaries. It is also evident at the provincial level, where Métis citizens within each province elect delegates to represent their regional interests. These regional representatives make up the executive decision-making body of each provincial Métis government. For example, the representative for one of the Manitoba Métis Federation's seven regions, Joan Ledoux, is the minister for education and therefore has the mandate to implement the MMF's education policy on behalf of the Métis citizens in Manitoba. In addition to local and regional representation, contemporary Métis governments also integrate women, youth, and elders into the overall governance framework of the Métis Nation in Canada.

Through deliberation, direct participation, and representation, democracy is exhibited in various aspects of Métis governance. To be sure, democracy is not unique to the Métis nor is it always uniformly applied. Some might disregard assemblies as mere requirements of the legislation under which Métis bodies are incorporated. Yet, in keeping with their historic prominence across the Métis Nation, we observe a continuing and deeply rooted commitment to assemblies at the community level. For example, there was a shared understanding that assemblies must continue to play a legitimizing role under a renewed governance structure during the community consultations that led to the restructuring of Métis governance in Saskatchewan. Support for the maintenance of assemblies was also readily apparent in the workshop discussions at the 2017 Manitoba Métis Federation Government Summit, where delegates emphasized the importance of democracy and accountability in any revamped governance structure.

Critics might also call into question the health of Métis democracy given the low voter turnout in Métis elections and the limited number of citizens who hold membership in provincial governing bodies. In Saskatchewan, for example, approximately five thousand Métis citizens of the approximate fifty thousand self-identified Métis population in the province participated in the 2017 MN-S election.[16] While this gap in participation certainly raises questions about the validity of Métis governments as representative political structures, it more squarely speaks to the challenge of building legitimate Métis governments in the wake of Canada's legacy of colonialism. Throughout this book, we point to the ways in which Métis leaders have sought to grapple with this legacy in advancing their self-government agenda.

Enhancing the legitimacy of Métis governments in the face of this history of colonialism and denial is not a simple task. Nor is it a task Métis leaders can achieve on their own in that the very existence of Métis governments challenges the status quo, which repudiates the sovereignty of the Métis as a distinct Indigenous nation and denies the existence of Métis rights. In Chapter 6, we discuss how recent developments are contributing to changing this status quo and draw attention to the impacts of these developments on the capacity, legitimacy, and effectiveness of Métis governments. In the absence of such changes, Métis leaders emphasize the importance of authority derived from the people while acknowledging the need to further strengthen electoral processes and enhance citizen engagement. In fact, these issues – how to further improve the electoral system and encourage more Métis to apply for citizenship and participate in elections, among others – constitute ongoing points of discussion at general assemblies across the Métis Nation.

For the Métis, the selection of leaders through a combination of deliberative, direct, and representative democratic processes enhances the political legitimacy of their governance practices. To observers like Ross (1957, 252), the Métis were too democratic: "they are all republicans in principle, and a licentious freedom is their besetting sin." Yet, for the Métis, each of these processes serves to ensure the legitimacy of what they refer to as *ka niikaaniichik* (those who lead us). Just as in the nineteenth century when Métis families (via heads of households) consented to participate in the hunt through public assemblies, and agreed to submit to the authority of the chief and council through elections, so contemporary Métis citizens approve the activities and programs of their governments through assemblies and ballot-box elections. While they remain imperfect and mired in the complex legacy of colonialism, democratic practices remain key tenets of Métis governance. Taken together, deliberative, direct, and representative democratic mechanisms contribute to the legitimacy of Métis governments by fostering a balance of power among the various components of Métis society. This is a key component of the fourth governance principle – the rule of law.

The Rule of Law: *Lii Lway di Michif* | Métis Law

In his address to the court at the time of his sentencing in 1885, Riel referenced the need for clear rules as a means of protecting freedom. He challenged the "irresponsible" nature of the Canadian government for its failure to represent the Métis of the Northwest (see Authers 2014). This choice of words was perhaps a play on the principle of responsible government embedded within the Westminster parliamentary tradition, which had failed the Métis. Riel argued that, by reneging on the commitments of the Manitoba Act, Canada did not honour the people's rights, despite the constitutional agreement to do so. As he declared, "I struggled not only for myself but I struggled for the rights, for the inauguration of the principles of responsible and constitutional government in Manitoba" (in Stanley et al. 1985, 554). Riel's words evoke the importance of acting not only out of self-interest but also for the good of the collective. Just as the laws surrounding the buffalo hunt were designed to protect the individual and communal dimensions of freedom, so the pursuit of rights was intended to secure the individual and collective freedom of the people of the Northwest. To achieve this goal, Riel, like other Métis leaders, was deeply committed to the rule of law (see Groarke 2014).

For the Métis, *lii lway di Michif* (Métis laws) are an expression of *ka ishi pimaatishiyaahk* (our way of life). As Métis elder Auguste Vermette recounts, the Laws of the Prairie were not written, but they were always practised during the buffalo hunt (in Ferland 2006, 119). They were not only intended to manage the hunt but also to protect the interests of the community as a whole. "[The laws] were the custom. They gave to each equal opportunity," explains Vermette (ibid., our translation). The protection of the collective good is evident in the Laws of the Hunt of 1840, which, in addition to regulating the manner in which the hunt was to take place, addressed social issues such as the consumption of alcohol and religious observance as well as the security of the camp (Ross 1957, 249; Weekes 1939, 51). *Lii lway di Michif* governed how the Métis lived together in the pursuit of common ends.

These laws are an expression of Métis constitutionalism insofar as they outline a comprehensive system of rules, processes, and institutions by which the Métis agree to live together. In his examination of early law and social control among the Métis, Barkwell (1991) traces the array of legal mechanisms used by the Métis to situate their actions within the rule of law, incorporating not only the laws passed by the provisional governments and councils in Manitoba and Saskatchewan but also the petitions, treaties, and resolutions that the Métis regularly engaged in as part of their political activities. These mechanisms confirm that the Métis recognized the need for an equitable system of justice through which self-determination could be achieved; as such, they were "developed by the people, operated by the people, and were by all accounts successful in maintaining social order and essentially harmonious social relations" (Corrigan 1991a, iv).

The Métis do not view laws in utilitarian terms as prescriptions intended to organize or coerce behaviour. Rather, as Barsh (1986) observes, Indigenous conceptions of law are best understood within a framework that privileges the moral equality of all beings, whereby each individual has a unique but complementary role. This role is given to them through creation and thus cannot be imposed on them by individuals or institutions since "each man alone is responsible for his own conduct" (Radin in Barsh 1986, 184). Political leaders interviewed for this project spoke of their connection to others and a responsibility for their welfare as persuasive societal forces. This understanding of collective accountability and responsibility underpins *lii lway di Michif* – the laws that were developed during the buffalo hunts, that guided the governance processes in the Red River and Saskatchewan settlements, and that persist to the present day.

The commitment of the Métis to *ka ishi pimaatishiyaahk* (our way of life) has also encouraged a flexible and adaptable approach to law as necessitated by evolving contexts. Larry Chartrand (2008, 151) traces the formalization of Métis governance processes through written laws and clear enforcement mechanisms in response to the threat posed by Canada's incursion onto Métis lands. Riel, for instance, urged the Convention of Forty to transform itself into a provisional government to give it more official standing during negotiations with Ottawa (Sprague 1988, 48). Throughout history, the Métis have developed various political structures to apply these laws, whether it be in the form of the buffalo hunt assemblies, councils, or provisional governments. Although these political structures and the ways in which the Métis developed and codified law evolved, their purpose – to enable *ka ishi pimaatishiyaahk* – has remained consistent.

Contemporary Métis leaders continue to demonstrate a commitment to constitutionalism and the rule of law. As Val Napoleon argues, Indigenous laws are not static but are adapted to new contexts and circumstances.[17] Métis laws have evolved to more effectively contribute to governance. Today, each Métis government is guided by a constitution or bylaws that express collective aspirations, responsibilities of elected leaders, and rules of conduct (Dubois 2015). The Métis have prioritized certain areas of law, notably harvesting and conservation, and have adopted policies and legislation to govern these sectors in concordance with their way of life. For example, Métis citizens in Manitoba can now apply for harvester cards and hunt according to the rules outlined in the Manitoba Métis Federation's harvesting laws (Saunders 2011). These Métis-made laws were formally recognized by the Province of Manitoba as a result of the Métis Harvesting Agreement negotiated in 2012. The Manitoba Métis Federation's harvesting laws reflect similar undertakings by Métis governments in Saskatchewan (the Métis Wildlife and Conservation Act, adopted by the Métis Nation-Saskatchewan Legislative Assembly in 1994) and Ontario (the Métis Nation of Ontario Harvesting Policy, first passed in 2004 and recognized by the Ontario government in the Interim Harvesting Agreement).

To ensure the equitable application of laws, the Métis have traditionally established checks and balances on the exercise of power. This occurred during the buffalo hunts as leadership positions – including those of guides, soldiers, guards, and sentries – rotated between groups of individuals as well as in the settlements, where elected officials sought periodic re-election by the people (Ross 1957, 248). With the dissolution of hunt councils, the Métis continued to apply the practices of these provisional governments and the principles they embodied in their everyday lives. In Riel's (1982, 204) words, "the Laws of the Prairie followed the Métis as the rules in mines follow the miners in their work."

This practice continued in Red River, where the provisional government included the separation of powers between legislative, administrative, executive, and judicial bodies – each of which had built-in checks and balances. In his final memoir, Riel (1982, 204) explains that the provisional government was formed for the "general good" – no one could derive individual benefit from it. Hall et al. describe how the provisional government was designed to be a responsible, representative entity made up of an elected cabinet and legislative council as well as appointed administrative and judicial structures – each of which included French and English representatives.[18] In contemporary Métis governments, power continues to be divided along executive, legislative, and judicial lines. In a general sense, Métis citizens take part in legislative affairs, for example by deciding what laws to adopt, which are then carried out by a provincially elected executive body and overseen by a council of elders selected from each region. These actors exercise their responsibilities according to the rules laid out in the constitution/bylaws of their respective governments.

While the Métis are committed to the rule of law, it is worth noting that this commitment only extends to those laws that they see as legitimate – that is to say, laws that were democratically agreed upon by their own people. For the Métis, the commitments that flow from democratic processes are binding on *ka niikaaniichik* (those who lead us). In his final memoirs, Riel deplores the Canadian government's failure to respect the rights that were promised to the Métis through the Manitoba Act. In taking up arms against Canada, Riel was expressing his refusal to submit to the laws of the Canadian state, which contradicted what had been agreed to by both parties. He asks: "What people, in their place, would not have done the same?" (Riel 1982, 209). As Blair Stonechild explains, Riel – like other Indigenous leaders – is "responding to a larger sense of injustice, one which exists at the level of the state" (in Kostash 2009, 196). For the Métis, *lii lway di Michif* (the laws of the Métis) are grounded in democracy and are directed towards the fulfillment of freedom and respect for kinship relations.

Provisionality: *Aen Ishi Wiichayaamitooyahk* | How We Live Together

The Métis have demonstrated their willingness to take whatever actions necessary to protect *ka ishi pimaatishiyaahk* (our way of life). Yet, as Riel (1982, 209) notes, "The Government [of Canada] neither protected [the Métis] nor gave them justice. It oppressed them." To redress this injustice, the Métis mobilized politically and developed formal governance structures. Governance contributes to what the Métis refer to as *aen ishi wiichayyaamitooyahk* (how we live together). Throughout history, the Métis have adopted different tactics (petitions, demonstrations, armed resistance, litigation) and put in place mechanisms (buffalo hunt councils, provisional governments, and contemporary governments) to secure their way of life as a distinct Indigenous people. Métis lawyer Jason Madden argues that the constant push for self-government through political action is a part of who the Métis are as a people: "We know that it's all of these things, whether it be the buffalo hunts, the Battle of Seven Oaks, the provisional governments, the MMF – all of those are elements of our Métis self-government."[19] From the historic buffalo hunts to the present day, the goal has remained the same: Métis self-government.

In pursuit of this goal, the Métis have had to navigate relationships with the Canadian state as well as with other Indigenous nations. Zoe Todd (2016) adds that reciprocal relationships with "more-than-human-beings," such as fish and the buffalo, also contributed to shape Métis governance. She examiness the ways in which the Métis negotiated governance through land-based relationships as well as relationships with First Nations as they moved within and across territories.

In reflecting on the wide variation of strategies and structures that have been adopted by the Métis in their pursuit of self-government, scholars like Sealy and Lussier have pointed to the provisionality of Métis political mobilization. For example, they write that

> Métis efforts to organize themselves had historically centered around a crisis and, when this had passed, the organization dissolved. In 1815–16, they organized under Cuthbert Grant to keep the pemmican trade open to all. In 1849, the focus was the Sayer trial and the attempt to free the fur trade from monopoly of the Hudson's Bay Company. They rallied again in 1869–70 in order to secure traditional land rights, while the last stand of Métis people to preserve their lands took place in 1885. In each instance the organizational model used was comparable to that developed for the buffalo hunt and, when the particular incident had passed, the organization disbanded as had the buffalo hunters. (Sealy and Lussier 1975, 163–64)

Similarly, Bumsted (1996, 84; 2003, 205) argues that the Provisional Government of Assiniboia was intended to be provisional so as to strengthen the residents of Red River's hand in their dealings with Canada.

While scholars aptly draw attention to the temporal character of Métis political organization, we argue that provisionality must be understood within the larger objective of self-determination as well as within the struggle to secure rights to land and to self-government on which this depends. For the Métis, provisionality is not a function of time but of purpose. The ultimate purpose of the Métis Nation is self-determination. It involves contending with the political realities to protect *aen ishi wiichayaamitooyahk* (how we live together).

The fact that governance for the Métis is directed towards maintaining their unique culture and traditions in changing circumstances explains why the power invested in leaders must be continuously renewed by the people through elections, assemblies, and other mechanisms. Democracy and the rule of law are not ends in themselves but, instead, contribute to the pursuit of *ka ishi pimaatishiyaahk* (our distinct way of life).[20] While political tactics, governance practices, and structures change according to the circumstances and resources at hand, they are linked to one another across time and space through the commitment to maintain *aen ishi wiichayaamitooyahk* (how we live together) as well as the enduring principles of freedom, kinship, democracy, and the rule of law. Thus, it is not the actual forms of political action that ultimately matter but, rather, the ways in which they support and augment the overarching desire of the Métis to remain a free and self-determining people.

The creation of provisional governments is one among many tools the Métis have used in their pursuit of self-government. Other tools include informal governance strategies such as the fostering of diplomatic relations and alliances. Such practices are illustrated in the gift exchange with the Sioux chief Terre qui brûle to amicably settle a military dispute as well as in the alliances developed with Plains Cree, Saulteaux, and Assiniboine as part of the *Nehiyaw Pwat* (Ross 1957, 265–66; Vrooman 2012, 8; Innes 2013, 59–62). Just as Métis leaders brokered agreements with First Nations, they sought to negotiate with provincial and federal governments to ensure the ongoing protection of their way of life. This was most notably evident in the negotiation of the Manitoba Act, but it can also be seen in subsequent attempts by Métis leaders to work with provincial and federal governments to achieve their goals (Barron 1997; Pitsula 1997; Quiring 2004; Dubois and Saunders 2017a).

The Métis have developed more permanent and representative political bodies to more effectively engage with state and non-state actors in a contemporary context (Dubois 2015). The increasingly formal institutionalization of Métis governance practices through these structures has led to practical and philosophical debates about how best to achieve collective objectives – how to live together (*aen ishi wiichayaamitooyahk*) – through the mechanisms of governance. This debate reached new heights in the context of Canada's constitutional crisis in the 1980s. One of the key participants in this conversation, Jim Sinclair, highlighted the difficulty of reconciling the desire to create formal, permanent, and visible political bodies that would garner legitimacy in the eyes of Métis citizens and the state with the recognition that these structures would need to evolve alongside the larger political context.[21] It is within this context that Métis leaders questioned whether power should be centralized within a national federated governance body or decentralized to Métis governments – a question that remains a point of contention in Métis political circles.[22]

Ongoing debates about the form and structure of Métis governance are nothing new; rather, they represent the contemporary manifestation of recurring efforts to address the question of how best to use the instruments at hand to protect their way of life. For the Métis, governance is one of the key ways to collectively maintain *ka ishi pimaatishiyaahk*. As described in Michif by Métis elder Norman Fleury, governance embodies the way the Métis think and live together as a nation – *aen ishi mamoonakatwayhtamaahk, aen ishi wiichayaamitooyahk* (personal communication, July 20, 2016). Whatever the path taken, the governance mechanisms and political structures put in place to achieve Riel's vision in the past and present are directed towards the continued existence of a free and self-determining Métis Nation.

Conclusion

From the buffalo hunt to the present day, the Métis have developed a distinct approach to governance. While the form of governance has changed, the practices that were first adopted in the early days of political organization continue to resonate in the structures that govern the Métis Nation. Contemporary political structures, like those that preceded them, are informed by principles of freedom, kinship, democracy, the rule of law, and provisionality. Together, these principles aim to protect what the Métis refer to as *ka ishi pimaatishiyaahk* (our way of life). In so doing, they contribute to the Métis' ongoing pursuit of self-determination.

Rooted in a distinctly Métis history, the governance practices that evolved from the hunt also reveal influences inherited from their Indigenous and European ancestors as well as from their American neighbours. Hall et al. describe how the proposals put forward to create a provisional government in Red River reflected the principles of responsible and representative government and also incorporated features of republican-style democracy with provisions to protect security, property, and freedom from oppression.[23] In a similar vein, Woodcock (2003, 11) describes the St. Laurent Council as a reminder of Riel's Provisional Government in Red River, with its "echoes of French and American revolutionary constitution making." In an effort to identify the origins of these influences, O'Byrne (2014) and O'Toole (2010) point to evidence of republicanism in Riel's political thought, while Barkwell and Goodon note the Scottish influences on Métis kinship practices.[24]

Principles such as freedom, kinship, and democracy have various ideological origins and are not unique to the Métis. Our objective in this chapter is not to deny the presence of these principles in other cultural practices, nor is it to trace the origins of each of these principles. Instead, it is to show how they interact with one another to give life to a distinctly Métis way of governing. At the same time, as Métis leaders reminded us, these principles are not absolute – they do not live independently of one another but instead bring to life a unique way of governing. Although some of the structures and practices have evolved in the face of changing circumstances and the realities of colonialism, we argue that the underlying principles of Métis governance have remained consistent. Then, as now, Métis approaches to governance are reflected in the principles of freedom, kinship, democracy, the rule of law, and provisionality, which together inform *ka ishi pimaatishiyaahk*.

3

Lii Goovarnimaan di Michif
Métis Governments

THE MÉTIS IN CANADA have long identified as a self-governing nation. They are *ka tipemishoshik* (the free people). Historically, the Métis not only organized and managed the internal affairs of their communities but also engaged in political action to protect what they refer to as *ka ishi pimaatishiyaahk* (our way of life). From the Laws of the Prairie to the provisional governments of Louis Riel and Gabriel Dumont that dotted the landscape of the Northwest, Samuel Corrigan (1991b, 197) notes that "there is a lengthy history of Métis organization and representation ... of organized Métis objecting successfully to externally-imposed restrictions upon their freedom." With the continuing encroachment on Indigenous lands by settlers, the Métis turned to political organization as a means of protecting their right to govern themselves, to hunt and trade freely, and to practise their distinctive culture. The quest for self-determination through political action has been a constant thread in Métis history.

The evolution and practice of Métis governance has occurred within the larger legislative and political context of the Canadian federation. As an Indigenous minority within Canada, the Métis have had to navigate their ongoing existence within the constraints imposed by the colonial state. The complex history of Canada-Métis relations has not only limited the ability of the Métis to achieve self-government but also, through state-imposed laws, policies, and discourse, has influenced the evolution of Métis governance bodies and processes (Sawchuk 1992, 1998, 2000).

At the same time, Métis leaders have found creative ways to "deal with the reality" of this colonial state context in a manner that reflects Métis history, culture, and principles of governance.[1] By charting their own path to self-government, Métis citizens have developed what Audra Simpson (2014) describes as a "nested" political order within the confines of state sovereignty.

Today, Métis citizens from Ontario westward are politically represented by five Métis governments: the Métis Nation of Ontario (MNO), the Manitoba Métis Federation (MMF), the Métis Nation-Saskatchewan (MN-S), the Métis Nation of Alberta (MNA), and the Métis Nation British Columbia (MNBC), which, in turn, are represented by a national body, the Métis National Council (MNC). The MNC describes the governance structures that it represents as "the contemporary expression of the centuries-old struggle of the Métis Nation to be self-determining within the Canadian federation."[2] Surrounded by the presidents of each Governing Member at the 2017 Crown-Métis Summit in Ottawa, Métis Nation president Clément Chartier explained: "The governments we lead are successors to Métis nationalist movements and governments that go back more than two centuries."[3] Described by one elder, the political structures that make up the MNC are all part of the Métis Nation's collective government – "our government, *nootr goovarnimaan*" (personal communication with Métis elder, July 20, 2016).

While they are recognized by state governments, the courts, and private actors as the political voice of the Métis Nation, the legitimacy of these governments as the political representatives of all Métis citizens has been called into question in some quarters. Critics of contemporary Métis governments aptly note that participation within these entities remains limited. This is evidenced by the fact that the self-identified Métis population is significantly higher than the registered population in each province. For example, the self-identified Métis population in British Columbia according to the last census was almost ninety thousand, 16,500 of which are provincially registered Métis citizens with the MNBC.[4] This gap is not all that surprising given the invisibility of the Métis since the early twentieth century and the confusion created by legal and administrative categories that fragmented Indigenous peoples in Canada.[5] Many of the issues related to Métis self-identification are tied to the historic unwillingness of federal and provincial governments to fully engage with the Métis as a distinct Indigenous nation, and to the purposeful misrecognition of the Métis as a hybrid offshoot of two races – "Indian" and "white" (P. Chartrand 2008; Chartrand and Giokas 2002; Andersen 2014, 6).

As "ordinary citizens with no special privileges" under Canadian law since Confederation, the Métis have long been marginalized from education, welfare, and social services provided by the state (Ens and Sawchuk 2016, 190). State racialization and denial, coupled with the lack of a recognized Métis land base outside of the Alberta Settlements, left Métis governments to rely upon their citizens to self-identify with the Métis Nation. Some Métis are unaware of their own heritage and the services that are offered by Métis governments. Others continue to see state governments as their primary representatives. Competition for the role of political representation means that Métis governments like the Manitoba Métis Federation "must at all times work to remain the government of choice for Métis in Manitoba."[6] MMF president David Chartrand has repeatedly spoken of the need to educate Métis citizens in Manitoba about the MMF, so that they turn first to their Métis government for the promotion of their interests rather than to provincial or federal governments. As they endeavour to enhance the legitimacy of their governments, Métis leaders like MNBC president Clara Morin Dal Col view their role as representing the well-being of all Métis people: "Our Métis people in this province – all [the self-identified population] are depending on us to look after their interests."[7]

In this chapter, we focus on the five Métis governments that represent Métis citizens from Ontario westward. Rooted in the early forms of Métis political organization that existed in the Historic Northwest, these governments have taken on the mandate to fulfill Riel's vision of a self-governing Métis Nation in Canada. Scholarship conducted by the Harvard Project has shown that self-government is most successful when Indigenous peoples exercise agency over their governance institutions (e.g., Cornell and Kalt 2007). Despite the ongoing challenges the Métis face in legitimizing their governance institutions, contemporary Métis governments are becoming increasingly recognized as partners in the Canadian federation. Yet little is known about their governance structures and processes. How are Métis governments organized? What are their political objectives? How do they interact with Métis citizens, the private sector, and with provincial and federal state actors? How are women, youth, and elders integrated into decision making? We explore these and related questions to better understand Métis governments as they become increasingly visible actors on the Canadian political scene.

Governing from the Grassroots

The Métis see themselves as united under *nootr goovarnimaan* (our government). At the same time, governance within the Métis Nation is designed along provincial lines. Métis Nation president Clément Chartier explains that the decision to adopt provincial governing structures reflects the political reality that Métis leaders had to contend with when these bodies were created.[8] Invisible in the eyes of the federal government, the Métis turned to provincial governments in the 1920s and 1930s to improve the social and economic situation of their people. Contemporary Métis governance began to take shape as leaders organized to draw attention to the plight of their communities.

The various political organizations and entities that emerged out of these mobilization efforts are both a product of the particular circumstances within which they were formed and a reflection of Métis traditions and history. As the MMF notes in its 2013–18 Strategic Plan, "the events of the Métis in Manitoba and the way by which they responded to those events give meaning to why the MMF exists, does the things it does and how it carries out its activities."[9] Since Confederation, the Métis have had to find creative ways to give meaning to their governance structures in a political context they did not fully control, reinforcing some traditions while strategically adopting others to advance their collective objectives. While there are differences in terms of how the Métis navigated this reality and structured their governing bodies, Métis governments all share the same commitment to the principles of governance first established during the buffalo hunts and the overriding goal of a self-governing Métis Nation.

Métis governments operate at local, regional, and provincial levels and are also represented nationally through the Métis National Council. Al Benoit, chief of staff to MMF president David Chartrand, describes the relationship between the three levels of Métis government (locals, regions, and provincial council) as akin to a Matrushka doll. Like this famous nesting doll, "the locals are the foundation for what's built around it, and like the dolls they fill the inside and make it solid. The locals help fill out the MMF and provide the foundation of the MMF."[10] Benoit's metaphor aptly describes how the three levels of government interact not only in Manitoba but across the Métis Nation.

To understand contemporary Métis governments, we must begin at the grassroots, where Métis citizens participate in the affairs of their government through community-level associations. As Figure 3.1 illustrates, the organization of Métis governments flows from the bottom up. Referred to as "chartered communities" in British Columbia, "locals" in Alberta, Saskatchewan, and Manitoba, and "chartered community councils" in Ontario, community-level associations are at the heart of Métis governance (Dubois 2013; Saunders 2013; Sawchuk 1998). The model of locals is not specific to the Métis; rather, it is borrowed from the labour movement. Using the tools available to them at the time, Métis leaders in the 1930s chose this model to build support for Métis organizations at the grassroots, reflecting the importance of democracy as a tradition of Métis governance (see also Dobbin 1981).

Every member of a Métis government belongs to a local association. Most of these associations are incorporated separately and are governed by a board elected by the members of that local – generally a president/chair, vice-president/chair, and secretary-treasurer. Local associations send their elected president or chair to regional meetings that are typically held each year as well as to the provincewide annual assemblies.[11] While the number varies within each jurisdiction, the roughly four hundred community-level associations that exist across the Métis Nation serve as the first point of contact for Métis citizens.[12]

With significant variation in size and capacity, local associations tend to focus on organizing cultural events within their communities (e.g., Métis days celebrations) and the delivery of programs and services

FIGURE 3.1 **Overview of the structure of Métis governments**

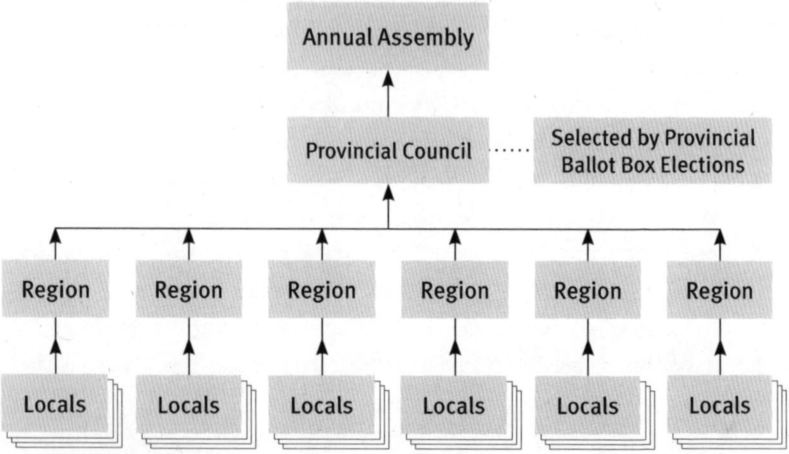

Source: Adapted from Jason Madden, John Graham, and Jake Wilson, "Exploring Options for Métis Governance in the 21st Century" (Ottawa, Institute on Governance, September 2005, 17), http://www.metisportals.ca/cons/wp-content/uploads/2009/02/metis-governance-in-the-21-century.pdf.

(e.g., Michif language courses, genealogy workshops, harvesting rights information sessions, and so forth). As Gerard Ens and Joe Sawchuk (2016, 374) note, locals have played a key role in ensuring the survival of Métis communities by fostering cultural identity while remaining under the radar of the Canadian state.

Although locals are foundational to Métis governance, the degree to which they participate in the governance affairs of the Métis Nation is variable. As Métis governance structures became increasingly formalized in the second half of the twentieth century, the role of locals in the echelons of decision making has come under debate. Some local leaders express feeling disconnected from their government and excluded from decision making.[13] Others advocate for more communication between provincial and local leaders and greater support from provincial leaders to enhance the resources and capacity of locals to engage in Métis politics.

While there is a consensus that locals are an important avenue for direct democracy, their representative role differs across Métis governments. In British Columbia and Ontario, where there are fewer locals, local representatives interact more directly with provincial leaders. This is in part by design – for example, locals in Ontario and British Columbia are incorporated under the MNO and the MNBC, respectively, whereas they are incorporated separately as their own entities in Manitoba, Saskatchewan, and Alberta.[14] It is also in part a function of political practice: MNO and MNBC provincial leaders work more closely with locals than do provincial leaders in the Prairie provinces who tend to collaborate more directly with regional leaders. Testifying to the discontent of some grassroots members, a spirited discussion took place at the 2017 MMF annual assembly on a motion to impose term limits for regional positions. The motion was primarily supported by local leaders who see limited opportunities to have their voices heard and to participate in executive-level decision-making processes.[15]

Locals are grouped into regions. The number of regions varies by province: 7 in British Columbia, 6 in Alberta, 12 in Saskatchewan, 7 in Manitoba, and 9 in Ontario. Each region is governed by some type of regional council, typically consisting of an elected president and vice-president and/or regional directors. In some provinces, such as Saskatchewan and Alberta, the presidents of the community-level associations, or locals, also sit on their respective regional councils. Each region maintains an office responsible for delivering programs and services to the citizens of that region, reviewing membership applications, and representing their local associations at the executive level (Saunders 2013, 359).

Regional leaders play a representative role within Métis governments. As regional officials have come to play a more direct role in Métis politics, some Métis citizens have expressed concerns that this enhanced power has not been accompanied by mechanisms of accountability. Proposals have been made to create deliberative spaces at the regional level to ensure fairness and transparency.[16] Regional officials have also come under greater scrutiny as they are tasked with delivering a greater number of programs and services, often with limited capacity. Undertaking these responsibilities is made more difficult as regional leaders are often called upon to participate in provincial-level consultations and meetings as well as by the fact that they are geographically dispersed and do not necessarily reside in the community where staff administer services. Since regional leaders do not receive remuneration as full-time employees, many are forced to juggle these responsibilities alongside other, paid employment. Although the political voice and responsibilities of regional leaders differs across the Homeland, regions have had to grapple with growing pains as they take on greater representative and deliberative roles within the democratic structure of Métis governments.

Above the regions, and constituting the next level of government, are provincial councils. Provincial councils are comprised of the provincial leadership (president, vice-president[s], and treasurer/secretary who are elected provincewide by all members), regional representatives, as well as representatives of youth and women. While the names of these Provincial Councils vary – in Manitoba and British Columbia, they are referred to as the Board of Directors; in Saskatchewan, the Provincial Métis Council; in Alberta, the Provincial Council; and in Ontario, the Provisional Council – they essentially serve the same purpose. It is within Provincial Councils that most executive decisions are made.[17] Operating as a type of cabinet, those elected to Provincial Councils are assigned responsibility for a ministry by the provincial president. In Manitoba, for example, the twenty-three-member Board of Directors contains ministers responsible for portfolios that include natural resources and agriculture, health and wellness, energy and infrastructure, Michif languages, employment and training, land claims, and tripartite self-government negotiations. While the name and scope of departments vary across governments, they generally involve such policy sectors as health, education, lands and resources, economic development, families, citizenship, culture, and Métis rights.

In contrast with local and regional representatives, who are elected by the citizens that reside in a given area, key leadership positions – including the provincial president, vice-president(s), and secretary/treasurer – are directly elected by the provincial membership. Elections within the Métis Nation are held every four years, with the rules governing the electoral process – in terms of who can vote and stand for office, the appointment of a chief electoral officer, dispute resolution mechanisms, and so forth – outlined in the constitution, bylaws, or legislation of each Métis government. To vote in an election, Métis citizens must be enrolled on the citizenship registry of their respective government. Voting procedures vary across provinces as some Métis governments have sought to modernize their electoral systems. In some jurisdictions, members vote in advance polls or attend a polling station set up across the regions on election day. To accommodate individuals living in remote areas, some Métis governments provide mail-in ballots and set up mobile polls. In other jurisdictions, voting is conducted electronically.

Despite provisions made to decrease barriers to voting, electoral turnout remains low across the Homeland. Close to five thousand Métis citizens cast their ballots in the 2017 MN-S election, a fraction of the almost fifty-eight thousand individuals who self-identify as Métis in Saskatchewan.[18] Some Métis governments have struggled to find candidates to run for office, leaving positions vacant for significant periods. In some cases, the low number of candidates leads some representatives to be acclaimed. In other cases, electoral races can be tight. For example, during the 2011 elections in Alberta, the provincial vice-president was elected by fewer than forty votes over the second-place candidate. Despite variations across Métis governments, leaders often emphasize that their legitimacy as representatives lies in their direct election by Métis citizens.

In addition to the direct election of their leaders, Métis governments are also noteworthy for the degree to which youth and women are represented.[19] The MNO, for example, has a youth council comprised of representatives elected in each of the province's nine regions, in addition to a youth representative (along with a postsecondary representative) on its Provisional Council.[20] These representatives, elected by Métis youth in Ontario aged sixteen to twenty-nine, play an active role in various MNO events and activities. Youth delegates were included as part of the MNO delegation (along with the MNBC delegation) to the 2016 General Assembly of the Métis National Council, where they successfully moved a resolution on the development of a national youth position paper. The purpose of the paper is to explore ways to "better integrate youth leadership across our Métis Governments," including the reactivation of the now defunct Métis National Youth Advisory Council.[21] As active political leaders in their communities, youth representatives like Mitchell Case have worked to make youth a priority for the Métis leadership. Case explains: "my strategy when I was elected was not only to contribute to 'youth' issues, but to the MNO as a whole."[22] This strategy has allowed youth representatives in Ontario to build relationships with the leadership and thus be in a better position to advance youth interests more broadly.

Métis women's organizations also exist in each of the five provinces that comprise the Métis Nation Homeland, and are similarly integrated into Métis governments.[23] A national organization, Les Femmes Michif Otipemisiwak, or Women of the Métis Nation, represents Métis women across the Homeland and works alongside the national president and Governing Members on a variety of issues affecting Métis women and children. While there have been national Métis women's organizations in Canada dating back to the 1980s, Women of the Métis Nation has held official status within the MNC since the Board of Governors passed a resolution enabling women "to take an active role within Métis Nation governance ... [and to] promote leadership by Métis women at the local, provincial, national and international levels."[24] The president of Women of the Métis Nation routinely participates in MNC Board of Governors meetings, Métis rights panel sessions, and general assemblies. Women of the Métis Nation is also engaged in intergovernmental fora on issues of relevance to Métis women. Recent examples include the Aboriginal affairs working groups on justice, economic development, and ending violence against Aboriginal women and girls.

Elders generally play advisory or judicial roles in Métis governments. The method of selection and role of elders varies across Governing Members. Within the MNO, four elected elders – referred to as "senators" – sit on the Provisional Council, where they share their knowledge, experience, and values with other elected officials. MNBC has a senate comprised of elders appointed in each of the regions that serves as its judicial arm. Their responsibilities include participation in ceremonial activities, dispute resolution, and mediation at the provincial, regional, and community levels, and appeals arising through the elections process.[25] In the case of the Manitoba Métis Federation, elders are incorporated through more informal mechanisms; for example, they are routinely invited to participate in assemblies, meetings, and other important events where they lead in prayer, oversee proceedings, and serve as a resource on Métis history, culture, and traditions.[26]

At the apex of contemporary Métis governance are the annual assemblies that occur across the Homeland. These assemblies are open to all citizens and reflect the Métis tradition of direct democracy. As such, they serve as an important means by which elected officials are held accountable to their citizens. Assemblies provide an opportunity for members to ask questions directly of their regional and provincial leaders and to bring forward their own resolutions for consideration. All legislation, bylaw, and constitutional amendments; financial and accounting statements; and significant policy decisions must be brought before the people gathered in assembly for discussion and approval through a consensus vote. Elected officials are expected to respect the "will of the people" in undertaking their responsibilities. However, as the example of the motion on term limits from the MMF annual assembly attests, the extent to which this actually occurs will depend on the question at hand and how willing, or not, leaders are to embrace the issue.

In many ways, contemporary Métis governments are the product of an ongoing negotiation with internal and external forces. As the conditions facing Indigenous nations have changed, Stephen Cornell (2007, 59) argues that so too have the tools available to address those conditions. Scholars have shown how Indigenous nations have actively resisted colonial rule by empowering their own leaders (Alfred 2005) and practising their own traditions and legal orders (Corntassel 2014; Borrows 2010). By relying on their own traditions and practices, the Métis have developed a "nested" political order within the confines of state sovereignty (Simpson 2014). While the Métis have found creative ways to exercise agency over their political structures, they have nevertheless had to contend with the realities of the colonial state context within which they operate.

Delivering Services and Programs

One of the key roles of Métis governments is to deliver programs and services. This is accomplished in partnership with a number of affiliates that range from economic development agencies such as Apeetogosan (Métis) Development Incorporated in Alberta, postsecondary educational institutions like the Gabriel Dumont Institute in Saskatchewan, and service-delivery organizations such as Métis Child and Family Services in Manitoba. The relationship between Métis governments and their various affiliated institutions is complex. This complexity is in large part a consequence of the not-for-profit legislation under which most Métis governments are incorporated and that prohibits them from being directly involved in some of the activities carried out by affiliates. For example, the MNA is incorporated under the Alberta Societies Act and therefore cannot pursue for-profit activities. To foster economic development, the MNA therefore works with Apeetogosan (Métis) Development Inc., which is incorporated independently as a business and, as such, can participate in profit-seeking activities. While Apeetogosan was created as an initiative of the MNA in 1984 and has a seat reserved for the MNA on its Board of Directors, it legally reports to the Government of Alberta and not to the Métis citizens in the province. Affiliates have the mandate to serve Métis people in their respective sectors but ultimately report to the provincial/federal governments under which they are incorporated.

In so far as affiliates function as distinct entities, they are a step removed from Métis governments. This allows affiliates to conduct their affairs without direct political interference, but it also undermines decision making and accountability across the various organizations and governments.[27] Unlike non-Indigenous service delivery organizations, which are created to carry out mandates determined by provincial and federal governments, Métis service delivery organizations have the mandate to serve Métis citizens but remain accountable to provincial/federal governments. Cognizant of the limitations imposed by their statutory requirements, affiliates and governance bodies have looked for creative ways to integrate each other into their decision-making processes.[28] For example, the bylaws of the Gabriel Dumont Institute stipulate that the MN-S minister of education sit as the chair of its Board of Governors, while the Métis Capital Housing Corporation, an affiliate that provides affordable quality homes to Alberta's Métis, has representatives from each region of the MNA on its Board of Directors.[29] Similarly, the governing board of the Louis Riel Institute, the cultural and educational authority of the Manitoba Métis Federation, is chaired by the MMF minister of education.[30] Such initiatives, which are evident across the Métis Nation, aim to promote the accountability of affiliates towards Métis citizens.

Advancing the Métis Nation's Political Agenda

The Métis National Council, which was established in 1983, is responsible for advancing the collective goals of the Métis Nation. Incorporated under the Canada Corporations Act, the MNC Secretariat Inc. is governed by a board of governors composed of the national president and the presidents of the five Governing Members. The national president is elected every three years by the MNC's General Assembly to serve as the common voice of the Métis Nation nationally and internationally. The president appoints ministers from among the Board of Governors who are assigned portfolios, including finance, economic development, health, environment, and Métis rights. The focus of the MNC is not program and service delivery; this is the responsibility of the Governing Members. Instead, the MNC is responsible for achieving consensus among the Governing Members on policy matters related to Métis rights, land claims, and other issues of importance to the Métis Nation as a whole. In addition to Board of Governors meetings, the work of the MNC occurs primarily through the General Assembly, which meets at least once every eighteen months. As outlined in the MNC Secretariat Inc. bylaws, the General Assembly is composed of fifty-five delegates; fifteen from each of the three Governing Members that originally founded the MNC (the MMF, the MN-S, and the MNA), and five each from the MNBC and the MNO.

The governance structure of the MNC in part reflects the context in which it emerged in 1983. It is based on a confederal model, with the balance of power largely contained within the three Prairie provinces that decided to break away from the Native Council of Canada to found a Métis-specific representative body in the context of the post-1982 constitutional conferences. Under the leadership of Smokey Bruyere, the Native Council of Canada's Board of Directors refused to allow a Métis representative to take one of the two seats allocated to the council at the First Ministers Conferences on Aboriginal Rights (Belcourt 2013, 131–32). This decision undermined the council's legitimacy in claiming to represent the Métis and triggered the creation of a Métis-specific representative body (ibid.).

As the MNC expanded to include Métis governments in Ontario and British Columbia, decision-making power remained largely concentrated in the hands of Prairie-based Métis governments. This is evidenced in the composition of voting delegates at the MNC General Assembly. In contrast with provincial general assemblies, voting rights at these events are not open to all Métis citizens. Instead, the MMF, the MN-S, and the MNA each has fifteen voting delegates, whereas the MNBC and the MNO each has five voting delegates. These fifty-five delegates vote on a number of matters, including the election of the national president, resolutions brought forward by the Governing Members, financial statements, and other issues of national importance. The composition of the voting delegates at the General Assembly has come under criticism, notably by the MNBC and the MNO, which have repeatedly called for an equal voice at the table.

Concerns have also been expressed about the role of the national president at the General Assembly. The president generally delivers a State of the Nation address to open the assembly and often intervenes in numerous agenda items, but she/he does not have a seat at the table as a delegate or have the right to vote. The president's legitimacy as the democratic national representative of the Métis Nation is also undermined by the fact that, unlike local, regional, and provincial leaders who are directly elected by Métis citizens, the national president of the MNC is elected indirectly by delegates to the General Assembly.

In order to enhance the democratic accountability of the MNC, the General Assembly passed a resolution in 2002 supporting in principle the direct election of the national president by a Homeland-wide ballot. Changes to the election process for the national president constitute one of the items up for debate in continuing discussions on the adoption of a national Métis constitution. For the current national president, a Métis constitution at the national level is a necessary step since it will enable the Métis National Council to engage in a government-to-government relationship with the state and to negotiate self-government on behalf of the Métis Nation.[31]

In a general sense, constitutions serve as political instruments that outline the rules by which political communities agree to make decisions, distribute and exercise authority, and engage with each other and the world around them (Cornell 2015, 2). As President Chartier argues: "As a distinct people and nation, with the right to self-determination, we should be governing ourselves under our own laws drawn from our own constitution rather than the bylaws of non-profit societies."[32] Echoing this argument at the provincial level, MNO president Margaret Froh notes: "Building a constitution brings a nation's citizens together to tell the world who they are, the fundamental rules and principles that guide our government, and how we plan to govern ourselves based on Métis law and traditions."[33]

Constitutions contribute to Métis self-government in two significant ways, from both an internal and an external perspective. First, constitution building represents a type of nation-building exercise that calls upon Métis citizens to reach a political consensus on such foundational questions as citizenship and boundaries of the Métis Nation Homeland. It thus contributes to nation building by providing a vehicle for Métis leaders and citizens to design institutions, rules, and procedures that are consistent with historical Métis governance practices. Second, the development of Métis constitutions helps to position Métis governments to negotiate with provincial and federal state actors. Significantly, the adoption of a constitution is a necessary prerequisite to the successful negotiation of self-government and land rights with the state since Canada requires Indigenous groups to have constitutions prior to concluding self-government agreements (for a discussion, see Dubois and Saunders 2017b).

Despite numerous efforts since 1983 to adopt a national constitution, ongoing debates surrounding citizenship in the Métis Nation, the boundaries of the Historic Métis Nation Homeland, and the relationship between the MNC and its Governing Members (among other sticking points) have made it difficult to move this agenda forward. While there is support across provincial Métis governments for a national constitution, there are concerns that it could vest too much power in a national government to the detriment of Governing Members that deliver programs and services at the community level and that, as a result, are more strongly connected to Métis citizens.

As debates surrounding a national constitution continue to unfold, Governing Members have engaged in their own constitutional development processes. The MN-S was the first to adopt a written constitution in 1993, which provided the groundwork for the establishment of a democratically accountable governance body outside of the confines of provincial legislation (Dubois 2013). The MNBC followed suit in 2003 with the passage of its own constitution. Other Métis governments are in various stages of developing constitutions and reinforcing democratic aspects of their governance structures. As Ontario moves forward on its constitution-building process, President Froh emphasizes the need to remove the MNO from its reliance on corporate structures for recognition and to instead develop a constitution by and for Ontario Métis.[34] While the path taken differs across Governing Members, the goal remains the same: the creation of democratically accountable governments, grounded in Métis laws and principles of governance, which can negotiate on a government-to-government basis to meet the needs of their citizens.[35]

Government-to-Government Relationships

While Métis leaders hope that constitution building will enable them to more effectively achieve self-government, their ability to enter into government-to-government relationships has depended in large part on the willingness of state actors to engage with Métis governing bodies as representative governments (Dubois 2015). While the federal government has historically refused to directly engage in political negotiations with the Métis Nation, a window of opportunity arose in the context of Canada's constitutional crisis (Dubois and Saunders 2017b). As a result of the instrumental lobbying efforts of such Métis leaders as Harry Daniels and Clément Chartier, the Métis gained constitutional recognition as one of Canada's Aboriginal peoples in section 35(2) of the Constitution

Act, 1982. Despite this achievement, Métis demands for rights to land and self-government remained unaddressed by Canada in the years that followed. It was not until the negotiation of the Charlottetown Accord in 1992 that progress was made on this front.

Significantly, attached to the Charlottetown Accord was the Métis Nation Accord, which had been negotiated by federal and Métis officials (Weinstein 2007). The proposed Métis Nation Accord would have addressed the constitutional place of the Métis Nation within the Canadian federation for the first time since 1870. It committed Canada and the provinces to enter into negotiations with the Métis Nation on self-government and land, and it provided a framework for the transition of Métis advocacy organizations into representative governments. However, the defeat of the Charlottetown Accord – and by extension the Métis Nation Accord – in a national referendum in 1992 left the question of the Métis' place within Canada's political framework unaddressed.

The Métis remained at the margins of federal political circles until the mid-2000s, when Canada and the Métis Nation signed the Métis Nation Framework Agreement. This agreement, which was negotiated in the context of the Kelowna Accord,[36] laid the foundation for a partnership between the Métis Nation and Canada based on mutual respect, responsibility, and sharing. These principles were further formalized in the 2008 Canada-Métis Nation Protocol, which established a bilateral process to address jurisdictional issues, including land and harvesting rights as well as economic development. Moreover, the Protocol committed the federal government to enter into multilateral discussions with the provinces and the Métis Nation on matters of joint interest such as health and justice. These developments led federal, provincial, and Métis bureaucrats to begin to work together to develop programs and services in designated areas. As they ventured into these unchartered waters, progress was slow, with some notable steps forward taken in economic and skills development (Dubois 2015).

The Protocol was renewed in 2013 with added provisions for Métis participation in intergovernmental processes at a political and policy level. Provisions for fiscal accountability were also added in the accompanying Governance and Financial Accountability Accord.[37] In many ways, the Métis Nation Protocol provided a general framework for the Métis Nation to participate within the formal mechanisms of intergovernmental relations. Yet, without the constitutional recognition of the Métis' place within the federal framework (as had been proposed in the 1992 Métis Nation Accord), developments that occurred under the Métis Nation Protocol were slow and generally depended on the willingness of state actors to engage with the Métis.

As with similar agreements, the implementation of the Métis Nation Protocol is contingent on a willing federal partner. Under the leadership of former Conservative prime minister Stephen Harper, negotiations were primarily limited to ad hoc, interest-based agreements like the Governance and Financial Accountability Accord and the Economic Development Accord. The incremental gains achieved through these accords opened up space for Métis leaders and bureaucrats to interact directly with their federal counterparts but remained restricted to those areas of mutual interest. For this reason, President Chartier highlighted the limited utility of these kinds of agreements in the absence of a more robust framework that recognizes the Métis Nation's right to self-government.[38] In practice, a more robust framework would entail a paradigm shift: moving away from a framework within which provincial/federal governments devolve funding and programs to Métis *organizations* and instead moving towards a framework that would enable the Métis to generate their own revenues (e.g., through resource-revenue agreements and the recognition of land title) and develop their own policies and programs as democratically accountable *governments* (Dubois 2015). To be sure, this shift would give rise to a host of challenges with which Métis and state governments would have to contend. Yet, without it, Métis governing bodies remain vulnerable to the political and financial volatility of the state.[39]

The need for a more formal and equitable relationship with the Métis Nation extends to the provinces as well. In light of their constitutional responsibilities for health and welfare, provinces have been somewhat more receptive than the federal government to working in tandem with Métis leaders on issues of mutual concern, albeit according to their own legislative and political frameworks (Dubois 2015). This can notably be observed in the aftermath of the Supreme Court of Canada's 2003 *Powley* decision, which affirmed for the first time that the Métis have a constitutionally protected Aboriginal right to harvest. This ruling, compounded by the numerous Métis harvesting cases that were winding their way through provincial court systems, led the governments of Alberta, Saskatchewan, Manitoba, and Ontario to re-examine provincial laws and enter into bilateral discussions with their respective Métis counterparts on harvesting rights.

The initial promise of these bilateral discussions – captured in agreements like the 2012 Harvesting Agreement in Manitoba and the 2004 Interim Harvesting Agreements in Ontario and Alberta – has receded in the face of continuing disputes over jurisdiction, funding, and land.[40] In spite of these ongoing challenges, the relationships established in the aftermath of *Powley* nevertheless created an opportunity for Métis governments to engage with provinces on issues that extend beyond harvesting, and have contributed to fostering a legislative and political environment more amenable to the Métis Nation's demands for self-determination.

Significantly, negotiations around Métis harvesting rights brought to light the need for more comprehensive frameworks to help guide Métis-provincial relations. To this end, several provinces have entered into formal political relationships with Métis governments. For example, in 2005 the MNBC and the Government of British Columbia formalized their commitment to close the gap between Métis citizens and other British Columbians in the Métis Nation Relationship Accord.[41] Similarly, the 2008 Framework Agreement between the MNO and the Government of Ontario (which has since been renewed) has led to positive developments in a number of areas, including the creation of a capital corporation, the Métis Voyageur Development Fund, in 2010.[42] In Manitoba, the provincial government worked with the MMF to develop a Métis policy that aims to empower the MMF in the delivery of programs and services to Métis citizens, and, most recently, it convened its own Provincial Crown Consultation Process with the MMF.[43] Through these types of protocols, agreements, and policies, the Métis Nation has pushed state actors to develop new rules and processes that extend the boundaries of multilevel governance in the country. In so doing, the Métis have successfully managed to carve out a space for their governments within the mechanisms of Canadian federalism (Dubois and Saunders 2013; Dubois 2015).

While important steps forward, these kinds of piecemeal and limited agreements with provincial and federal actors fall short of the kind of macro-level, constitutional change necessary for the Métis Nation to fully realize its social, political, and economic goals. For President Chartier, this kind of change requires the development of a clear legislative framework at the federal level – one that acknowledges Métis rights to land and to self-government– to replace the patchwork approach currently in place. The likelihood of such a scenario increased in the wake of several important developments since the election of Liberal prime minister Justin Trudeau. In keeping with his electoral promise to establish a renewed nation-to-nation relationship with the Métis, Prime Minister Trudeau and his cabinet convened a Métis Nation-Crown Summit with the MNC and the Governing Members (which we discuss in detail in Chapter 6). A key outcome of the summit was the signing of the Canada-Métis Nation Accord and the creation of a permanent bilateral mechanism designed, in part, to "advance reconciliation of the rights, claims, interests and aspirations of the Métis Nation."[44] While negotiations are still under way, Métis leaders are hopeful that the accord will serve to "reset" the relationship between Canada and the Métis Nation. As the vice-president of the MN-S, Gerald Morin, declared: "This Accord, and the Permanent Bilateral Mechanism it creates, will be a foundational process to facilitate the resolution of outstanding grievances of the Métis Nation."[45]

Canada also signed framework agreements on advancing reconciliation with the Métis governments. For the president of the MNA, Audrey Poitras, this opens the door to a government-to-government relationship with Canada to address Métis rights, lands, and self-government.[46] As the president of the MNO remarked, "The fact that we've got a federal government that acknowledges us ... is a remarkable shift."[47] While the federal government has a leadership role to play in developing the legislative space to advance Métis rights, the ministerial special representative on reconciliation with Métis, Thomas Isaac, adds, "Canada should also engage the provinces and territories on a Section 35 Métis rights framework and ... seek to develop a cooperative and coordinated approach to Métis and their constitutionally protected rights."[48] Given the priorities of Métis citizens, there is a need for both levels of government to be at the table.[49] Some provinces appear to be stepping up to the plate, as witnessed by the signing of a ten-year framework agreement between the provincial and Métis governments in Alberta in February 2017 that takes a "whole-of-government" approach to Métis issues.[50]

While such agreements are indeed historic, they are largely contingent on the willingness of state actors to devote the human and financial capital necessary to fully operationalize their goals. As President Chartier remarked, "We know that governments change and so do fundamental policies."[51] The developments currently unfolding across the Métis Nation are reminiscent of the excitement that followed the 2003 *Powley* decision as provincial governments sat down with Métis governments to discuss the implementation of hunting rights – discussions that remain unfinished and that are now expected to be taken up within these new political frameworks. A number of Métis leaders argue that their governments will continue to be subject to the ebb and flow of the goodwill of state governments in the absence of a comprehensive approach to Métis-state relations. Specifically, they argue that, without a legislative and political framework that clarifies the nature of Métis-Canada relations and that meaningfully recognizes the Métis' right to govern themselves across provincial-federal jurisdictions, their self-government objectives will remain relegated to the margins of state processes and structures.[52]

Conclusion

The innovations in governance demonstrated by the Métis Nation in the last quarter century are consistent with historical efforts to remain *ka tipaymishooyahk* (we who own ourselves). Since the emergence of *la noovel Naasyoon* over two hundred years ago, Métis leaders have engaged in pragmatic and principled actions to govern their social, political, and economic future and to fulfill Riel's vision of a self-determining Métis

Nation. The creation of governance institutions and the adoption of practices grounded in democracy and the rule of law have allowed the Métis Nation to move its self-government agenda forward.

Despite the gains made through Métis participation in formal and informal governance processes, the Métis Nation's aspirations to self-government continue to be limited by the ambiguous position it occupies within Canada's political and legislative framework. Addressing this legacy is no small feat. Yet, as the minister's special representative on reconciliation with Métis writes: "Simply because a task is difficult or challenging or may have some ambiguities around its edges, cannot be a reasonable reason for not addressing what is a constitutional imperative and an important matter of public policy."[53] In the face of uncertainty, the Métis have taken a pragmatic approach to building relationships of mutual benefit on a sector-by-sector basis.

These incremental gains, together with advancements made through the courts, have helped to pave the way for a renewed nation-to-nation relationship with Canada. At the same time, the Métis Nation remains vulnerable to the goodwill of provincial and federal governments. The signing of the 2017 Canada-Métis Nation Accord and the establishment of bilateral tables on section 35 rights with Governing Members suggest that Canada is taking action to give life to a nation-to-nation relationship with the Métis. Time will tell whether these latest initiatives will live up to their promise of advancing reconciliation with the Métis Nation in Canada.

4

Kiihtwaam Ooshtaahk lii Goovarnimaan di Michif

(Re)building a Métis Civil Service

WHAT SHOULD MÉTIS GOVERNANCE in Manitoba look like moving forward? This question was posed to over one hundred local, regional, and provincial Métis delegates and leaders at the Métis Government Summit. Gathered in Winnipeg for this inaugural event, participants deliberated on the future of Métis political institutions, constitutionalism, and self-government through a series of themed workshops and presentations by Métis leaders and experts. The objective of the summit, as Manitoba Métis Federation president David Chartrand stated in his opening comments, was to prepare for "the next phase of our government." Marked by the signing of a historic framework agreement between the MMF and Canada in November 2016, this next phase asks Métis citizens to reflect on the road ahead as the Métis government in Manitoba engages in self-government negotiations with Canada. As President Chartrand affirmed, "change is coming, coming quick, we need to be ready for it."[1]

The theme of change has been a perpetual characteristic of Métis governance as Métis leaders have sought to capitalize on emerging opportunities to advance their self-government agenda. Confronted with shifting political and legal circumstances, Métis leaders have had to continually adapt their governance structures to better position themselves in Canada's increasingly robust system of multilevel governance. These efforts have been accelerated by the steady devolution of programs and services from provincial and federal governments to Métis governing bodies. From Ontario to British Columbia, contemporary Métis governments and affiliated agencies deliver an array of programs to their citizens, ranging from health care and education to skills training and business development. They also provide justice and parole services, build social housing, oversee child and family service agencies, and manage Métis harvesting laws and conservation programs. These activities have required the creation of a Métis civil service comprised of staff skilled in policy development, implementation and evaluation, human resources and financial management, and front line program delivery – all within a context that is sensitive to Métis history, culture, and identity.

As Métis governments assume greater responsibilities, engage with stakeholders, and strive to meet the pressing needs of their communities, they have had to develop the internal capacity and acquire the resources and tools necessary to offer effective and efficient governance to their citizens. Using the Manitoba Métis Federation as a case study, we reflect on how Métis governments have undertaken the process of building an organizational structure rooted in the spirit of *aen ishi mamoonakatwayhtamaahk* (the way we think together). Specifically, we investigate some of the issues involved in public-sector capacity building within the context of Métis governance, and we consider the challenges that the MMF and other Métis governments have encountered in their attempts to reconcile Canadian-style organizational practices with Métis traditions and ways of knowing. We also explore the ongoing evolution of the MMF as Métis leaders and citizens in the province respond to the significant possibilities presented by the Supreme Court of Canada's ruling in *Manitoba Métis Federation Inc. v. Canada* and the Trudeau government's commitment to reconciliation with the Métis Nation. The process of adaptation currently under way in Manitoba is consistent with ongoing efforts to build governance structures that best reflect *aen ishi wiichayaamitooyahk* (how we live together), and it speaks to the various ways the Métis continue to engage in political action to fulfill Riel's vision of a free and self-determining Métis people in Canada.

The Manitoba Métis Federation

The MMF was established in December 1967 as a not-for-profit corporation under Manitoba's Companies (later Corporations) Act. Emerging from various community-based organizations scattered throughout southern and central Manitoba, the creation of the MMF provided a means for the leaders of these "locals" to meet on a provincewide basis (Ens and Sawchuk 2016, 371). Initially comprised of a five-member board of directors supported by seven staff members (three office staff along with four field workers), the MMF relied on donations from churches and the private sector as well as on a small grant from the Province of Manitoba to fund its operations.[2] Today, the MMF has a staff complement of more than seven hundred people and oversees an annual budget of approximately $84 million.[3] With a voting membership of over fifty-three thousand people, the MMF represents a community in excess of 140,000 Métis citizens in Manitoba.[4]

The membership requirements and governance structure of the MMF are set out in its Constitution and accompanying bylaws, which are amended as necessary through the General Assembly process to reflect the ongoing evolution of the MMF and the changing needs of its citizens. The rules surrounding membership in the MMF have been modified several times over the past fifty years. Past provisions included different types of membership (affiliate, associate, and honorary memberships) along with evolving eligibility criteria. From its formation in 1967 until 1992, membership in the MMF was open to any person of mixed Aboriginal ancestry who was not a registered or treaty Indian. In 1992, the requirements for membership were amended to include only those Métis persons whose ancestors had taken scrip or land grants in Manitoba as well as individuals accepted as Métis by the community.[5] In 2003, the MMF General Assembly adopted the National Definition approved by the General Assembly of the Métis National Council the previous year. Under these guidelines, in order to become a member of the MMF, an individual must: self-identify as Métis, submit a genealogy that demonstrates his/her ancestral connection to the historic Métis community, and be accepted by the Métis Nation.[6] Once accepted for membership, citizens of the Métis Nation in Manitoba can vote and run as candidates in MMF elections at the local, regional, and provincial levels; attend general assemblies; and participate in MMF events. The electoral process is overseen by a chief electoral officer, who, for the past few elections, has been a retired chief justice of Manitoba (Saunders 2013, 362).

The issue of membership has been challenging for the MMF and, indeed, for other Métis governments in Canada. In mobilizing their citizens, Métis leaders have had to contend not only with the damaging impacts of discrimination but also with the consequences of the misrepresentation of the Métis in state policy and law. As Chris Andersen (2014, 36–39) argues, the understanding of Métis as "mixed, diluted missives" of "more legitimate" peoples – First Nation and White – has been internalized by many Métis themselves. He writes: "Métis are viewed as hybrid – and I imagine far too many Métis understand ourselves to be hybrid – because more than a century of imposed colonial classification that sought to name us as such has produced the perception that it sought to merely describe" (39). Moreover, the lack of a recognized land base has added to the challenge of identifying Métis citizens. Given the complex legacy of colonialism, many Métis in Canada are just beginning to discover their heritage and to self-identify as Métis, let alone seek membership in Métis governing bodies. As a result, Métis governments like the MMF have devoted a considerable amount of their resources to reaching out to potential members and to increasing awareness of Métis identity, culture, and governance.[7]

Given the legislative and political framework within which Métis governments operate, the gap between those who self-identify as Métis and those who register as members of Métis governments presents practical challenges. Métis governments have a mandate to represent all Métis citizens in their respective jurisdictions, but they are constituted under provincial laws that make membership in these entities entirely voluntary.[8] Hence, while membership and political participation are restricted to those individuals who wish to join the MMF and meet the National Definition, state government funding agencies tend to insist on "inclusivity," which means that the programs and services they fund cannot be limited to only members of the MMF. As a result, the MMF typically provides services to anyone who self-identifies as Métis, with programs in some cases delivered to all Aboriginal people living off reserve.[9] This has complicated the ability of the MMF to clearly identify its target constituency as it is called upon to serve its own members, those who self-identify as Métis but who have not chosen or are illegible to join the MMF, and off-reserve Aboriginal people to whom it is required to provide services.

The programs and services delivered by the MMF are chiefly administered at the regional level. Reflecting both its historical development and the requirements of its legal status as a non-profit corporation under the Manitoba Corporations Act, the MMF is divided into seven regions spanning the entire province, with each region separately incorporated. As a result, each region exerts a wide measure of autonomy under the leadership of a regionally elected vice-president and two board members, elected to four-year terms. In addition to overseeing each of their respective regions, these elected representatives also serve on the executive governing body of the MMF, legally referred to as the Board of Directors. Functioning much like a cabinet in the Westminster parliamentary system, representatives on the Board of Directors are assigned an area of responsibility by the provincial president.

There are two types of portfolios that exist within the MMF cabinet: those that are supported by departments and those that exist in policy.[10] The department/policy division is largely driven by whether the MMF delivers programs and services in that area. Thus, while health, employment and training, and natural resources are departments (involving the delivery of specific programs to Métis citizens), heritage, sports, and youth constitute policy portfolios. While the MMF does not necessarily offer services to its citizens in these policy areas, they nonetheless remain important issues of concern warranting executive-level attention. Not surprisingly, departments typically have larger staffs and budgets than policy portfolios.

Finding a Métis Approach to Good Governance

As outlined in its Constitution and bylaws, one of the core objectives of the MMF is "to provide responsible and accountable governance on behalf of the Manitoba Métis Community."[11] What constitutes good governance, and what does this look like in the Métis context? What kinds of institutions and processes help facilitate the provision of good governance? In addressing these questions, Métis leaders have sought to adapt traditional governance practices and values to meet the ongoing needs of their people. As Métis scholar Larry Chartrand argues, "We must take care to outline principles of Aboriginal governance that go beyond 'traditional' practices of good governance that pre-date European arrival in Canada ... they must recognize the contemporary relationships, realities and values of Aboriginal communities."[12] Articulating a Métis approach to good governance thus requires giving consideration to the realities imposed by colonization and the dominant political structures within which the Métis have had to operate. Key in this respect is the legal structure that governs the operations of the MMF and, indeed, Métis governments across the Métis Nation Homeland.

The long history of the Métis as Canada's forgotten people, coupled with the federal government's long-standing refusal to accept fiduciary responsibility for the Métis under section 91(24) of the Constitution Act, 1867, meant that Métis governing bodies were not recognized by the state. The Métis Settlements in Alberta remain the only governing entity to have powers recognized in provincial statute. While the provinces of Saskatchewan and Ontario have adopted legislation acknowledging Métis governing bodies outside of not-for-profit corporation legislation, these are not explicitly recognized as representative governments.[13] In order for Métis governments like the MMF to hold assets, secure loans, and receive government grants, the only legal option available to them was to incorporate as a non-profit corporation under provincial legislation as this was a familiar form to banks, state governments, and creditors. Incorporating in this manner also ensured that individual representatives of the MMF would not be held legally responsible for monies and assets; instead, assets are held by the corporate body. While corporation legislation may have served the MMF reasonably well in the past, Murray Trachtenberg, legal counsel to the MMF, notes that it is not an effective model in the transition to Métis self-government in Manitoba.[14]

The first drawback of corporation legislation is that it forces Métis governments to be legally accountable to the provinces under which they are incorporated rather than to their own people. While most Métis governments across the Homeland have adopted constitutions (typically developed through democratic processes and reflecting Métis traditions and culture), these constitutions are superseded by provincial corporation law, a legal reality that continues to restrain their ability to act as true representative governments on behalf of their citizens. Métis governments are required to comply with the requirements contained in these laws, which can be altered at any time by the respective provinces, regardless of what is contained within their own constitutions.

As explored in more detail below, a second shortcoming of corporation law relates to the language and structures that are imposed through this business-driven model. Rather than being guided by the language of constitutionalism, governance, and citizenship, the MMF remains legally bound in its legislation by problematic terms such as "bylaws," "board of directors," "organization," and "members." The confines of corporation legislation are not intended for self-governing Indigenous nations and impose requirements that are impractical for Métis governments. Speaking about the ill fit of corporation legislation in Ontario, for example, Métis leader France Picotte remarks that it does not allow youth to sit on the executive council. She adds that it also dictates the annual election of board members, which not only involves significant human and financial resources but is unrealistic given the breadth of the mandate given to Métis leaders through democratic elections. Since these legislative requirements do not reflect Métis ways of governing, Picotte remarks: "It doesn't work for us."[15]

A third deficiency of the legislative framework with which Métis governments have been forced to comply is the limited ability for coordinated decision making. Corporation law necessitates the creation of discrete legal entities. Hence, locals, affiliates, and other institutions that together comprise governing bodies like the MMF are all separately incorporated in order to hold assets and receive grants. To enhance their ability to speak with one voice, the MMF and other Métis governments have adopted various measures such as having Métis ministers sit as board members of affiliates that work in their area of responsibility. Yet the very necessity of having these boards of directors adds complexity for Métis governments and affiliates that are already struggling with limited capacity and resources.

Trachtenberg concludes that the continued imposition of corporation law circumvents the ability of the Métis to be "masters in their own house" in terms of determining for themselves how their governments should be structured. In order for self-government to be meaningful, Métis leaders have argued that Métis citizens must derive rights from their own constitution. In the words of Métis Nation-Saskatchewan vice-president Gerald Morin: "We need to remove ourselves from this oppressive legislation which was not meant to apply to a self-governing people with aspirations of self-determination."[16]

Métis governments such as the MMF not only represent a unique amalgam of Métis culture, values, and history (and, within this, distinct evolutionary patterns within each of the provinces) but are also reflections of and responses to the realities of Canadian federalism and law. In developing their own approach to governance, the Métis have created organizational structures that look and function differently from the typical Westminster model found in provincial and federal governments in Canada while still meeting the legal requirements of the legislation under which they are incorporated.[17] The Métis have had to navigate between the political structures of the dominant society, the legal requirements of the corporate legislation that oversees their activities, and their own historical traditions – a set of requirements that has proven to be particularly challenging for Métis leaders.

An anecdote shared by a former senior official in the MMF speaks to the difficulties of reconciling Métis governance practices with the realities of their legal status.[18] As this individual notes, if the MMF wants to be seen as a government by Manitoba and Canada, and, most important, by the Métis people in the province, then that means "we have to act like a government and not [like] a not-for-profit corporation," a structure that has been forced upon the Métis by the state. He describes how the recasting of the MMF as a vehicle for self-government rather than as a non-profit advocacy organization led to the search for new terminology among MMF leaders. For instance, the MMF has increasingly adopted the term "cabinet" to describe its executive body rather than "board of directors," which is the common name used in corporation legislation.[19] However, as the former official explains, this change in vocabulary carries with it its own difficulties.

> "Minister" is a British word; it's not a Métis word. But calling our leaders "directors of the board" doesn't fit either. We really don't have a traditional concept for these kinds of executive positions. Métis provisional governments in the 1800s used the term "councillors," but we don't want people to think we are the same as municipalities and local governments. Trying to find different language that reflects who we are but that isn't colonialist hasn't been easy.[20]

The clash between Métis and Canadian/corporate approaches to governance extends beyond semantics and affects the organizational behaviour of the MMF. For example, the preferred approach to decision making around the cabinet table is consensus – a practice that dates back to the days of the buffalo hunts. By ensuring ample time for discussion and consideration of various opinions and positions, the president's goal within the MMF is to try to reach unanimous agreement among ministers without the need for formal votes.[21] Moreover, in line with the practices of the buffalo hunt, whereby the captains of the hunt were empowered to exercise judgment within their agreed-upon areas of responsibility by the chiefs of the hunt and those who elected them, the more culturally appropriate tendency is to allocate discretionary decision-making power to ministers. Yet the corporation model's emphasis on centralization and hierarchy as opposed to participation and dialogue works against these traditional approaches. As one former senior civil servant in the MMF pointed out, this model forces leaders to run the organization like a CEO rather than as a democratically elected head of a consensus government.[22]

The corporate governance model can also impede the ability of elected officials within Métis governments to successfully fulfill their responsibilities. While the MMF cabinet/board of directors sets broad direction in terms of priorities and policy during its monthly meetings, ministers are sometimes not able to provide the kind of oversight and direction to their departments that they would like.[23] This is in part because the majority of ministers reside in the seven regions that comprise the MMF, making it difficult to interact on a daily basis with their senior staff members who are headquartered at the MMF Home Office in Winnipeg.

Geographic barriers are compounded by the fact that, as a result of funding constraints, only eight of the twenty-three members of cabinet (the president and the seven regionally elected vice-presidents) are full-time salaried positions. With limited human and financial resources, one minister admits, "I am technically in charge of my department but more often than not I am one of the last ones to know what is happening."[24] While ministers are responsible for approving departmental expenditures and providing reports to funders (provincial and federal governments), the reporting mechanisms between departmental staff and cabinet members are difficult to sustain since most ministers are not available on a consistent basis. The ongoing operation of ministries therefore falls to the managers of each department (who are similar to deputy ministers) and to the executive director (who is similar to the clerk of the Privy Council), who primarily reports to the provincial president rather than to the cabinet as a whole.

In spite of these and other challenges, one official noted that, even if it were to shed the yoke of corporation legislation, the MMF would still require some kind of structure that, while reformed in some aspects, would probably look largely similar to what already exists. As this person commented, "We have created, with the limited corporate tools that we have, our own body, our own government that is in most cases already there ... I'm not saying it's perfect, but I think we are doing a very good job considering we have had very little in terms of resources."[25] Indeed, the MMF has shown a remarkable ability to adapt to changing circumstances, to push the boundaries of the legislation under which it is incorporated, and to position itself to negotiate with state actors on a government-to-government basis. This is evident in the way in which provincial and federal governments interact with the MMF, most notably in the Government of Manitoba's development of its Métis Policy as well as in the Government of Canada's negotiations with the MMF as the representative body of Métis section 31 land grantees. The courts have also increasingly recognized the MMF as a de facto government for Métis citizens in Manitoba rather than as a mere not-for-profit organization. However, as Trachtenberg notes, this recognition "can only go so far."[26]

Funding

Funding remains one of the biggest – and perennial – issues facing Indigenous communities across the country. The majority of funding agreements between Indigenous peoples and provincial and federal governments remain woefully inadequate, inefficient, and more reflective of state interests than of community priorities.[27] The Métis Nation faces a particular barrier in light of long-standing jurisdictional squabbles between federal and provincial governments. Canada's historical denial of responsibility for the Métis resulted in their exclusion from many of the funding streams available to First Nations and Inuit, thereby forcing the Métis to turn to the provinces for financial assistance.[28] As a former senior official in the federal government testified before the Senate Standing Committee on Aboriginal Peoples in 2013:

> Canada's relationship with Métis is distinct from that with First Nations or Inuit. For example, living off-reserve, Métis receive most of their basic social programming from provinces and not from the federal government. Provinces have their own deep relations with Métis people and organizations, especially in Western Canada. There are also no federal Métis acts, no federal registry of Métis people and no Métis reserves. (Elizabeth Tromp, Assistant Deputy Minister of Métis and Non-status Relations Directorate, Aboriginal Affairs and Northern Development Canada, in SSCAP 2013, 46)

The funding that is provided to Métis governments is largely distributed on an ad hoc basis, generally for the purposes of program and service delivery (Dubois 2015). In addition to being program-specific, funds tend to be awarded yearly rather than on a multi-year basis, within parameters largely set and controlled by state governments. The cumbersome reporting mechanisms that accompany program-driven funding agreements require civil servants within the MMF to spend "an inordinate amount of time having to juggle our finances, defer one project or another or lay off staff in one area to cover costs in another area."[29] This means that officials have less time to spend on policy and program development, staff training and upgrading, and responding to the needs of Métis citizens.

The conditions under which funding is distributed also limits the ability of Métis governments to plan for the future and to provide for the effective and ongoing management of their programs over the long term. In the words of one department manager, "The ways in which funding is provided by the provincial and federal government really ties our hands. We live in constant uncertainty, not knowing from year to year whether the money will be there to deliver many of our programs and services."[30] A recent example of this occurred in the fall of 2016, when the Province of Manitoba decided to eliminate $650,000 in funding for healthcare workers who were employed by the MMF and who helped deliver services to Métis communities. In his reaction to the news, MMF president Chartrand said he felt "blindsided" by the province's decision, which came in the absence of any prior notice or consultation with the MMF. He indicated that, as a result of this, his government would "now be on the hook for six months' worth of salaries."[31] The consequences of this financial uncertainty are exacerbated by the fact that the MMF receives only a limited amount of core funding to maintain its overall operations.[32]

This challenge is echoed across the Métis Nation. As one local president in Saskatchewan remarked, "Where we struggle is in the core dollars."[33] Beyond core funding, Métis governments like the MMF rely on the small (typically 10 to 15 percent) administrative fees they are able to collect for the programs they administer on behalf of the federal and provincial governments. These funds help to pay for the costs associated with building a government and a bureaucracy, including financial and human resources, maintaining the president's office, providing stipends to board members, and undergoing staff development and training. This puts the ongoing functioning of Métis governments in a constant state of financial uncertainty and leaves them at the mercy of political and bureaucratic actors. To illustrate, a past official within the MMF recalled a time when the federal government decided, without warning, to not only refuse to pay the standard 15 percent administrative fee for the delivery of a program but also to wait until the middle of the year to inform the MMF of this – and to make its decision retroactive to the start of the year. As this official concluded, "We were nearly bankrupted because of these actions, which we had no control over."[34]

Joe Sawchuk (1998, 72–91) likens the funding relationship between Indigenous organizations and the state to one of client and patron. Rather than a nation-to-nation relationship of equals, he contends that the capacity of the state to fund programs creates an imbalance in the relationship. He adds that this, in turn, leads to all kinds of distortions, not the least of which is the creation of structures, programs, and activities that favour state priorities over functional goals. This argument finds resonance in the question posed by Roger Maaka and Augie Fleras (2005, 270) as to whether self-determination for Indigenous peoples can occur within the existing foundational structures of a settler constitutional order, notably when "vested interests" are at play.

Métis leaders have long argued that meaningful self-determination involves political as well as economic sovereignty. As Stephen Cornell and Joseph Kalt (2007) demonstrate, Indigenous peoples can more readily foster economic development when they have stable, fair, effective, and reliable governing institutions. The MMF's reliance on state funding inhibits its ability to meet the needs of its citizens and to fully engage in self-government. One senior public servant admits that, given that the MMF is not allowed to carry over a surplus from year to year and therefore risks losing funding provided for specific programs, the MMF has undertaken projects that either were not a priority for it at the time or that had to be completed within such a short time frame that their value was rendered meaningless.[35] In some cases, the alignment of priorities between the MMF and state governments has led to fruitful working relationships

– notably, in economic development and labour market training – but these relationships often develop according to timelines set by the state. Hence, advancements that were made in health and education under former Liberal prime minister Paul Martin took a back seat when his successor, former Conservative prime minister Stephen Harper, set his sights on economic development. As one interviewee remarks, this did not mean that Métis governments stopped caring about health and education; rather, as a result of the change in government in Ottawa, they were limited with regard to how far they could move forward on these files. He adds that, for Métis governments with limited self-source revenues but an abundance of needs, "We have to dance with the partner we've got."[36]

Métis leaders remain hopeful that the Trudeau government's financial investments in Métis governance in the 2018 federal budget will pave the way towards a more stable fiscal arrangement. Yet progress on this front has been slow; notwithstanding the Supreme Court of Canada's ruling in *Daniels*, the federal government's underfunding of Métis compared to other Indigenous groups in Canada continues. Of the $11.8 billion invested in Indigenous peoples in the 2016 and 2017 federal budgets, less than 1 percent was allocated to the Métis Nation, despite the fact that Métis make up over 30 percent of the Indigenous population in Canada.[37] While it is certainly the case that all Indigenous governments and organizations suffer from a chronic lack of funding (e.g., Palmater 2011), the issue for Métis leaders is that the particular needs and unique circumstances of the Métis are not taken into consideration in large-scale federal spending on Indigenous peoples. The absence of attention to the community's needs in federal decision making, a criticism also leveraged by other Indigenous leaders, is particularly concerning for the Métis given their historic exclusion from federal policy circles.

The Métis have long advocated for a distinctions-based approach that considers their particular circumstances in a way that is not adequately captured in broader, pan-Indigenous approaches typically favoured by state decision makers. Calling the situation "simply not acceptable," following the release of the 2017 federal budget, Métis Nation president Clément Chartier expressed his disappointment in a letter he sent to the prime minister.[38] He noted that, despite record "Indigenous" spending in the Trudeau government's previous two budgets, "We the Métis find ourselves pushed to the margins once again."[39] In response to these criticisms, the prime minister acknowledged that his promised commitment to a distinctions-based approach to the Métis was not reflected in the 2017 budget and assured Métis leaders: "this will be corrected."[40] Marking a break with past practices, Métis-specific funding allocated to key areas, most notably governance and housing in the 2018 federal budget and the distinctions-based approach included in the 2019 federal budget, suggests that the prime minister is putting the mechanisms in place to follow through on this commitment.

Staff Recruitment and Training

The lack of access to stable and secure funding not only detrimentally affects the kinds of programs and services the MMF and other Métis governments are able to offer their citizens but also inhibits their ability to adequately recruit and train staff. A study on Métis governance, prepared for the Institute on Governance by Métis lawyer and advisor Jason Madden and his colleagues John Graham and Jake Wilson, identified a number of obstacles to building a strong and productive Métis civil service, including the following:

- inability to offer competitive compensation packages to qualified candidates (i.e., the federal and provincial governments being able to offer significantly more money in salaries, a lack of pension plans, a lack of defined grids for salary reviews, and so forth);
- inability to offer long-term employment contracts to qualified candidates due to the project-based nature of funding received from other governments;
- lack of effective and ongoing training for staff in order to upgrade skills throughout their career;

- lack of job security due to the political nature of these organizations where there may be elections every 3-4 years and political factions on provincial boards; and
- a lack of clearly defined organizational structures, job descriptions, expectations and career planning within the organizations.[41]

As a result of these factors, the authors conclude that some qualified individuals may not see a career with the Métis Nation as a long-term option. While this report was prepared in 2005, the challenges it identifies remain in place today. This is evidenced by the ongoing high turnover of civil service staff at the MMF. As several interviewees noted, no sooner is a qualified individual recruited and trained for a position than it seems that he or she is recruited by federal and provincial governments or by the private sector, where salaries and benefits are more attractive. This is, of course, contingent on the existence of a pool of qualified individuals from which the MMF can hire in the first place.

While the Métis have a higher postsecondary education rate than First Nations and Inuit, they are underrepresented compared to the non-Aboriginal population in Canada. According to the 2016 census data, over half (55 percent) of Métis aged 25 to 34 have a postsecondary qualification (12 percent trades certificate, 24 percent college diploma, 14 percent bachelor's degree, 3.5 percent university diploma above the bachelor's level). In comparison, almost two-thirds (70 percent) of the non-Aboriginal population aged 25 to 34 have a postsecondary qualification (10 percent trades certificate, 22 percent college diploma, 26 percent bachelor's degree, 11 percent university diploma above the bachelor's level).

The limited postsecondary education of the Métis workforce places a premium on staff training and development, notably in the areas of program and policy design, accounting, program evaluation, and service delivery. Yet the precarious nature of much of the MMF's funding renders this kind of staff development nearly impossible: "When you are juggling so many demands as an expanding government, you simply don't have the time or the resources to train your employees the way that you would like," commented one former senior official.[42] This leads to sub-optimal outcomes in terms of operations and service delivery and creates inconsistencies in organizational culture (due to an unstable and ever-changing staff complement) that makes it difficult to retain institutional knowledge across the organization.

Not only is staff training limited, so too is training for new ministers. While Allison Loat and Michael MacMillan (2014) find a similar lack of preparation for new members of Parliament in the Canadian parliamentary system, the situation takes on added dimensions in the case of Métis governments. Once elected, ministers have little time to "ramp up" and master their portfolios in the face of pressing needs from their communities – a challenge that is difficult to meet given that most cabinet members are not compensated for full-time work and must therefore retain outside employment in addition to their MMF duties. Together, these factors restrict the ability of Métis governments to carry out priorities on behalf of its citizens.

"We Need to Be Ready for Self-Government"

Like many Métis governments across the Métis Nation Homeland, the MMF has experienced phenomenal growth in recent years. In the mid-1990s, the organization was in receivership, operating with a core staff of roughly half a dozen people; today, the MMF has a staff of over seven hundred people who oversee a wide range of programs and services involving a diverse set of economic and social policy sectors, and it is responsible for managing an annual budget of $84 million.[43] While its achievements to date have been nothing short of monumental, the veritable explosion of the MMF in terms of responsibilities, staff, and budgets in such a relatively short period of time has not been without a few bumps. In many ways, the MMF has experienced a "big bang" approach to self-government, something pursued by many First Nations, whereby they assume full jurisdiction in areas where they have little or no capacity or governance experience (Madden 2008, 376). Rather than a slower, more evolutionary approach to self-government, however, President Chartrand highlights what the MMF has been able to achieve in the course of a few short decades. As he expresses with understandable pride, the MMF has "accomplished many things that could only be dreamt about a generation ago."[44] When we look to the future and to the implementation of the Supreme Court of Canada's decisions in *Daniels v. Canada* and *Manitoba Métis Federation Inc. v. Canada*, it is clear that the march towards self-government will only quicken in pace.

The considerable growth in the size and scope of the MMF has been a mixed blessing. On the face of it, it is a concrete manifestation of the Métis Nation's right to self-government as the MMF takes increasing responsibility for the well-being of its citizens. At the same time, this growth has not been accompanied either by the necessary funding or by adequate capacity building.[45] A number of regional offices and associated locals lack the infrastructure to effectively deliver programs and services to their citizens, many of whom continue to suffer the ill effects of colonization and discrimination.[46] As Richard Missens warns, sovereignty without the capacity for governance will have very little impact on the socio-economic lives of Indigenous peoples.[47] While the Métis have historically seized opportunities to push forward with their ambitious agenda, there is a recognition that "we need to be ready for self-government."[48] Self-government not only depends on competent leadership but also on healthy communities. In the words of a former Manitoba government official, "Good governance requires good citizens, but people must be in a good place to be good citizens."[49]

Managing the relationships between the regions and the Home Office in Winnipeg, building capacity across communities, recruiting and training staff, improving communication, seeking out new revenue-generating opportunities, and empowering elected officials – the to-do list facing the MMF and other Métis governments is daunting. Added to this is the need to balance capacity building with a culturally grounded government that reflects *aen ishi mamoonakatwayhtamaahk* (how we think together). Research undertaken by the Harvard Project on American Indian Economic Development points to the importance of grounding assertions of sovereignty in capable institutions of culturally appropriate governance (e.g., Cornell and Kalt 1998). As such, self-government requires more than the implementation of stable political institutions and decision-making processes, the establishment of capable and well-functioning bureaucracies, and the separation of politics from day-to-day business and program management. It also requires incorporating Métis ways of knowing and adapting each of these activities to the reality of Métis communities. While Métis leaders are committed to community involvement, decentralization, and the representation of elders, youth, and women, these commitments add complexity to decision making and to the overall apparatus of Métis government.

Conclusion

In the words of MMF president Chartrand: "We are entering a historic time for the Métis Nation's Manitoba Métis Community. Our record of accomplishments cannot be ignored and our vision for the future is one that our People can clearly see."[50] Whether it be in the area of health and social programs, harvesting rights, education and training, or economic development, it is clear that the MMF is building the mechanisms of self-government from the ground up. Métis elder and past MMF president John Morrisseau reminds us of how far Métis governments like the MMF have come:

> It wasn't too long ago that our people were shot at, called traitors and forced to go underground and hide in shame simply because they were Métis. Now, we are sitting across the table from Prime Ministers negotiating agreements, passing our own laws and winning victories at the Supreme Court. We cannot lose sight of how far we have come with so few tools at our disposal.[51]

The MMF's path to success is contingent on a number of factors. Significant challenges remain in terms of institution building and capacity development, and much will depend on ongoing negotiations with private-sector corporations and Manitoba Hydro in the areas of natural resources, hydro development, and the MMF's Métis Economic Development Fund (a venture capital fund to support the development of Métis entrepreneurs and businesses). Also key will be the ability of the MMF to shed the yoke of its provincial corporation status and derive its governance legitimacy from a constitution developed by its own citizens and reflecting its own traditions.

One of the key stepping-stones in moving the MMF's self-government agenda forward hinges on the state's response to the Supreme Court of Canada in *Manitoba Métis Federation Inc. v. Canada.* The Court issued a declaration to assist the MMF in negotiations with the Crown towards reconciliation and emphasized the need for a meaningful response. Asked to help chart a path forward, the minister's special representative, Thomas Isaac, concluded, "There can be no doubt that based on the [Supreme Court of Canada]'s statements in the MMF Decision, that the MMF represents the Métis in Manitoba and can forthrightly represent Métis interests in respect of any discussions or negotiations relating to the implementation of [this declaration]."[52] Isaac called on Canada, the MMF, and the Province of Manitoba to immediately engage in discussions to negotiate a framework agreement to guide negotiations.

To its credit, the Trudeau government has moved expeditiously on this front. Shortly after assuming office, negotiations began between the Crown and the MMF on a memorandum of understanding (MOU) on advancing reconciliation and, in particular, resolving the outstanding claim of the Manitoba Métis against Canada.[53] Following the signing of the MOU in May 2016, work continued on the negotiation of a framework agreement, which was completed six months later – a record achievement in terms of federal-Indigenous land claims negotiations. Contained within the Framework Agreement are several shared objectives between Canada and the MMF. These include the recognition and support of a Manitoba Métis government with law-making authority and acknowledged jurisdiction; the facilitation of a nation-to-nation, government-to-government relationship; and improvements in the cultural, social, physical, emotional, and economic well-being of the Manitoba Métis Community.[54]

On November 16, 2016, at a graveside ceremony marking the 131st anniversary of Canada's execution of Louis Riel, President Chartrand symbolically presented Riel with the signed Framework Agreement. Speaking to this momentous occasion, Chartrand noted that, after more than 140 years, three decades of court battles, and numerous consultations with Métis citizens, the solemn promise made to Riel at the time of the Manitoba Act would finally be resolved. Seen as a precursor to the negotiation of a modern day self-government treaty with Canada, for the MMF, the vision of Riel has come full circle. As Chartrand declared: "This Agreement is the culmination of the hope, hardship and struggle of the Métis. We never quit fighting for what Riel gave his life for."[55]

These latest developments are a testimony to the resilience and fortitude of the Métis Nation to stay the course in advancing its goal of self-determination. The systematic approach taken by Métis leaders also speaks to the value of incremental change in building self-government from the ground up. While much work remains to be done, the Métis in Manitoba have won the necessary battles to gain legal and political recognition of their rights to land and to self-government. The next step is to negotiate the implementation of these rights alongside federal actors in a government-to-government relationship. As President Chartrand summed up: "This is a monumental and historic time for Manitoba's Métis."[56]

5

Lii Faam di Naasyoon di Michif
Mothers of the Métis Nation[1]

It is true that our Indian origin is humble, but it is indeed just that we honour our mothers as well as our fathers.

– LOUIS RIEL (1982, 200)

DENISE THOMAS, MINISTER of tripartite self-government negotiations and consultation for the Manitoba Métis Federation, was one of seven elders recently honoured by an Indigenous community organization for her role as a knowledge keeper of the Métis Nation and her long-standing commitment to the Métis people of Manitoba. In accepting her award, Thomas spoke of her life-long devotion to the struggle for Métis rights: "I always knew I would become a leader in fighting for the Métis," she said. Reflecting on the changes that have occurred during the three decades that she has served as an elected representative of the Métis community in Manitoba, she added, "I've been involved with the MMF Board since 1988, and now they call me Minister, because the Métis are a government – a government that fights Nation to Nation."[2] Instrumental in the creation of the Louis Riel Capital Corporation and the Louis Riel Institute, two key institutions that aid Métis business development and education in Manitoba, Thomas also serves as the alternate to the MMF president on the Métis National Council Board of Governors.

The achievements of Minister Thomas, while commendable, are not unusual when we look at the active engagement of women in Métis governments across the Homeland. Women play key roles in Métis politics and governance; they run the majority of local and community organizations and hold almost half of all elected executive positions in Métis governments. In 2018, three out of the five Métis governments in Canada (Métis Nation British Columbia, the Métis Nation of Alberta, and the Métis Nation of Ontario) are led by female presidents. What accounts for the ongoing prominence of women in Métis politics? Melanie Omeniho, the president of the national organization that represents Métis women, explains that "Métis women have been equal partners in the development of Métis communities politically, socially and economically, and have always held the esteemed role of keepers of traditional knowledge."[3] Yet, as Nathalie Kermoal (2016) notes, relatively little research has been devoted to Métis women and to the knowledge they contribute to their communities.

In this chapter, we place women at the centre of our analysis of Métis politics and governance. We begin by tracing the importance of women in early Métis society and in the development of Métis identity. Our analysis of the historical literature reveals that the various roles held by Métis women in the fur trade economy were integral to the emergence of a distinct culture among the Métis. In addition to highlighting women's contributions to what the Métis refer to as *ka ishi pimaatishiyaahk* (our way of life), we draw attention to the central role of women in the formation of kinship networks that are at the heart of Métis governance. Through kinship, women also contributed to keeping Métis identity, history, and culture alive, notably during the period of *le grand silence,* which followed the defeat at Batoche and the hanging of Louis Riel. Consistent with this history, Métis women continue to occupy conspicuous positions in the Métis Nation.

To deepen our understanding of the contributions of women to contemporary Métis politics, we conducted interviews with close to a dozen female leaders and engaged in several informal conversations with other political representatives, community organizers, and elders. Their stories revealed a marked continuity in the historic and contemporary contributions of Métis women. In this chapter, we take note of the ongoing participation of women at all levels of Métis governance and examine the critical roles women occupy in the social, economic, and political life of the Métis Nation. As some of those interviewed reminded us, the impressive number of women elected to Métis governing bodies does not mean that Métis women do not still struggle with the legacies of sexism and patriarchy that accompany colonization. Despite these ongoing challenges, we assert that Métis women occupy prominent roles in all levels of contemporary Métis governments. Following Kim Anderson (2016, 15), we are interested in understanding how Métis women have come to hold and maintain power in spite of oppression. Borrowing the language of Métis women, we argue that the ongoing, dominant presence of women in Métis politics stands as a testament to their historic and contemporary role as "mothers of the Métis Nation."

The Representation of Women in Métis Politics

Women have contributed to advance Métis self-government through their presence in the political affairs of their nation. The women we interviewed stated that they chose to get involved in politics to promote Métis culture and rights. "We can do better for our people," one participant from Saskatchewan commented. "I want my children and grandchildren to be proud of who they are, I don't want them to suffer as I did [as a Métis person], sent off to residential schools and told I'm no good."[4] Many of these women view political participation as a means of advancing the interests of the Métis Nation as a whole. Interestingly, none of the participants identified the promotion of women's rights as their primary goal; instead, they situate their political activities within the larger context of Métis nationhood. As described by one participant from Manitoba, "the best way to promote Métis women's rights is to promote the rights of all our people."[5] This point of view is consistent with Métis understandings of individual and collective freedom, whereby individual freedom depends on the freedom and well-being of the Métis Nation as a whole (see Chapter 2).

Women's organizations are integrated in the affairs of Métis governments across the Métis Nation Homeland. As we note in Chapter 3, each Governing Member works alongside a Métis women's organization whose spokesperson sits on its executive body.[6] At the same time, women who are members of Métis governments (Métis Nation British Columbia, the Métis Nation of Alberta, Métis Nation-Saskatchewan, the Manitoba Métis Federation, and the Métis Nation of Ontario) are also able to join the women's group in their home province, participate in its events, and run for its executive leadership. For example, the Métis women's group in Manitoba, Infinity Women, an affiliate of the MMF, aims to promote, empower, and enhance the social, cultural, and economic well-being of Métis women in Manitoba.[7] Its activities are overseen by an eight-person Board of Directors, comprised of representatives elected in each of the MMF's seven regions, along with a provincial spokesperson who is elected provincewide. Members of Infinity Women hold a general assembly each year, in addition to regular meetings and events. Métis women's organizations in other provinces function in a similar fashion (see Table 5.1).

TABLE 5.1 Métis women's organizations by province

Province	Organization
British Columbia	Métis Women of British Columbia
Alberta	New Dawn Métis Women's Society
Saskatchewan	Filles de Madeleine Association Inc. (Métis Women of Saskatchewan)
Manitoba	Infinity Women Secretariat Inc.
Ontario	Women's Secretariat of the Métis Nation of Ontario

Together, the heads of each provincial Métis women's organization (or its designated representative) serve on the board of a national Métis women's organization, Les Femmes Michif Otipemisiwak, which operates under the working title Women of the Métis Nation. Its priorities include such goals as economic development (notably, supporting Métis women's entrepreneurship); education (specifically with regard to Métis culture, traditions, and Michif language); health (improving the gaps in care for Métis women, synergizing traditional healing practices with Western medicine, and strengthening mental health and addiction services); and combatting violence against Métis women and girls.[8] While not a Governing Member of the Métis National Council, the president of

Women of the Métis Nation is widely consulted on virtually all matters affecting the Métis Nation as a whole and is regularly invited to attend assemblies, meetings, and events across the Homeland.[9]

Women also hold a substantial number of elected positions in all levels of Métis governments, including key executive positions (see Table 5.2). Three of the five Governing Members (in British Columbia, Alberta, and Ontario) currently have a female president. In the MN-S's May 2017 election, women were elected in eight out of the sixteen seats on the Provincial Métis Council, the executive governing body of the MN-S.[10] In 2018, the eleven-member Board of Directors of the MNBC, which serves as its executive decision-making body, was composed of six women, while in the MNO, three of the top executive positions – president, chair, and vice-chair – were held by women.[11] In the MMF, women have constituted on average 43 percent of all representatives elected to the Board of Directors since ballot-box elections began in 1984.[12] In 2018, five of the MMF's seven vice-presidents were women, with high-profile ministerial portfolios that include finance, economic development, justice, health, and self-government negotiations. Audrey Poitras, who has held the position of provincial president of the MNA since 1996, also served as interim president and national spokesperson of the Métis National Council in 2003 during a particularly difficult time in its history.

TABLE 5.2 Number of women on Métis provincial executive councils in 2017

Executive council	Number of women
Métis Nation British Columbia	6 of 11 (55%)
Métis Nation of Alberta	7 of 14 (50%)
Métis Nation-Saskatchewan	10 of 16 (63%)
Manitoba Métis Federation	9 of 23 (39%)
Métis Nation of Ontario	8 of 19 (42%)

In addition to occupying high-profile elected positions at the regional and provincial levels, Métis women are also prominent in leadership roles at the community level. Jim Sinclair, a pre-eminent leader in the Métis rights movement in the 1970s and 1980s, recounts: "in our heyday, we had more than half the women in our locals and communities [as] leaders."[13] Since the establishment of the MMF in 1967, women have continuously made up a majority of locally elected representatives in addition to their strong presence as regional directors and vice-presidents. In the words of Anita Campbell, the spokesperson for Infinity Women, "women make up the backbone of the MMF."[14] It would be a mistake to regard this kind of community-level involvement as less worthy or relevant than that of other elected positions. Not only can locals, through annual assemblies, exert a significant degree of influence in policy making and constitutional change, they can also serve as an effective entry point and training ground for women in subsequent regional and provincial elections. Métis women's participation in politics, however, does not end at the grassroots level. Indeed, most of the participants interviewed referenced how they got their start in politics by becoming involved with the Métis local in their area. "I didn't see myself as wanting to get into politics," commented one participant from Saskatchewan. "I just wanted to help other Métis in my community, to give them a voice, and getting involved in my local seemed a good place to do that."[15]

In addition to being well represented in elected office, Métis women carry out important functions behind the scenes. Reflecting on the political mobilization of Métis communities in the 1970s and 1980s, former MN-S president Jim Durocher remembers that women were the main organizers of important events at the grassroots level – efforts that supported and gave voice to the national political agenda. From helping to establish local Indian and Métis Friendship Centres to organizing bingos, Christmas dinners, and clothing drives, Métis women take pride in their community involvement and view these activities as integral to the overall advancement of the Métis Nation and its citizens. "We [women] are the ones that do most of the organizing for things like Métis Days and other cultural events; even things like annual general assemblies and regional meetings we do most of the work," declared one participant from Manitoba. "Without us, a lot of these things wouldn't happen."[16]

Situating Métis Women in Historical Perspective

Our discussions with contemporary female leaders revealed the extent to which they see their presence in politics as a means of carrying on the legacy bestowed upon them by their maternal forebears. While historical accounts of the fur trade in pre-Confederation Canada have remained largely silent on the role of women, recent scholarship supports the argument that Métis women held economic, social, and political power in their communities that was unparalleled in the lives of their European counterparts (Blady 1997; Brown 1980; Barter 2007; Payment 1996, 2009; Peterson 1981; Murphy 2003; Iseke-Barnes 2009; White 2006). Métis women not only played a central role in the fur trade economy through their labour and kinship connections but were also seminal in the enduring existence of their people as the firekeepers of Métis culture and identity.

Despite their absence in much of the historical record, First Nation and Métis women occupied critical positions in the economy of the Northwest. Scholars who have studied the fur trade have helped illuminate the seminal role of Indigenous women. As Sylvia Van Kirk (2006, 70) explains, the fur trade was predicated "on a mutual exchange and dependency between Indian and white." Within fur trade society, marked by little division between the public and private spheres, women were active agents in the survival of their communities and in the economic development of the region. Indigenous women within these communities were integral to teaching traders arriving from Europe and eastern parts of Canada how to survive in the interior, serving as interpreters, guides, and goodwill ambassadors. European traders thus sought out unions with Indigenous women as a way of building alliances, achieving economic gain, and ensuring their physical survival (Peterson 1978). Our understanding of the complexities of the fur trade economy has been enhanced by historical and anthropological studies that focus on Indigenous women in the Great Lakes region (see especially Sleeper-Smith 2001).

Unions between Indigenous women and European men, from which the Métis Nation took root in the Historic Northwest, were not merely based on happenstance or sexual motive; rather, they were motivated by strategic considerations on the part of both parties. Indigenous women often incorporated their European husbands into societies structured by

Indigenous custom and tradition. As they took on the traditional role of serving as godmothers to each other's children, women could and did translate these familial connections into strategic alliances that worked to their advantage. For Indigenous women, alliances with European traders were a means of extending their authority.

In addition to their role in creating strategic alliances, Indigenous women were instrumental to the success of the buffalo hunts and the fur trade economy itself. Working alongside men, they performed a variety of tasks; these included building buffalo pounds, serving as scouts and guides, preparing the meat after the hunts, making pemmican, dressing the furs and tanning the hides, drying fruit and smoking fish, netting snowshoes, and helping with the production of birch bark canoes (Brown 1980; de Trémaudan 1982, 9–10; Payment 2009; White 2006). As the functions performed by both men and women were necessary to the physical and economic well-being of families and communities, they were seen as complementary rather than hierarchical, with neither role considered to be more important than the other. The value of this sharing of responsibilities was subsequently transmitted to their children.

The transmission of values along the maternal line became especially important to the development of a distinct Métis way of life. It was the persistence of a heritage of productivity and practical value, Brown (1983, 31) notes, that was to sharply contrast Métis women with "the relative frailty and oft-idolized economic uselessness of their 'fairer' sisterhood" (the white settler women who would later populate the Northwest). As Anderson (2016, 57) argues, Indigenous women shared a common sense of power that was not part of European women's experience.

The power held by Métis women is particularly evident in the various roles they occupied in the fur trade. Through social network analysis, Brenda Macdougall and Nicole St-Onge (2013) illustrate how women took on leadership roles through their participation in the construction of Métis hunt brigades. These brigades were based on networks of men drawn together through marriage to sisters and other female relatives from the same families. Upon the death of their husbands, some women would become independent traders by relying on their kin networks to establish economic alliances. It is in large part through social and economic activities in which women were pivotal that the Métis developed a shared sense of identity as a distinct Indigenous nation (St-Onge, Podruchny, and Macdougall 2012).

The Agency of Métis Women

Métis women took a pragmatic approach to their existence within the fur trade economy, seeking to enlarge their role in economic production as opportunities arose. The economic functions performed by Indian and Métis women in fur trade society, which allowed them to assume positions of genuine power, reflected the simple fact that European traders had to adapt to the Indigenous way of life if they were to survive in the Northwest. Hence, while "women's roles were defined in terms of their relationships to men: wife, mother, daughter or worker," Van Kirk (1980, 7) argues that, "within these spheres, women did act to make the most of the opportunities available to them." This was especially evident in the area of skilled needlework and clothing production.

Sewing served as a focal point from which Métis women gained access to the economy as entrepreneurs. Their proficiency with a needle, which translated into coats and other items of clothing, moccasins, and the netting of snowshoes, rendered Métis women indispensable to survival in the interior. In addition to producing these goods for their own families, Métis women sold them to the steady stream of men coming through the Northwest as travellers, adventurers, and hunters, creating a vibrant market for Métis free traders (Racette 2009, 289). Through their extensive kinship relations, Métis women sold their products to national and international markets, receiving cash, credit, or goods in exchange for their work.

As the fur trade began to wane, needlework became a necessary means for women to supplement their families' incomes (Racette 2005, 40). While the decline of the fur trade marked the end of the social and economic infrastructure created by the network of posts, it did not mark the end of women's economic activity. Métis women, like their male counterparts, adapted to the dramatic shifts in the economy, transforming their production to suit changing circumstances (Racette 2009; Haggarty 2013). Continuing subsistence production for their household's needs, these women produced goods for the clothing and souvenir markets, managing both the resources and the means of production. Métis women thus gained unparalleled economic power. As Sherry Farrell Racette (2005, 41) argues, "while women across Indigenous North America produced useful and beautiful clothing and other decorative items, no other group of women had their work commodified to the same extent."

Firekeepers of Métis Identity

Métis women applied their skills not only to ensure a source of income and a status beyond the domestic sphere but also to bolster their role as key players in the dissemination of Métis identity and culture. Peterson (1978) asserts that Métis identity was not based on racial distinctions but on occupation, mobility, and cultural practices (including style of dress), all of which separated Métis from Europeans and First Nations. Particularly important in this respect was the material representation and expression of Métis cultural identity through beadwork and embroidery. As the Métis came into increasing conflict with the incoming Euro-Canadian settler population, Métis beadwork functioned as a vehicle of political resistance to this encroachment. Sharon Blady (1997, 179) goes so far as to argue that "beadwork was an act of cultural defiance and pre-feminism." Wearing beaded and embroidered garments was a demonstration of pride in being Métis. Moreover, it signalled a refusal on the part of the Métis to abandon their Indigenous roots and assimilate into the dominant European culture (Blady 1996, 135).

Blady's work examining the symbolism of beadwork as both an expression of Métis identity and as an act of political resistance speaks to the importance of women in fostering among the Métis a sense of themselves as a distinct people. As Brown and others have revealed, the salience of Métis women in their historic communities went beyond their activities in the fur trade economy: women were also integral to the ethnogenesis of the Métis Nation and the formation of Métis identity (Brown 1980, 1983; Payment 1996, 2009; Macdougall 2010; St-Onge, Podruchny, and Macdougall 2012). The findings of these scholars reveal that Métis women became firekeepers of Métis identity as they carried out responsibilities related to maintaining *miyeu waahkootoowin* (good relations).

The crucial role of women in maintaining Métis identity is in large part due to the fact that Métis societies were matrilineal and matrilocal (Macdougall 2010). The centrality of women is evident in the way families developed in the context of the fur trade. In keeping with the custom of the country, the initial unions that occurred between voyageurs and Indigenous women in the Northwest tended to be fluid and seasonal. The mobility of the voyageurs kept them away from their wives and offspring for extended periods of time. Upon their return, many voyageurs did not go back to their original families, instead "turning off" their first wives and taking up residence with others (Payment 2009, 123). Some men chose to return east rather than to reunite with their families in the interior (Podruchny 2006; Van Kirk 1980; Brown 1983). The men who did return to their families often became cut off from European relatives, looking to their wife's kinship networks for familial connectedness (Brown 1980). Regardless of the particular circumstances, women were often left to raise children. The Métis, therefore, saw a significant part of their identity and unity as a distinct people originating from matrilineal associations that fundamentally differed from the practices of the dominant anglophone society (Blady 1996, 134). Summing up and reflecting on this history, MMF president David Chartrand declared: "We are a maternal nation. It was our mothers who kept us; it was our fathers who left us."[17]

The custom of matrilocality, whereby dual-heritage offspring developed strong connections to and identification with their mothers and their mothers' families, was greatly accelerated from the 1820s to the 1860s – a tumultuous time in the Northwest marked in particular by the merger of the North West Company and the Hudson's Bay Company in 1821. The HBC's transformation into both a monopoly over the fur trade and the de facto colonial government had significant consequences for the Métis population and the role of women as firekeepers of Métis identity. The rise of a capitalist economy and the increased colonization of the region by European settlers brought about what Catharine Cavanaugh (1997, 503) describes as "a shift in the social order, one that would ensure elite Euro-Canadian men's hegemony in the new West."

The realignment of political and economic forces led to a new social stratification based on Euro-Canadian and Catholic gender ideals that would permeate all levels of Métis society. Under the direction of Governor George Simpson, trading post families were required to incorporate British civilities and religion into daily domestic life. British law as applied in the territory did not recognize paternity in "illegitimate" marriages, which included most of the "country" marriages between European men and Indigenous women. The rise of racial discrimination and the economic, social, and political marginality of dual-heritage children helped set the stage for the birth of Métis nationalism.

In the European drive to clearly demarcate social categories, Sarah Carter (2007, 81) contends that "those who did not appear to suit the requirements of the emerging order, or potentially stood in the way of it, were singled out for criticism by those who did stand to profit." The Métis – the largest demographic cohort and the most prominent of the groups that could lay claim to the Red River – stood out as the most obvious target. Sensitive to these newly imposed class and racial distinctions, many of those who had the financial and social means sent their children away to be educated in the mores of European values and culture (as was the case of Louis Riel's father, Jean-Louis Riel, who was educated in Berthier, Quebec). For those who chose not to or could not afford to do so, the opportunities for economic security or upward social mobility were constrained. It is in this context that dual-heritage descendants began to develop their own collective consciousness.

Efforts by colonial powers to police Métis identity based on ancestry or cultural traits have been adamantly resisted by Métis leaders, both historically and today. Recent scholarship has elucidated the intergenerational consequences of the ongoing imposition of race-based understandings of Métis identity (Andersen 2014; Gaudry and Andersen 2016; Vowel and Leroux 2016; Gaudry and Leroux 2017). These scholars note that the reliance on an Indigenous ancestor to legitimize and, by extension, to delegitimize claims to Métis identity fails to acknowledge the complex kinship connections that are at the heart of the shared consciousness that unite the Métis as a distinct nation. Jennifer Adese (2016) contends that the Canadian state has repeatedly – with strategic intentions – failed to recognize the way in which the Métis Nation defines itself through kinship connections and a shared political consciousness.

Ultimately, as Gaudry and Andersen (2016, 28) remind us, "determining who belongs to Indigenous political communities is the purview of those political communities."

Women in Action across the Métis Nation Homeland

Our understanding of the role of women as the firekeepers of Métis identity has been enhanced by case studies of women in historic Métis communities in Manitoba, Saskatchewan, and Montana. In recounting the life histories of Métis women in Saint-Eustache, Manitoba, for example, Nicole St-Onge (2008) draws attention to these women's strong identification with Métis identity and culture and their equally strong sense of the "Other" (notably, their French Canadian neighbours) in terms of social status and material wealth. Moreover, Brenda Macdougall's (2006, 2010) examination of Métis communities in northwestern Saskatchewan reveals that the physical location of many Métis communities in maternal lands reflects the fact that women became a centrifugal force in incorporating successive waves of outsider males. She explains that "Aboriginal women – Cree, Dene and then Métis – grounded their families in their homelands, creating for them a sense of belonging to the territory through a regionally defined matrilocal residency pattern and, therefore, female-centred family networks."[18]

In addition to their central position in identity-production, Métis women played an influential role in the decision-making practices and structures that historically governed their societies. As we discuss in earlier chapters, Métis governments and the laws and processes that they embrace were inspired by the traditions of the hunt and the harvest. Métis social organization was both communal and democratic, with laws that had been passed down orally, ratified or changed at public assemblies. It is through these democratic fora that social values and traditions, such as respect for the authority of elders, care for the sick and infirm, the adoption of children, and divorce (or the "turning off" of spouses) were also subjected to moral persuasion and community control. Métis women – indeed, like many Indigenous women – were not excluded from these fora, which were based on egalitarian ideals that did not have a parallel in European society. While formal political positions tended to be held by men, because of the complementary nature of their socio-economic roles and their central place within family and kinship networks, women were nonetheless able to assert their influence (Troupe 2009, 61). As a Métis woman from Alberta noted, "Women, especially the grandmothers, were always asked their opinion by the men in our community. As women we weren't showy like the men, but when asked our opinion, we gave it and our words were valued."[19]

Cheryl Troupe's (2009, 107) examination of Métis women's activism in Saskatchewan reveals their ongoing influence in the political mobilization that occurred in the province in the 1930s. Women attended meetings, visited with friends and relatives to garner support for emerging political associations, and, within Métis communities, organized social events that were political in nature. In speaking about her motivations to become active in Métis politics in Saskatchewan in the 1970s, Nora Cummings, a respected Métis elder and the founder of the Saskatchewan Native Women's Association, draws attention to how political work was not seen as the sole domain of men. Senator Cummings stated that, "we as women, as Métis women, and it goes back in history, we were always equal with our men and we worked with our men."[20] The need for men and women to work together was viewed as essential if the Métis Nation was to survive. An interviewee from Alberta described how the Métis as a group were historically shunned by both their First Nations and European relatives. She spoke of how this marginalization, coupled with their exclusion from state policies and assistance programs, led Métis men and women to rely on one another – in her words, "as the Road Allowance People, we only had each other."[21] The efforts that women undertook alongside men to protect Métis identity and culture were constitutive of a distinct Métis way of life. They are embodied in what Métis refer to as *aen ishi wiichayaamitooyahk* (how we live together).

Situating Gender Relations in Indigenous Societies

The traditional influence wielded by Métis women is reflective of the power held by other Indigenous women prior to European contact. In their examination of historical Indigenous groups in Canada, Menno

Boldt and J. Anthony Long argue that Indigenous societies were collectively ruled according to values that favoured consensus among men and women over hierarchy (1984, 543). Gender roles were perceived as complementary rather than dichotomous, with no human being – not even the community's leader – deemed to have control over the life of another (Stark 2013; see also Bastien 1996, 127–29; Baskin 1982, 43). The political authority of women was tied to the value placed on gathering input from all members of the community and to their role as nourishers of future generations (Anderson 2016, 65–72). Jeanette Armstrong (1996, ix) speaks of the "immense power" of women in traditional Indigenous communities as being a result of their ability to bring forth life: "The earliest instruments of governance and law to ensure social order came from the quality mothering of children."

Despite the power held by Indigenous women, scholars caution against the dangers of overly romanticizing the status of Indigenous women in pre-contact societies. Métis scholar Emma LaRocque (1996, 4), for example, points out: "We cannot assume that all Aboriginal traditions universally respected and honoured women ... It should not be assumed, even in those original societies that were structured along matriarchal lines, that matriarchies necessarily prevented men from oppressing women." The power held by women in Indigenous societies cannot solely be measured by the political positions they hold but should also take into account their role in the governance of the community as a whole.

The role of women in Indigenous governance has varied throughout history (RCAP 1996b; Voyageur 2008; Anderson 2009). While many First Nations had male chiefs, in some societies, such as the Haudenosaunee, women exercised key decision-making powers (Childs 1998, 154). Kiera Ladner explains that, in Blackfoot society, governance was largely consensual, with power wielded collectively and horizontally by men and women. Though most women remained in camp and were responsible for camp life, Ladner (2009, 70) argues that this seemingly gendered division of labour is guided by principles of interrelatedness and responsibility and thus "cannot be equated with inequality, subordination or oppression." Viewed as equal and valued persons in their own right, women were consistently consulted on matters affecting the community, "as good decisions are said to have begun and ended with women" (71).

In many respects, the prominence of women in contemporary Métis politics is consistent with the responsibilities women have traditionally held in Indigenous societies generally and in Métis society in particular. The fact that Métis women are represented at all levels of contemporary Métis governments, that the majority of Métis governments are currently led by female presidents, and that women hold high-profile portfolios like finance and self-government demonstrate that Métis women are prominent political actors in contemporary Métis governments. These roles are consistent with the historical responsibilities of Métis women, who were integral to *kȧ ishi pimaatishiyaahk* (our way of life) through the kinship relations they nurtured. They are also constitutive of *aen ishi wiichayaamitooyahk* (how we live together) as Métis women assumed economic, social, and political responsibilities.

Keepers of the Nation

Our understanding of the cardinal role that women have come to occupy as keepers of the Métis Nation has been enhanced by anthropological and historical studies (Van Kirk 1980; Peterson 1985; Payment 1996; Sleeper-Smith 2001; Devine 2001, 2004; St-Onge 2008; Macdougall 2010). Notably, Diane Payment's extensive research of the Métis community of Batoche, Saskatchewan, reveals that Métis women actively served in the war effort as helpmates and military strategists in the Resistance of 1885. Indeed, Métis oral history tells of women scrambling during the Battle of Batoche to melt pots, cutlery, and whatever else they could find to fashion bullets. Nor were Métis women afraid to join their fathers and brothers in battle. During the Battle of Grand Coteau in 1851, Isabelle Falcon Trottier, the daughter of Pierre Falcon, took up her brother's gun and fought in his place while he served as captain of the brigade.[22]

The women of Batoche were also not afraid to openly express their political views, "especially if they were contrary to those of their fathers or husbands" (Payment 1996, 27). Most of the victims of the Métis resistance movements were men who left behind widows with large families.

As Métis women rose to the challenge of supporting their families and rebuilding their communities during the period of *le grand silence*, they kept the flames of Métis identity burning. In contrast with the dominant society, in which the status of women had become greatly eroded by the promulgation of Euro-Christian values by the end of the 1800s, Payment (1996, 20) argues that the "persistence and pride" of Métis women ensured the survival of Métis communities like Batoche. Female kinship ties would prove essential in keeping Métis communities alive after 1885 (Troupe 2009, 65).

Payment pays particular tribute to the prominence of grandmothers in cementing Métis identity among children, notably during the dark decades that followed the Northwest Resistance (see also Kermoal 2016). She writes: "Transmission of cultural values took place at home and generally was done by grandmothers, or kokums, who were 'the real teachers' … they were the bosses in the homes and were responsible for the education and survival of future generations" (Payment 2009, 253–55). Other Métis women have also commented on the seminal role played by grandmothers and great-grandmothers in keeping Métis knowledge, cultural traditions, and kinship relations flourishing, a power that extended beyond the immediate family. For example, Maria Campbell describes her great-grandmother as the head of not only her family but also of all the extended families of her offspring, which gave her tremendous influence over the community (in Anderson 2016, 136). She explains: "No decision was made without her first giving her blessing. My dad and uncles would sit down and talk to her when they were going to do something. If she said no, nobody questioned it" (in Anderson 2016, 68). The stories of Métis women, while less known than those of their male counterparts, are nonetheless essential because they provide us with a more complete account of the lives of the Métis (Iseke-Barnes 2009, 70). As Métis scholar Lorraine Mayer (2007, 73) poignantly writes: "We Métis carry the stories our grandmothers told. We carry them and we survive."

Many of the women who shared their stories with us spoke of the influence of their grandmothers and great-grandmothers in shaping their political consciousness and informing their commitment to participate in Métis political life. One interviewee from Manitoba recounted one of her strongest memories as a child sitting beside her great-grandmother on wagon rides into the bush: "All of the kids would fight for the chance to sit beside her. She would tell us stories about Louis Riel, who was her cousin, and about how he had fought for Métis people. She would tell us all about how we had to be proud of who we were, and to never be ashamed of being Métis."[23] Another woman active in Métis politics spoke of her grandmother's impact in forming her political awareness. She described her grandmother as someone who was not directly involved in Métis politics but who was very powerful in her own right due to the high esteem in which she was held by the family and the community. Her grandmother's brother was one of the first organizers of the Métis in Saskatchewan. "As a little girl it was my job to help clean up after Uncle had one of his political meetings. When I would ask my grandma why I had to do it, she told me to listen to what the people were talking about, to learn about the Métis and their struggles. 'You are the keeper of the family,' she told me. I never forgot that."[24]

Conclusion

Women play a key role as mothers of the Métis Nation. As Métis elder Verna DeMontigny reminds us, "women are the ones who keep the community together."[25] In this chapter, we contend that the historic centrality of women in the fur trade economy and in the birth of Métis identity and nationhood lives on in contemporary political practice. Today, women are active agents in all aspects of Métis politics. In addition to their involvement in women's organizations, a significant number of women hold elected and executive positions within Métis governments across the Homeland. As we show in Chapter 3, neglect by provincial and federal governments provided the Métis with the opportunity to design political structures that more fully reflected their values and traditions. Although not without their own set of challenges, these structures created space for the continued inclusion of Métis women in political life in ways that reflect their historical influence.

However, as LaRocque (1996, 11) reminds us, "colonization has taken its toll on all Native peoples, but perhaps it has taken its greatest toll on women." In this, Métis women are no exception. The fact that they occupy a significant portion of the seats around the political table is not meant to suggest that Métis women have not suffered from the effects of patriarchy, marginalization, and sexism within their own governments. Several of the women interviewed recounted the chauvinism and resistance they encountered as elected representatives, notably as they rose to the upper echelons of executive power within their respective governments. Even though she has been an elected official for several years, one of the participants interviewed described being treated differently by her male counterparts, some of whom perceive her as a threat.[26] Another interviewee from Alberta recounted the pushback she encountered by her male colleagues when she first tried to get programs started for women and children in her community. "The men didn't see these things as a priority when there were larger battles to be fought over rights and land claims," she noted.[27]

While acknowledging the sexist comments she and other female leaders have experienced, a participant from Saskatchewan spoke earnestly about the situation in which the Métis Nation finds itself. "Our men are still hurting," she stated. "They are scared of our inner strength, when they feel they have been made powerless [by the colonization of the Canadian state]."[28] In the face of the sexism and patriarchy that continues to exist not only in Métis governments but in all contemporary political structures, Kim Anderson (2016, 157) calls for the reclamation of Indigenous tradition, "the picking up of these things that were left scattered along the path of colonization." It is through a return to ancestral traditions, customs, and ways of being, she contends, that Indigenous women can foster a feminine identity that "moves us away from the western patriarchal model."

For Lee Maracle (2006), the "rematriation" of governance structures is not secondary but, rather, integral to rebuilding Indigenous nations. LaRocque, however, warns against the danger of overly focusing on maternalism. As she argues, Indigenous women should not saddle themselves with the staggering responsibility of teaching or nurturing the whole world; nor should they assume sole responsibility for "healing" or "nurturing" Aboriginal men (LaRocque 2007, 65). To do so sets up a troubling dichotomy: "Native women are 'honoured' as 'keepers' of tradition, defined as nurturing/healing, while Native men control political power" (66).

Métis women are continually called upon to navigate the legacy of patriarchy and sexism that accompanied colonization. In so doing, they can rely on the legacy of success and power of the Métis women who preceded them. All of the female Métis political leaders interviewed spoke of the legacy of the women who came before them; indeed, they see their political successes as nothing out of the ordinary but, rather, as the continuation of the vital position that previous generations of Métis women held in their communities and in the survival of their nation. Significantly, the well-being of Métis women is seen as intrinsically tied to the success of the Métis Nation as a whole. In the words of one participant from Manitoba, "I'm doing what my mother and grandmother taught me, to fight for the rights of the Métis and to be proud of our identity."[29]

6

Li Shmayn ishi Tipaymishoohk

The Road to Métis Self-Government

ON APRIL 13, 2017, leaders from the Métis Nation and Canada gathered in Ottawa for the inaugural Métis Nation-Crown Summit. In a joint news release with Métis Nation president Clément Chartier, Prime Minister Justin Trudeau stated: "Last December, I made the promise that federal ministers and Métis Nation leaders would work together to solve important challenges. We did not take that commitment lightly."[1] Surrounded by members of the federal cabinet and the five Métis Government presidents, the prime minister and the leaders of the Métis Nation signed the Canada-Métis Nation Accord.[2] Described by the Métis National Council as a "turning point for Canada and the Métis Nation," the accord lays the foundation for a new government-to-government relationship based on the recognition of rights, respect, cooperation, and partnership.[3]

The accord is ground-breaking for two reasons. First, it charts a path towards reconciliation between the Métis Nation and Canada through the implementation of Métis section 35 rights and the resolution of outstanding grievances. To this end, the accord outlines the ways in which the Government of Canada will work with the Métis National Council and its Governing Members to develop policies. To facilitate this new relationship, the accord creates a permanent bilateral mechanism consisting of annual meetings between Métis leaders and the prime minister, in addition to bilateral and quarterly meetings between federal and Métis cabinet members and departmental officials. With the creation of this new mechanism, Canada has committed to implementing Métis constitutional rights and to setting up a specific process towards achieving this goal. No longer relegated to the sidelines, Métis leaders now sit at the table with their federal counterparts on a nation-to-nation, government-to-government basis for the first time since Confederation.

Second, while the Canada-Métis Nation Accord looks to the future, it also pays homage to the historical struggle of the Métis to remain *ka tipemishoshik* (the free people). The accord represents the culmination of the collective efforts of the Métis over the past century and a half to bring to life their inherent right to self-government and to force Canada's hand in acknowledging and implementing this right. The promise of the accord to complete the unfinished business of Confederation stands as testimony to the decades of political negotiations, legal battles, and nation-building efforts in which the Métis Nation has continuously engaged to reach this point. As such, it speaks to two arguments advanced throughout this book: (1) that since their emergence as a distinct Indigenous nation the Métis have asserted agency to remain self-governing and (2) that they have used whatever tools available in the pursuit of this objective. The Métis have demonstrated an ongoing willingness to adapt to the circumstances at hand and to develop governance structures and processes to achieve self-government.

In this chapter, we discuss the significance of the Canada-Métis Nation Accord and the potential it holds for the advancement of Métis self-government. In so doing we highlight some of the key legal and political milestones that led to this historic moment in Canada-Métis Nation relations and that are reflected in the accord itself. We also consider challenges in fostering reconciliation between the Métis Nation and Canada; in particular, we discuss issues related to citizenship, boundaries, and the relationship between the Métis National Council and its Governing Members. We conclude that the promise of the accord ultimately depends on the actions of Métis, provincial, and federal leaders as they navigate *li shmayn ishi tipaymishoohk* (the road to self-government).

The Canada-Métis Nation Accord: A Long Journey to a New Way Forward

The Canada-Métis Nation Accord does not introduce new ideas about the Métis. Many of the accord's provisions, including the commitment to negotiate agreements on issues of priority, were proposed in the context of the 1992 Charlottetown Accord. The novelty of the Canada-Métis Accord lies in the fact that it affirms what the Métis have been advancing for years – something that previous governments have refused to acknowledge in any meaningful sense. As Métis Nation of Ontario president Margaret Froh notes, "Our communities have long been self-governing based on Métis laws, traditions, customs and kinship." She adds: "the notion of formally recognized Métis self-government – by other orders of government – that is new."[4] Significantly, the accord brings to an end 150 years of state denial regarding Métis constitutional rights and acknowledges the need to politically negotiate these rights on a government-to-government basis. This is reflected in the accord's opening preamble, which recognizes the emergence of the Métis as a distinct Aboriginal people in the Historic Northwest, with their own collective identity and way of life, who continue to "exercise [their] right to self-determination[,] including self-government within Canada."[5]

Beginning with the inclusion of the Métis in section 35 of the Constitution Act, 1982, the Canada-Métis Accord traces the legal victories of the Métis as they engaged with the courts to advance their rights-based agenda. These victories include the Supreme Court of Canada's 2003 recognition in *Powley* that Métis communities that emerged prior to effective control possess constitutionally protected Métis rights, the Court's 2013 ruling in *Manitoba Métis Federation Inc. v. Canada* that the Crown has fiduciary obligations to the Métis, as well as its 2016 decision in *Daniels* that the Métis fall within the constitutional jurisdiction of the federal government.

The accord goes a step further than merely acknowledging the existence of Métis constitutional rights. It asserts Canada's commitment to a renewed relationship with the Métis National Council's Governing Members in order to "further Métis self-government, while respecting Métis rights and ending the status quo."[6] With the accord, Canada commits to engage in the political negotiation of these rights and to the fulfillment of the federal government's fiduciary obligations towards the Métis. It can rely on the newly established mechanisms to facilitate these outcomes. Yet, as with any political agreement, its success depends on the willingness of the parties to honour their promises.

For the leaders gathered at the Métis Nation-Crown Summit, the goal has remained the same as that of their forebears in Red River and Batoche. Then, as now, Métis leaders aspire not only to have their rights affirmed but also to have the ability to negotiate these rights in a political forum in partnership with Canada. The signing of the Canada-Métis Nation Accord opens the door for Métis and federal leaders to politically engage with one another in a formal and concrete manner. As Métis Nation of Alberta president Audrey Poitras attests, the accord "demonstrates the commitment of Prime Minister Trudeau to working with the Métis Nation on a government to government basis."[7]

The parties already have a foundation on which to base these government-to-government negotiations. Significant in this respect are advances in the legal sphere (notably Supreme Court rulings in *Powley, Manitoba Métis Federation Inc.*, and *Daniels*); the findings of the 2016 report of the ministerial special representative on reconciliation with Métis, Thomas Isaac; as well as the work undertaken by the Métis to enhance and strengthen their own governance structures. In keeping with these developments, the prime minister announced a new engagement process with First Nations, Inuit, and the Métis Nation in February 2018, which is expected to include new legislation on Indigenous rights as well as a new distinctions-based policy to replace the current Comprehensive Land Claims Policy and the Inherent Right to Self-Government Policy.[8] In order to assess what lies ahead as Métis and federal leaders engage in this new political relationship, we look back at some of these developments and consider their implications moving forward.

Turning to the Courts to Achieve Political Outcomes

The signing of the Canada-Métis Nation Accord demonstrates the success of the Métis' purposeful strategy to use litigation to force Canada's hand to return to the bargaining table. The accord was notably made possible by the inclusion of the Métis in section 35 of the Constitution Act, 1982. Hailed at the time as a monumental triumph for the Métis, the promise of section 35 constitutional rights did not materialize. The constitutional conferences designed to clarify "existing Aboriginal and treaty rights" were instead followed by what Jean Teillet (2012, 339) refers to as "the full box/empty box debate." On one side, the Métis asserted that the section 35 rights box was full and that the federal government therefore had an obligation to recognize and affirm those rights. Canada took an opposing perspective, steadfastly arguing that section 35 was devoid of meaning until filled in by court-determined rights.

Hope that Métis constitutional rights would be addressed in the political, rather than the legal, sphere was raised yet again in the early 1990s during negotiations on the Charlottetown Accord. Contained within the constitutional amendments agreed to by the first ministers and Métis leaders in Charlottetown was the Canada-Métis Nation Accord. Significantly, the accord would have recognized the Métis as "Indians" within the meaning of section 91(24) of the Constitution Act, 1867, thus acknowledging the federal government's constitutional responsibility for the Métis. The accord also promised negotiations towards Métis self-government. This promise was abandoned following the rejection of the Charlottetown Accord in a national referendum in 1992. As President Chartier stated before the House of Commons Standing Committee on Aboriginal Affairs and Northern Development, "the defeat of the Charlottetown Accord in the national referendum of October 1992 dashed our hopes for a negotiated settlement of our outstanding rights and forced us into the courts."[9]

Jason Madden, legal counsel to several Métis governments, explains the frustration of Métis leaders over Canada's unwillingness to negotiate with them in the wake of the failed constitutional reform process. Confronted with state intransigence, the Métis had little choice but to change tactics: "When you have no other option, when you don't have a partner on the other side, you turn to the courts to resolve your problems."[10] The goal in adopting a legal strategy, he adds, "was to throw enough pebbles at the window to crack it" and thus force the government back to the bargaining table. A critical step in this legal strategy was the affirmation in *R. v. Powley* that the Métis hold existing Aboriginal rights under section 35 of the Constitution Act, 1982.

In *Powley*, the Supreme Court outlined three criteria to identify section 35 Métis rights-holders. In what came to be known as the Powley Test, the Court specified that, in order to claim Métis rights, a person must self-identify as Métis, hold membership in a present-day Métis community, and be connected to a historic Métis community. As such, not everyone of mixed Aboriginal ancestry is a Métis rights-holder. The Court clarified that "the term 'Métis' in section 35 does not encompass all individuals with mixed Indian and European heritage; rather, it refers to distinctive peoples who, in addition to their mixed ancestry, developed their own customs, way of life, and recognizable group identity separate from their Indian or Inuit and European forebears."[11]

One of the most significant political outcomes of *Powley* for the Métis Nation was the federal government's decision in 2004 to make funding available to facilitate the development of a standardized, national registry process through the Powley Initiative. This decision was a response to what the Supreme Court described as the "urgent" need for a more systematic approach to identifying Métis section 35 rights-holders.[12] Métis governments used the funding provided by Canada under the Powley Initiative to strengthen and standardize their citizenship registries. To this end, provincial registry offices were established by each Governing Member to assist applicants in obtaining the necessary documents – long-form birth certificates, marriage certificates, and baptismal registers and scrip records – that show proof of intergenerational links to the historic Métis community.[13] In developing these registries, Governing Members unanimously agreed that individuals who applied for citizenship must meet the National Definition adopted in 2002. As Métis Nation of Alberta president Poitras asserts, "One of the fundamental aspects of Métis rights is our ability to define ourselves. It's not up to the government, or non-Métis people, to define who is Métis. Only the Métis Nation itself can make those kinds of distinctions."[14] Manitoba Métis Federation president Chartrand echoes this sentiment, declaring: "no one other than the Métis People can define our Nation."[15] Rather than defining who is Métis – a right that lies with the Métis Nation itself – *Powley* drew attention to the need for capacity building within Métis governments to enable the identification of section 35 rights-holders.

Despite this development, the lack of stable funding made it difficult for some Métis governments to maintain their registries and to respond to the growing backlog of applications in a timely manner. Speaking to these challenges, Isaac argues that it is in the "public interest" to have transparent, legally correct, and objectively verifiable Métis registries.[16] Predictable and long-term investments to support the governance capacity of Métis governments is not only consistent with principles of good governance but, as Isaac contends, also contributes to the fulfillment of Métis constitutional rights. In the 2017 budget, the federal government responded to the Métis Nation's call for predictable, long-term, and stable funding with the promise of $84.9 million over the next five years; this funding is specifically targeted to building the governance capacity of the Métis National Council and its Governing Members and supporting Métis identification registries.[17]

In addition to assisting with the development of Métis registries, *Powley* was enthusiastically welcomed by Métis leaders for providing a much-needed analytical framework to prove the existence of Métis constitutional rights. As Catherine Bell and Clayton Leonard (2004, 31–32) recall, "Before *Powley*, debates and uncertainty – about the possible nature and scope of Métis rights, the legal effects of scrip on Métis Aboriginal rights and title, Métis constitutional identity, federal and provincial jurisdiction for Métis, and the appropriate modern legal entities with whom to negotiate Métis rights – created barriers to consultation and negotiation." *Powley* fostered negotiations between Canada and the Métis by imposing obligations on the Crown to consult and accommodate in good faith as a way of minimizing the infringement of proven Métis constitutional rights (Bell and Seaman 2015).

The promise of *Powley* as a catalyst to clarify and negotiate Métis section 35 rights more broadly failed to materialize in political circles. The absence of a policy framework to negotiate Métis rights and disagreements among provinces and courts about the proper application of *Powley* led to varied and sometimes contradictory approaches to Métis rights, particularly with respect to harvesting (see discussion in Bell and Leonard 2004; Weinstein 2007, 58).

In the absence of a political framework for negotiations with Canada, the Métis continued to use the courts to advance their section 35 rights. This proved to be a tedious avenue as Métis claimants sought to prove the existence of historical Métis communities in various parts of the Historic Northwest as required by the Powley Test. An analysis of the arguments presented in lower courts reveals that the Crown and the Métis do not perceive communities in the same way. While the Crown insists that localized communities prove site-specific rights, Métis claimants argue that there is a single Métis Nation characterized by mobility and kinship networks whose territory covers the entire Prairies (Gagné, Larcher, and Grammond 2014; Grammond, Lantagne, and Gagné 2016). The heart of the problem, as Teillet (2012, 345) explains, is that the political and legal framework in place does not take into account the historic or contemporary reality of the Métis:

> Finding the boundaries of a physical settlement that can be called a Métis community is an exercise in futility. This is not to say that there were no Métis settlements. Red River (now Winnipeg), Fort Edmonton, Lac Ste. Anne, Batoche, St. Laurent, Rainy River and Sault Ste. Marie are just a few well-known Métis settlements. But for many Métis these settlements were not where they lived. If they were fur traders in the boreal forest they spent most of their time en route. If they were buffalo hunters they spent the bulk of their time on the plains. They built temporary wintering cabins in sheltered spots such as Cypress Hills, Wood Mountain and Turtle Mountain. Settlements were primarily for the acquisition of necessaries. But life for many Métis was one of mobility. It is in these circumstances that the current problem of Métis litigation arises. How does one geographically define a historical Métis community when the people were so mobile?

Thus, even with the Supreme Court's ruling in *Powley*, the Métis were forced to return to the courts time and again to fight for their rights on an "inch-by-inch" basis.[18]

With the existence of Métis constitutional rights confirmed in the *Powley* decision, the second goal of Métis legal strategy was to seek affirmation that the Métis have outstanding claims against the Crown. In an address to the Senate of Canada in 2011, President Chartier described the absence of a political solution to Métis rights as a consequence of "Ottawa's persistent refusal to accept historical, constitutional and moral responsibility for dealing with the Métis people as a distinct Aboriginal people and nation."[19] At the top of Métis grievances is Canada's long-standing position that the scrip system extinguished any claims to Métis land title, a position that Métis leaders disputed in *Morin v. Canada and Saskatchewan* and *Manitoba Métis Federation Inc. v. Canada*. While the *Morin* case (which was filed in 1994) is still pending, in its 2013 ruling on *Manitoba Métis Federation Inc. v. Canada*, the Supreme Court of Canada found that promises of land made to the Métis in section 31 of the Manitoba Act, 1870 engaged the honour of the Crown and imposed constitutional obligations that were not fulfilled.[20] As long as these promises remain unresolved, the Court added, the goal of reconciliation recognized in section 35 of the Constitution Act, 1982, and that underlies section 31 of the Manitoba Act, remain unachieved. Bell and Seaman (2015, 5) explain that the decision in *Manitoba Métis Federation Inc.* "emphasizes the ongoing process of reconciliation by taking the focus away from proof of rights and putting it on negotiation and enforcement of solemn promises and the constitutional principle of the honour of the Crown." Significantly, the Court acknowledged that negotiations should occur with Métis governments and, in particular, with the Manitoba Métis Federation.[21]

Having confirmed that Métis hold constitutional rights and that the Crown has a fiduciary obligation to fulfill those constitutional rights, Métis leaders subsequently sought to clarify the federal government's constitutional relationship with the Métis. Specifically, they sought direction from the Court as to the constitutional responsibility of the federal government towards the Métis. While the Métis were constitutionally recognized as one of Canada's three Aboriginal peoples in section 35 of the Constitution Act, 1982, provincial and federal governments continued to treat the Métis differently, sidelining them from programs and policies and calling on them to meet state-imposed categories as a condition of the recognition of their rights (Andersen 2014; Grammond 2009; Chartrand 2004; P. Chartrand 2008; Chartrand and Giokas 2002). Canada's refusal to accept jurisdictional responsibility for the Métis led to what the Supreme Court of Canada describes as a "legislative vacuum" with neither level of government willing to adopt legislation to address the needs of the Métis.[22] Finally bringing this long-standing game of jurisdictional football between provincial and federal governments to an end in *Daniels v. Canada*, the Supreme Court of Canada confirmed that the Métis fall under the meaning of "Indians" in section 91(24) of the Constitution Act, 1867, and are therefore under federal jurisdiction. The Court acknowledged that the disagreement between the federal government and the provinces over who bears legislative authority for the Métis has resulted in the Métis people having been deprived of much needed programs and services. This led the Court to conclude that granting a declaration that assigns constitutional authority to make laws affecting the Métis and non-status Indians to the federal government would have "enormous practical utility."[23]

The implication of this ruling is that the Métis are no longer left wondering about where to turn for policy redress. The Court provided certainty by confirming the federal government's constitutional authority to pass laws that deal with Métis rights and needs. At the same time, the Court acknowledged that the provinces still have a role to play.[24] Isaac, the minister's special representative on reconciliation with Métis, contends that the role of provinces with respect to the Métis is tied to reconciliation. As embodiments of the Crown, federal and provincial governments have an obligation to act in good faith in their dealings with Indigenous peoples as required by the honour of the Crown. Isaac argues that it is in the public interest for both levels of government to engage with the Métis.

For leaders like Métis Nation president Chartier, the value of legal decisions such as *Powley*, *Manitoba Métis Federation Inc.*, and *Daniels* does not rest in the details of the legal texts but in the potential they hold for advancing Métis rights and bringing about larger changes in Canada-Métis relations.[25] As Manitoba Métis Federation president Chartrand reminded the delegates gathered in Winnipeg for the MMF Government Summit, the goal of *Manitoba Métis Federation Inc.* was, from the very beginning, to bring the government to the negotiating table.[26] Métis elder John Morrisseau, who was one of the first organizers for the MMF, recalls that negotiating land was on the table from the first days of Métis political organization in Manitoba.[27] Described by Madden as the "trifecta of Métis case law," *Powley*, *Manitoba Métis Federation Inc.*, and *Daniels* give the Métis added leverage in overcoming the reluctance of federal and provincial leaders to politically negotiate a settlement regarding outstanding grievances and to move forward on the development of a true government-to-government relationship.[28]

The success of this relationship will depend on the implementation of section 35 Métis rights and the settlement of outstanding grievances. This conclusion was clear in the 2016 report of the minister's special representative on reconciliation with Métis. Appointed by the preceding Conservative government, Isaac was given the dual mandate to map out a process for dialogue on section 35 Métis rights as well as a framework for negotiations with the MMF in response to the Supreme Court of Canada's decision in *Manitoba Métis Federation Inc.* As Métis Nation president Chartier announced at the time of Isaac's appointment, "We are entering into a new era based on the principle that the sovereignty of Canada should be reconciled with the rights and interests of the Métis Nation."[29]

Following a series of meetings with Métis Nation governments, provinces, territories, and other interested parties in order to assess the current state of affairs and provide independent advice on a path forward, Isaac concluded that reconciliation flows from the constitutionally protected rights of the Métis.[30] He added that the design and implementation of a section 35 Métis rights framework must take *Powley* as the starting point.[31] The question incumbent on federal and provincial leaders is not whether the Métis have rights but, rather, how best to implement Métis constitutional rights – reiterating what Métis leaders have been advancing all along. As Isaac notes, reconciliation is more than "platitudes and recognition," it requires "practical actions."[32]

Moving beyond Myths

The Canada-Métis Nation Accord provides a framework to put in motion actions that will lead to the implementation of Métis rights. The existence of this framework, however, does not mean that these rights will automatically exist in any real sense. Isaac observes that there are a number of steps that must be taken to bring about reconciliation between Canada and the Métis. At the top of this list is the need for federal and provincial governments to address the deficiencies of existing legislation that has been built on myths and misconceptions about the Métis. It is telling that the first recommendation of the Isaac Report aims to address the "gap in knowledge" about the Métis that exists at the provincial and federal levels.[33] Specifically, Isaac calls for the immediate establishment of programs to educate government employees about the history of the Métis, their contributions to Canada, Métis culture and traditions, and Canadian law related to Métis rights. According to Isaac, this education is vital to the establishment of a common understanding of Métis identity and rights that is needed to bring about meaningful reconciliation.

This gap in knowledge about the Métis has been exacerbated by the historical refusal of federal and provincial governments to assume constitutional responsibility for the Métis. The Supreme Court of Canada notes in *Cunningham* that it was not until the adoption of the Constitution Act, 1982, that the Métis received legal recognition as a unique Aboriginal people in Canada:

> The Métis considered themselves as one of three Aboriginal groups in Canada, but this was not recognized until the Constitution Act, 1982. Unlike Indians, however, they enjoyed no land base from which to strengthen their identity and culture or govern themselves. Nor did they enjoy the protection of an equivalent to the Indian Act. Their aboriginality, in a word, was not legally acknowledged or protected ... the Métis have struggled for more than two centuries for recognition of their own unique identity, culture and governance.[34]

As evidenced by the pursuit of the *Daniels* case, one of the key deficiencies that the Métis have sought to address is their exclusion from the federal land claims processes established for First Nations and Inuit. This was confirmed in a 2015 report by another ministerial special representative, Douglas Eyford, who was tasked with giving direction on Canada's land claims policy. Eyford observed that Canada's policies related to land remain silent on Métis rights.[35]

Isaac calls on the federal government to take action to address the policy gaps with respect to the Métis. This call is consistent with the declaration of the Supreme Court of Canada in *Daniels*, which sought to give the Métis tools for policy redress. The Court acknowledged that the recognition of Métis under section 91(24) aimed to provide certainty and accountability and thus to be of practical utility in the resolution of long-standing jurisdictional disputes. While this declaration provides clarification about who can take legislative action, it does not give rise to a duty to legislate.[36] Constitutionally, it is ultimately up to the federal government to decide whether to act on the jurisdiction it holds with respect to the Métis. In his report, Isaac recommends that Canada adopt legislation that is directed specifically to the Métis. In practice, this could involve amending existing policy or adopting a new policy to expressly address Métis claims to land – a step that would require the federal government to reverse its long-standing position that denies Métis rights to land.

Although the accord provides the framework to move in this direction, the respect of Métis rights is not guaranteed. Significant and substantive changes are required for the federal government to fully engage with the Métis. These include changes in attitude through the education of civil servants as well as structural changes through the modification and adoption of legislation.

Ongoing attitudinal and structural challenges were apparent in the early meetings that took place as part of the new bilateral mechanism. To date, discussions have been productive, leading to advancements in the areas of economic development, skills and employment training, early learning and childcare, and housing.[37] At the same time, Métis officials note that discussions have been constrained by the focus on what needs to be done immediately.[38] They argue that it takes time to build relationships of trust and to learn to work together.[39] While acknowledging the federal government's willingness to engage with them, Métis officials caution against moving too quickly and emphasize the need to build a strong foundation for a lasting relationship with the federal government.

The success of this relationship will depend on the parties' commitment to give life to the accord. In so far as provinces and the federal government are engaged by the honour of the Crown, they have an obligation to act in good faith to advance reconciliation with the Métis. For Isaac, this implies that federal and provincial governments provide support to democratically elected and rights-based Métis governments. This is necessary, he notes, in order for Canada and the provinces to have duly mandated, democratic, and transparent Métis governments with whom to deal in advancing reconciliation.[40]

Recent actions of the Trudeau government suggest that Canada has taken note of the direction provided by the Supreme Court in its various rulings concerning the Métis, along with the recommendations contained in the Isaac Report. Following the signing of the Canada-Métis Nation Accord, the federal government signed memoranda of understanding on advancing reconciliation with each of the Métis governments. These MOUs provide a mechanism for advancing section 35 rights through bilateral and trilateral relationships. In particular, they lay the groundwork for negotiations on mutually agreeable subject matters, including Métis self-government, lands, rights, and outstanding claims against the Crown. According to Métis Nation of Alberta president Audrey Poitras, "For many years at the federal level, we have been on the outside looking in." She adds that the advancements made "open the door for us to finally put in place the government-to-government relationship with Canada our people have sought for generations as well as [to] begin to address the pressing issues of our citizens and communities in Alberta, including dealing with Métis rights, lands and self-government."[41]

While discussions are still at the exploratory stage in some provinces, the MOU signed by Canada and the Manitoba Métis Federation in May 2016 has already led to negotiations.[42] As we note in Chapter 4, the purpose of the MOU was to set the stage for exploratory talks on reconciliation in response to the Supreme Court of Canada's *Manitoba Métis Federation Inc. v. Canada* decision and to clarify section 35 rights more broadly.[43] This has led to the signing of framework agreements between Canada and Métis governments in Manitoba, Alberta, Saskatchewan, and Ontario.

Discussions taking place across the Métis Nation Homeland are consistent with the policy priorities expressed in the Canada-Métis Nation Accord. While policy priorities are to be jointly established through the bilateral mechanism, the accord highlights a number of areas for negotiation, including employment and training, education, housing, and homelessness.[44] As Isaac explains, "It is in the best interests of Canada that it designate programs and services, or parts thereof, as may be appropriate, as Métis-specific so as to be able to track success on the road to reconciliation with Métis peoples and treat Métis as distinct Section 35 rights-bearing peoples."[45] While there is still work to be done for state governments to move beyond myths that deny the constitutional rights of the Métis as a distinct Indigenous nation, recent developments suggest that Canada is committed to working directly with the Métis Nation to take action on Métis rights.

Opportunities and Challenges on the Road Ahead

In addition to affirming the existence of Métis section 35 rights, and creating a mechanism for the reconciliation of these rights with the Crown, the Canada-Métis Nation Accord also recognizes the efforts in which the Métis have engaged over the past several decades to enhance their own governance capacity. As the accord acknowledges, "through their registries and democratically elected governance structures at the local, regional and provincial levels, [the Governing Members that comprise the Métis National Council] are mandated and authorized to represent the citizens who comprise the Métis Nation."[46] This includes the mandate to deal with collectively held Métis rights, interests, and outstanding claims against the Crown.

Acknowledging this in his opening comments at the 2017 Métis Nation-Crown Summit, Prime Minister Trudeau admitted that the federal government has not been a good partner to the Métis Nation in the past and expressed a desire to change this situation. He added that the Métis Nation has fought for a long time to be recognized and to be treated as a legitimate government to serve its people, but now, having won, it was no longer necessary to continue this fight.[47] This acknowledgement represents a crucial victory for the Métis and their systems of governance as it brings to an end a century and a half of denial by the Crown. The prime minister's words, along with the references contained within the accord, stand as testament to Canada's recognition that the governing bodies that have been created by the Métis – the Governing Members that comprise the Métis National Council – are legitimate governments representative of Métis citizens.

The prime minister's remarks also pay homage to the ways in which the Métis have steadily been building the mechanisms of self-government from the ground up. Along with seeking redress through the legal system, Métis leaders committed to "just doing it" as a conscious strategy to advance their self-government agenda in the face of Canada's ongoing refusal to recognize Métis rights and governance processes (Dubois and Saunders 2013). This involved transforming their political bodies from advocacy organizations into representative governments in four key aspects: (1) the delivery of programs and services to Métis citizens, (2) the strengthening of existing and the creation of new governance institutions, (3) the passage of Métis-specific legislation in key policy areas such as harvesting, and (4) the pursuit of economic development opportunities designed to increase economic self-sufficiency and self-determination.

In the process of building the Métis Nation from within, leaders have had to consider what good governance looks like from a Métis perspective. In Chapter 2, we identify some of the long-standing principles that have shaped Métis governance. A number of these principles are consistent with what the Royal Commission on Aboriginal Peoples identifies as the core traditions of Indigenous governance. These include the centrality of the land; individual autonomy; the rule of law; the role of women and elders; leadership and accountability; and consensus-based decision making.[48] Building on these ideas at the 2017 Manitoba Métis Federation Government Summit, Al Benoit, chief of staff to MMF president David Chartrand, proposed eight characteristics of good governance designed to contribute to "moving our Métis government forward."[49] These include a Métis government that is participatory, consensus-oriented, accountable, transparent, responsive, effective and efficient, equitable and inclusive, and that follows the rule of law and strives for justice. These principles reflect Métis understandings of self-government. As he stated, self-government is about implementing Métis culture, about who the Métis are as a people: "It's about being able to assert your independence, your identity, being able to act as a collective."[50]

In addition to reflecting on the principles that serve as the foundation of their governing systems, Métis leaders are called upon to embrace modified forms of governance as they chart a new path forward. Isaac reminds us that "different forms of governance are not only practical but represent an opportunity for Canada to engage and not be bound by past historical models of governance."[51] While this new beginning presents an opportunity, it also carries uncertainty and risk. What will self-government look like? What will be the role of local communities? Provincial councils? Elders? Youth? Should there be a public government structure? How will power be exercised within and across Métis governments? These are questions that Métis leaders have already begun to explore.

Consultations with Métis citizens on the structures and mechanisms to advance self-government have been under way for some time. Some of these discussions date back to the early 1990s, with provincewide consultations held prior to the restructuring of the Métis Nation-Saskatchewan, and extend to ongoing consultations in Manitoba inaugurated by the MMF Government Summit held in March 2017. They also include consultations undertaken by the Métis Nation of Alberta in 2016 and the Métis Nation of Ontario in 2017. Testifying to the breadth and depth of its reflection on the future of Métis self-government, the MNO has established a seven-member commission on Métis rights and self-government to gather information on how to move forward on harvesting and self-government in ways that "better reflect Métis community, identity and culture."[52] The consultations that took place in twenty-nine communities across Ontario from February to June

2017 were preceded by telephone town halls attended by hundreds of Métis citizens. At the penultimate consultation meeting in St. Catharines, MNO chair France Picotte invited Métis citizens to help guide the MNO's negotiation with provincial and federal governments. In response, Métis citizens spoke of the immediate need for programs to support families and children but also called on the MNO to secure their right to decide for themselves how to govern their health and families in the long term.

There are still important decisions ahead for the Métis. In his 2013 State of the Nation address, President Chartier warned: "We will be condemned by future generations if we blow the opportunity to make the breakthrough on our rights."[53] At the same time, Chartier acknowledges that there are "stumbling blocks" that must be overcome in order to "capitalize on the opportunities for self-government currently unfolding before us."[54] He is alluding to ongoing internal debates about identity and land that have stirred tensions within the Métis Nation. The national leadership, along with the Governing Members, argues that the National Definition agreed to in 2002 must be used in moving the Métis Nation's self-government agenda forward. While enforcing the National Definition for individuals who apply for citizenship post 2002 is a relatively straightforward process, what to do with existing members is more problematic.

Governing Members of the Métis National Council have undertaken a lengthy re-registration process of existing members to ensure compliance with the revised definition. There remain disagreements about this process and, more specifically, about whether to grandfather in existing members. Tony Belcourt (2013, 137), the founding president of the MNO, argues that grandfathering-in is "the right thing to do" not only in the context of the history of Métis political mobilization in Ontario but also as a reflection of the Métis custom of "making relatives." Belcourt's position, which is criticized by the national leadership and many Governing Members, is a reminder that many Métis organizations once welcomed into their ranks non-status Indians and people of mixed Indigenous ancestry.

As the Métis National Council and its Governing Members continue to work towards achieving a consensus on citizenship within the Métis

Nation, the issue at stake is not simply one of applying the National Definition of who is Métis but also one of reconciling this definition with the complex historical, legal, political, and emotional realities that surround questions of identity and citizenship. Despite the fact that the five Métis governments unanimously agreed on a National Definition in 2002, some take issue with the overt focus on "Red River" Métis – or what Jacqueline Peterson and Jennifer Brown (1985, 173) have called "Red River myopia" (SSCAP 2013, 66). Others criticize the preclusion of dual (First Nation and Métis) membership as inconsistent with the historic realities of Métis existence on the plains (Belcourt 2013). During a Senate-led inquiry on Métis identity, one mother described the pain of knowing that her child, born to a Métis woman and a status Indian father, "is being denied the right to be Métis because he is on an Indian registry."[55] The personal stories heard by the Senate committee are a reminder that membership in the Métis Nation is a deeply emotional question that cannot be separated from the consequences of colonialism. Governing Members face a fractious choice mired in the complex legacy of colonialism: to exclude individuals from their membership registries – people who may have identified as Métis their whole lives but who do not meet the 2002 criteria – or allow them to remain, thus creating a two-tier system of citizenship.[56]

Related to this has been the equally difficult challenge of more clearly articulating the boundaries of the Métis Nation Homeland, which is a necessary task if self-government negotiations (and land claims processes) are to move forward under the current federal framework. Contentious in this respect has been the delineation of the eastern boundary of the Homeland and, more specifically, whether the Métis Nation extends throughout Ontario (and beyond). As Paul Chartrand (2008, 64) argues, identity and Homeland are intertwined: "the Homeland cannot be defined more specifically without deciding more specifically who the Métis are." Far from resolved, these questions continue to be the source of much debate – and controversy – among the political leadership.

In addition to difficult conversations about citizenship and land has been the proposed development of a Métis Nation constitution. President Chartier has long viewed a national constitution as a necessary step in advancing Métis self-government. The idea of a Métis Nation constitution dates back to the very creation of the Métis National Council in 1983 with the recognition by political leaders at the time of the need for a political instrument that would guide their internal development as well as their negotiations with the state (Dubois and Saunders 2017b). More than three decades later, the Métis Nation is still engaged in constitution-building efforts. Ongoing discussions among Governing Members have focused on questions related to structure and process: Should the president of the Métis National Council be directly elected by the citizens of the Métis Nation or continue to be elected by delegates from Métis governments? Should all Métis governments have the same number of votes at the General Assembly? What should be the separation of powers between the Métis National Council and its Governing Members? Beyond these debates about semantics and procedure, however, the main sticking points remain how best to identify, protect, and govern the citizens and boundaries of the Métis Nation.

In his State of the Nation address to the Métis National Council General Assembly in April 2017, President Chartier highlighted what he saw as three priority areas for the Métis Nation moving forward. The first consists of strengthening the Métis Nation's "whole of government approach" to ensure a united voice on important policy priorities and in its dealings with the federal government. The second involves the more effective mobilization of resources to enable the MNC, Governing Members, and their affiliates "to collaborate on the groundwork required on policy priorities" through the new permanent bilateral mechanism created by the Canada-Métis Nation Accord. The third entails the development of a national constitution "that fully respects the jurisdictions of the Métis governments in the provinces but also enables the Métis people to act collectively on matters of national and international importance."[57] While Métis leaders have their sights set on moving forward, the future of the Métis Nation remains, in many ways, tethered to its past.

As Métis leaders continue to engage with each other and with communities to chart a path forward, they face difficult choices about the nature of governance across the Métis Nation. Telling in this respect will be whether Métis leaders choose to advance self-government at the level of the Métis Nation through a national constitution or whether they will continue to work with their Crown representatives through bilateral relationships at the provincial level as set out in recent framework agreements. In paving the path forward, Métis leaders and citizens have resources at their disposal. They may choose to borrow certain elements and to learn from the experiences of other Indigenous peoples. Most meaningful, however, are their own governance practices on which they rely in the pursuit of self-government.

Conclusion

Speaking in the wake of the *Manitoba Métis Federation Inc.* decision in 2013, Métis Nation president Chartier declared: "We stand on the edge of a new frontier for Métis Nation self-government."[58] The Métis have made significant gains towards this goal. Building on more than a century of efforts to steadily build their systems of governance from the ground up, recent legal and political developments have accelerated progress towards Métis self-government. Significant in this respect was the confirmation by the highest court in the country that the Métis hold constitutionally protected rights in *Powley*, its recognition of the Crown's failure to carry out promises of Métis constitutional rights in *Manitoba Métis Federation Inc.*, and its clarification of the federal government's constitutional responsibility for the Métis in *Daniels*. While this trifecta of Métis case law marks important legal advances, it is its political consequences that are most significant. As intended, these decisions have allowed Métis leaders to force Canada's hand at the bargaining table.

Also critical in advancing the Métis self-government agenda has been the report of the minister's special representative on advancing reconciliation with Métis, Thomas Isaac. The report gives credence to many of the arguments that Métis leaders have been advancing for years but that fell on the deaf ears of successive governments in Ottawa. As President Chartier notes, Isaac's recommendations, in calling for a fundamental change in the mindsets of federal and provincial governments in their dealings with the Métis Nation, "has rendered a valuable service" for the Métis people. "The central message," Chartier adds, "is that these governments and their administrations have to start respecting the Métis as section 35 rights holders and to realign their attitudes and actions with this reality."[59]

Sitting alongside Prime Minister Trudeau, Métis leaders signed a momentous Canada-Métis Nation Accord in 2017. This accord marks a break from the past and offers promise for the future by committing the federal government to engage with Métis governments and putting in place mechanisms to advance Métis constitutional rights. Speaking after the 2017 Métis Nation-Crown Summit, Manitoba Métis Federation president David Chartrand commented: "As equal partners of Confederation, it is important we renew and strengthen the Métis Nation-Crown relationship upon the principles of cooperation, respect for rights, [and] equality."[60] The strengthening of this relationship will require federal and provincial governments to move beyond myths that deny the rights of the Métis Nation and to take action towards the implementation of these rights.

The future of Métis-Crown relations will also depend on developments set to unfold within the Métis Nation. Métis leaders are in a unique position to shape the future of Métis self-government in Canada. The extent to which this is done in collaboration with one another and with the participation of Métis citizens will be determinative of the scope, nature, and structure of Métis self-government. Speaking to the obstacles that lie ahead, President Chartrand reminds Métis citizens of the stakes involved: "Friends, these are exciting times for the Métis. Let us remain vigilant. Let us not allow petty differences and short-sighted gains cloud our judgment as we work to finally secure the lasting place in Canada that was promised to us and our children so very long ago."[61] Although *li shmayn ishi tipaymishoohk* (the road to self-government) is laden with challenges, Métis leaders are entering a new political chapter that holds significant promise.

Conclusion

Lii Drway di Naasyoon di Michif Ka Paashpiiwahk

The Ongoing Struggle for Métis Rights

SPEAKING TO THE GENERAL ASSEMBLY on the 200th anniversary of the *Viktwayr daan la Plenn di Goornouyayr* (the Victory at Frog Plain) in June 2016, Métis Nation president Chartier spoke of the long-lasting struggle by the Métis to govern their lands and their lives: "The same fighting spirit of the Métis who fought in the Victory at Frog Plain is the same spirit that guided the provisional governments of Riel in Manitoba and Saskatchewan." And it was this same spirit, Chartier added, that has "guided our struggles since then to achieve resolution of our historical claims and the implementation of the inherent right of the Métis Nation to self-government."[1]

Following President Chartier's comments, representatives of each Governing Member rose in turn to report on the progress made in their respective province towards the goal of self-government. They spoke of partnership agreements signed with private-sector companies, negotiations with provincial and federal governments on resource management and land claims, and advancements in curriculum development that acknowledged Métis history and culture. They celebrated the success of their youth, welcomed the then newly elected female president from Ontario, and reasserted their status as the legitimate representatives of Métis citizens in Canada.[2] Métis leaders also spoke of the challenges they continued to face in their respective jurisdictions – the lack of stable funding, unresolved battles in the courts over hunting rights, and the need to improve the health outcomes of their citizens. As they work with the tools at hand to govern the affairs of their nation, contemporary Métis leaders remain engaged in the ongoing struggle for self-government that began some two hundred years ago.

The Métis emerged as a distinct Indigenous nation through political organization. Beginning with the organization of the buffalo hunts and extending to the protest of the *Bois-brûlés* against trade sanctions under the leadership of Cuthbert Grant, the Métis emerged as *la noovel Naasyoon* (the new nation). The Métis Nation united under a provisional government to negotiate the protection of its rights with the Canadian state.

For the Métis, political action is not an end in itself but is, instead, a way to protect *ka ishi pimaatishiyaahk* (our way of life). In speaking with those involved in Métis politics, we have come to understand political organization as a deeply personal experience and source of empowerment for the Métis Nation as whole. The formation of organizations like the Association des Métis d'Alberta et des Territoires du Nord-Ouest in 1932 was a way for the Métis to lift the "blanket of shame" that accompanied *le grand silence* and find a way back to who they are as Riel's people (Campbell 1973, 137). Political activity provided a means through which the Métis could promote rights and opportunities as well as foster a sense of pride in their culture. Remembering his early involvement with the Manitoba Métis Federation, Métis elder George Fleury speaks of the feeling of self-worth he felt in representing Métis people,[3] while elder John Morrisseau explains that "the drive we had in standing up for ourselves gave us a lot of determination as a people."[4]

For many Métis leaders, this drive comes from Riel's vision of a self-determining Métis Nation. The commitment to protect self-determination led the Métis to take up arms against Canada's incursion into their lands in Duck Lake and Fish Creek. At the last stand against Canadian troops in Batoche in 1885, Riel (1886, 186) is purported to have said, "We may fail. But the rights for which we contend will not die." Riel, along with Métis soldiers like Isidore Dumont Jr., Jos Vermette, Damase Carrière, André Letendre, and Calixte Tourond, sacrificed his life to protect the Métis Nation's right to land and self-government.[5] After his death, subsequent generations of Métis leaders have carried on this struggle. As Riel's people, they share in the belief that *lii drway di Naasyoon di Michif ka paashpiiwahk* (the rights of the Métis Nation will survive).

Exercising Métis Rights through Governance

Above all else, Riel desired freedom for his people – the freedom of the Métis to live, trade, and organize as they wished. From the fur trade to the present, the Métis have developed various governance structures to achieve freedom and remain *ka tipaymishooyahk* (we who own ourselves). Far from usurping their commitment to self-government, the encroachment on Métis lands and economic rights by external forces – most notably, the Hudson's Bay Company in the events leading to the *Viktwayr daan la Plenn di Goornouyayr* and Canada's subsequent assertion of sovereignty over Rupert's Land and the Northwest – served as catalysts for political mobilization and nation building among the Métis. The sustained efforts of women as the keepers of knowledge helped the Métis Nation to survive through the darkest days of resistance and repression.

Turning to political action as a means of protecting their way of life, the structures and practices adopted to administer their activities evolved as the Métis transitioned to new economies and adapted to the changing reality of Canada's colonial context. Hence, the rules and processes developed by the Métis to oversee the buffalo hunts would inform the provisional governments established at Red River and St. Laurent de Grandin, which, in turn, would inspire the emergence of Métis organizations across western Canada in the 1920s and 1930s. In the face of Canada's shifting economic, political, and social landscape, these organizations evolved into the five Governing Members that currently make up the Métis National Council.

Today, Métis governments from British Columbia to Ontario offer an array of programs and services to their citizens, negotiate with their provincial and federal counterparts, and engage in revenue-generating activities that could only have been dreamed of decades earlier. While the structures have changed, these governing bodies continue to be informed by the principles of freedom, kinship, democracy, rule of law, and provisionality through which citizens of the Métis Nation have continually sought to exercise their inherent right to self-government. Originating in the collective practices that governed the hunt, the Métis apply these principles to fulfill the same overriding objective: self-determination. In describing the role of contemporary political leaders, Métis Nation president Clément Chartier explains: "We are doing the same thing that Riel did, just in a different context. What Riel picked up and ran with, hasn't been completed" (in Saunders 2015, 77).

The Ongoing Quest for Self-Government

The ability of the Métis Nation to achieve self-government within the context of the Canadian state has been constrained by a legislative framework that historically denied the very existence of the Métis and that marginalized them from the levers of power within the state system. The Métis elude the racial binaries enforced by the Canadian state: neither "Indian" nor "white," the Métis were relegated to the category of Canada's forgotten people. In the face of this denial and misrecognition, the Métis have continually mobilized to push the boundaries of a state that has historically disregarded their aspirations as a people. While the marginalization of the Métis from federal policy and law has had devastating repercussions, it also allowed the Métis to imagine for themselves what self-government could look like. This led to the creation of local, provincial, and national organizations that work together as what is referred to in Michif as *nootr goovarnimaan di Michif* (our Métis government).

Métis governments have positioned themselves to work alongside state and non-state actors to advance their self-government agenda. Operating in conjunction with a network of institutes, affiliates, and organizations, Métis governments are actively involved in various sectors, including health, child and family services, justice, labour market training, and education. Through partnerships with Métis capital corporations, bilateral agreements with the private sector, investments in entrepreneurship, and skills development, Métis governments have increasingly positioned themselves as key actors in the economy. Focusing on areas of mutual interests, Métis and state governments have found ways to act within the confines of existing legislation to advance their self-government agenda – albeit in limited ways. Despite these developments, the Métis continue to see the lack of a recognized land base as an impediment to their full participation in the economy and to the fulfillment of their right to self-government.

The Métis have been steadily building the framework of self-government from the ground up. Central to this endeavour have been *lii faam di Naasyoon di Michif* (mothers of the Métis Nation). Since the fur trade era, Métis women have played a key role as firekeepers of Métis identity and continue to ensure the survival of the Métis as a distinct Indigenous nation. Métis women are present in contemporary political life as organizers in their communities and as elected officials within their governments. Their participation in formal and informal aspects of politics is central to the collective pursuit of Métis self-government. Through their actions, Métis women contribute to the goals of the Métis Nation as a whole.

Building Self-Government from the Grassroots

In *Manitoba Métis Federation Inc. v. Canada*, the Supreme Court of Canada stated that "the unfinished business of reconciliation of the Métis people with Canadian sovereignty is a matter of national and constitutional import."[6] One of the seminal milestones in beginning dialogue on reconciliation was the constitutional recognition, in 1982, of the Métis as a rights-bearing Aboriginal people. This change in Canada's constitutional landscape led Métis citizens to pursue cases that call on federal and provincial governments to recognize their rights and to negotiate their implementation. State responses have been slow in coming.

Most Métis governments continue to operate under legislation designed for not-for-profit entities, and the Métis Nation continues to be excluded from the legislative frameworks created to advance Indigenous claims for self-government and land. Tasked with proposing a path forward, the minister's special representative on reconciliation with Métis, Thomas Isaac, outlined seventeen recommendations to build a renewed relationship between Canada and the Métis. A significant challenge to fulfilling this relationship, according to Isaac, is the ongoing lack of knowledge about the Métis. Isaac categorically argues that confusion over who is Métis and what rights they hold cannot be used to further delay the implementation of these rights. Instead, he calls on provincial and federal governments to educate the civil service about the Métis and to immediately enter into negotiations to respect the constitutionally recognized rights of the Métis to land and to self-government.

The success of this undertaking will depend on the good faith of all parties. In *Daniels v. Canada*, the Supreme Court of Canada noted that the federal government has a key role to play in shaping Canada's relationship with the Métis. Clarifying that the federal government has constitutional responsibility for the Métis, the Court opened the door for Canada to adopt enabling legislation that recognizes and allows Métis governments to represent the interests of their citizens. At the same time, the Court acknowledged that provinces have a role to play. Achieving reconciliation within the complex contemporary reality of Canada, according to Isaac, will require the cooperation of Métis, provincial, and federal governments.

Expectations for a renewed nation-to-nation relationship between Canada and the Métis based on cooperation, respect for rights, and equality have been heightened with the signing of the 2017 Canada-Métis Nation Accord. The accord proposes to move this relationship forward by committing the federal government to engage with Métis governments and putting in place mechanisms to advance Métis constitutional rights. As Métis leaders are invited by Canada to negotiate their place within the country for the first time in 150 years, they are also called upon to address challenges internal to the Métis Nation. Given that there is no single model of Métis self-government, it will be up to Métis leaders and citizens to make decisions about the structures and processes of self-government moving forward. This means addressing divisive debates about the boundaries of identity, land, and citizenship within the Métis Nation. It also involves difficult decisions about the relationship between the Métis National Council and its Governing Members. The path forward will require an honest engagement with the past and a concerted effort to address the deep-seated legacies of colonialism.

The members of the Métis Nation have demonstrated a sustained commitment to remain true to their right to govern their lands and their people. Just as they organized to safeguard their ability to trade freely and to govern themselves in Red River and Batoche, the Métis continue to work towards the fulfillment of their rights through their contemporary governing structures. Using the tools available to them, the Métis have shown determination in pursuing self-government from the bottom up despite having little control over the context within which they operate. While some are hopeful that the Canada-Métis Nation Accord will reset the Métis Nation's relationship with Canada, Métis governments across the Homeland have made clear that they will not wait for permission from the Crown to exercise their inherent rights. Instead, they will continue to pass their own laws, build bureaucracies, refine their electoral processes, and seek out revenue-generating opportunities to reduce their financial dependence on the state. This "just do it" approach has allowed the Métis to assert their place as legitimate actors in the Canadian federation and to further establish themselves as a self-governing Indigenous people.

As the Métis Nation negotiates its relationship with the Canadian state, Riel's words upon his surrender to Canada in 1885 find resonance: "I have fought for liberty, and if liberty is not worth fighting for, it is not worth winning" (Riel 1982, 148). It is through their struggles and their unrelenting commitment to political action that the leaders and citizens of the Métis Nation live up to the name they give themselves – *ka tipaymishooyahk* (we who own ourselves). As leaders enter a new political chapter with Canada, the Métis – Riel's people – are one step closer to realizing their goal of a self-determining and free Métis Nation. As the Métis look to the future, elder George Fleury offers the following advice: "Follow the vision that began with Riel."[7]

Notes

FOREWORD

1 The Manitoba Métis Federation-Canada Framework Agreement on Advancing Reconciliation was signed on November 15, 2016, the Métis Nation of Alberta-Canada Framework Agreement on Advancing Reconciliation was signed on November 16, 2017, while the Métis Nation of Ontario-Canada-Ontario Framework Agreement on Advancing Reconciliation and the Métis Nation of Ontario-Canada Agreement on Advancing Reconciliation with the North-western Ontario Métis Community were both signed on December 11, 2017.

INTRODUCTION

1 "Oath of Office," Manitoba Métis Federation, July 24, 2014.

2 "Office of the President Annual Report," Manitoba Métis Federation Annual General Assembly, Annual General Report, November 15, 2014, 21, http://www.mmf.mb.ca/docs/AGA_2014_OCT28.pdf.

3 Michif expressions are presented in the first person plural because that is how they were most commonly expressed to us. We occasionally use the third person when we refer to how others perceive the Métis (e.g., *ka tipemishoshik,* the free people), but the Métis generally use the first person plural, *ka tipaymishooyaahk* (we who own ourselves). Other phrases, such as *ki tipemishoonaan* (we are all free), are also used to express their collective identity as a free people. The Michif dialect (and spelling) we use is one of many. It has been shared and developed by Métis elders, including Norman Fleury, Verna DeMontigny, and Maria Campbell. While we are not fluent Michif speakers and continue to learn, we feel it is important to engage with the language as encouraged by elders.

4 See, for example, Bumsted (1996, 2001, 2003); Ens (1996); Flanagan (2000); Foster (1994); Giraud (1984); Morton (1967); Peterson and Brown (1985); Sealy and Lussier (1975); Sprague (1988); Stanley (1963); de Trémaudan (1982); and Woodcock (2003).

5 On law, see Bell (1994, 1999, 2015); L. Chartrand (2004, 2008); Chartrand and Giokas (2002); P. Chartrand (2008); Teillet (2007, 2008, 2013); Grammond and Groulx (2012); and Wilson and Mallet (2008). On identity, see Andersen (2008, 2014). On culture and history, see Devine (2004); Douaud

(2007); Ens and Sawchuk (2016); Hogue (2015); Macdougall (2010); Payment (2009); and St-Onge (2004). On the enduring significance of Riel, see Saunders (2014, 2015) and Reid (2008). For edited volumes, see St-Onge, Podruchny, and Macdougall (2012); Adams, Dahl, and Peach (2013); Lischke and McNab (2007); and Peterson and Brown (1985).

6 A notable exception is found in works by Sawchuk (1978, 1998, 2000) and Ens and Sawchuk (2016). Recent editions of *Topia* (no. 36) and *aboriginal policy studies* (especially vol. 6 no. 2) feature legal and political scholarship related to the Métis. Interestingly, some of the most informative accounts of Métis politics have been published in non-peer reviewed works (Campbell 1973; Chartier 1988; Adams 1975; Dobbin 1981; Morrison 1995; Purich 1988; and Weinstein 2007).

7 President Clément Chartier, in "Seven Oaks Two Centuries After," Métis Nation, Métis National Council Newsletter, July 2016, http://www.metisnation.ca/index.php/news/seven-oaks-two-centuries-after.

8 Described as the Battle of Seven Oaks in historical records, this 1816 battle was referred to in French as *la victoire des Bois-Brûlés*, the Victory of the Métis, or *la bataille de la Grenouillère*, the Battle at Frog Plain. It is referred to in Michif as *la Viktwayr daan la Plenn di Goornouyayr*, or the Victory at Frog Plain. We use "Métis" to denote the people that emerged from these struggles.

9 This point has been repeatedly made by Paul Chartrand. See, for example, Chartrand (2017).

10 "Current Government Structure and Local Governance," presentation by Al Benoit at the Manitoba Métis Federation Government Summit, Winnipeg, March 10, 2017.

11 Interview with Margaret Froh, March 18, 2017.

12 Interview with George Fleury, June 15, 2017

13 "Negotiation and Self-Government," presentation by Jason Madden to the Manitoba Métis Government Summit, March 12, 2017.

14 "Métis National Council," Métis Nation, Liberal Party of Canada, modified September 21, 2015, http://www.metisnation.ca/wp-content/uploads/2015/09/Liberal-Party-Response-Sept-21-2015-.pdf. See also Dubois and Saunders (2017c).

15 "Message from the President," Métis Nation, Métis National Council Newsletter, August 2016, http://www.metisnation.ca/wp-content/uploads/2016/08/Newsletter-August-2016.pdf.

16 Referred to as Rupert's Land and the North-Western Territory by the British, the Northwest was a vast territory extending from the Hudson Bay basin in the north, across present-day Manitoba, most of Saskatchewan, and parts of Alberta, Ontario, British Columbia, and the northern United States.

17 The authors would like to thank an anonymous reviewer for suggesting this formulation and emphasizing this argument.

18 Note that the official name of the Manitoba Métis Federation does not use "é" over the word "Métis," although it is used by the Métis National Council and the other Governing Members. For ease and as a reflection of this majority usage, we have chosen to use "é" throughout the book.

19 Given the scholarship that already exists in this area, we have chosen not to include a discussion of the Métis Settlement Councils and General Council in Alberta, which represent Métis in the only recognized land base in Canada (see, for example, Pocklington 1991; Bell 1994, 1999). As the ministerial special representative on reconciliation notes, governments in Métis communities have taken two forms: (1) geographic governments like the Métis Settlements in Alberta and (2) governments that have the legal authority to represent their constituents' interest and, in particular, their Section 35 rights. Our analysis focuses on the governments that fall within this second category. See "A Matter of National and Constitutional Import: Report of the Minister's Special Representative on Reconciliation with Métis: Section 35 Métis Rights and the *Manitoba Métis Federation* Decision," Indigenous and Northern Affairs Canada, June 14, 2016, 13, http://publications.gc.ca/collections/collection_2016/aanc-inac/R5-123-2016-eng.pdf.

20 "Canada-Métis Nation Accord," Métis Nation, April 13, 2017, http://www.metisnation.ca/wp-content/uploads/2017/04/Canada-Métis-Nation-Accord En.pdf.

21 "A Matter of National and Constitutional Import: Report of the Minister's Special Representative on Reconciliation with Métis: Section 35 Métis Rights and the *Manitoba Métis Federation* Decision," Indigenous and Northern Affairs Canada, June 14, 2016, 14, http://publications.gc.ca/collections/collection_2016/aanc-inac/R5-123-2016-eng.pdf.

22 "Principles of Ethical Métis Research," National Aboriginal Health Organization, viewed November 5 2018, https://achh.ca/wp-content/.../Guide_Ethics_NAHOMetisCentre.pdf.

23 Interview with John Morrisseau, November 21, 2009.

CHAPTER 1: MÉTIS POLITICAL ORGANIZATION IN HISTORICAL PERSPECTIVE

1 Adam Gaudry notes that it is in the pages of this memoir that Riel provides the most comprehensive insight into Métis political history. He writes: "The Last Memoir is an important document, not just because it is the last piece of writing of a great Indigenous leader, but because it articulates a comprehensive Métis political philosophy at a time when Riel's thought was at its most developed stage. Equally important is its presentation of a Métis historical narrative that stands in stark contrast to how this history is usually understood today, especially by non-Métis scholars" (Gaudry 2014, 5).

2 "Correspondence from J.P. Brady to J.F. Dion," James Brady Fonds, M-125-27, Glenbow Archives, April 21, 1940, http://www.glenbow.org/collections/search

/findingAids/archhtm/extras/brady/m-125-27.pdf. This expression is taken up by Dobbin (1981).

3 See, for example, Ens (1996, 40) and Ross (1957, 248–9). The terms used to describe the roles of various actors involved in the hunt varies. For example, Anderson (2006) refers to the chief of the hunt as "president" or "governor," while Riel uses "chief" (1982, 203). The number of council members also varies in different accounts. Riel (1982, 203) refers to twelve councillors, as do Charette (1980, 39) and Morton (1967, 79), but Ross (1957, 248) refers to ten captains in his account of the 1840 hunt. McLean (1987) uses the term "lieutenants" instead of "captains." Vermette's recollection of the hunt suggests that the numbers of hunters varied daily and averaged twenty-five (in Ferland 2006, 122), which is a much smaller number than the four hundred reported in the 1840 hunt.

4 "Bison Hunting," Patrick Young and Darren R. Préfontaine, Gabriel Dumont Institute, May 30, 2003, http://www.metismuseum.ca/resource.php/00716.

5 See Charette (1980, 24); Sawchuk (1981, 17); and "Bison Hunting," Patrick Young and Darren R. Préfontaine, Gabriel Dumont Institute, May 30, 2003, http://www.metismuseum.ca/resource.php/00716.

6 See Sprague (1988, 20). For a critical discussion of the Royal Charter, see O'Toole (2010, 91–98) and Gaudry (2016a).

7 See Purich (1988, 38); Saunders (2013); Goulet and Goulet (2006); Ens (2012); and Ens and Sawchuk (2016) for discussions of the impact of this battle on Métis nationalism.

8 This was evident during commemoration events held in Winnipeg on June 18 and 19, 2016, to celebrate the two hundredth anniversary of *la Viktwayr daan la Plenn di Goornouyayr* (the Victory at Frog Plain).

9 See Ens (1994); and "A History of the Legislative Assembly of Assiniboia/le Conseil du Gouvernement Provisoire," paper prepared by Norma Hall with Clifford P. Hall and Erin Verrier for Indian and Northern Affairs Canada, Manitoba Métis Federation, and the Province of Manitoba, 2010, 2, https://www.gov.mb.ca/ana/major-initiatives/pubs/laa%20essay%20eng.pdf.

10 See "List of Rights c. 5 December 1869," Provisional Government of Assiniboia, published October 21, 2014, https://hallnjean2.wordpress.com/chronology-during-1869/the-convention-of-twenty-four/list-of-rights-c-5-december-1869/.

11 "Declaration of the People of Rupert's Land and the North West," University of Manitoba Libraries, Archives of Manitoba, MG3 A1–6.

12 Initially, there were twelve representatives, but two were added to represent the capital. See "A History of the Legislative Assembly of Assiniboia/le Conseil du Gouvernement Provisoire," paper prepared by Norma Hall with Clifford P. Hall and Erin Verrier for Indian and Northern Affairs Canada, Manitoba Métis Federation, and the Province of Manitoba, 2010, 6, https://www.gov.mb.ca/ana/major-initiatives/pubs/laa%20essay%20eng.pdf.

13 Ibid., 1.

14 "An Act to amend and continue the Act 32 and 33 Victoria, chapter 3; and to establish and provide for the Government of the Province of Manitoba," Library and Archives Canada, Statutes of Canada 1870, c. 3, p. 26, https://www.collectionscanada.gc.ca/confederation/023001-7118.06-e.html.

15 In *Manitoba Métis Federation Inc. v. Canada*, the Supreme Court ruled that "the federal Crown failed to implement the land grant provision set out in s. 31 of the *Manitoba Act, 1870* in accordance with the honour of the Crown" (2013 SCC 14 at para. 154). For a discussion of the misappropriation of Métis scrip, see Sawchuk (1981); Chartrand (1991). For an alternate perspective, see Flanagan (1991, 2000).

16 See Sprague (1988, 83). Ens (1988) argues that the Métis movement out of Red River, which had already begun prior to 1870, was also a response to new economic opportunities, notably the opening of new fur markets.

17 "Copy of the Laws and Regulations established for the Colony of St. Laurent on the Saskatchewan," Gabriel Dumont Institute, May 27, 2008, http://www.metismuseum.ca/resource.php/12631. See also Payment (2009, 124–25).

18 Interview with John Morrisseau, November 21, 2009. See also Saunders (2015).

19 In a presentation at the Manitoba Métis Federation Government Summit in March 2017, Louis Riel's great grandniece, Jean Teillet, explained that this term was used in her family papers.

20 "Métis Land Rights and Self-Government," Leah Dorion and Darren Préfontaine, Gabriel Dumont Institute, May 30, 2003, http://www.metismuseum.ca/resource.php/00725.

21 "History of the Métis Organization of Saskatchewan," paper prepared by Wesley Budd for the Gabriel Dumont Institute, 2007, 6, http://www.metismuseum.ca/resource.php/05845.

22 "Road Allowance Communities Represented by the Northern Halfbreed Association," Gabriel Dumont Institute, Lawrence Barkwell, January 28, 2009, http://www.metismuseum.ca/media/document.php/10286.Road%20Allowance%20Communities.pdf.

23 For an overview of Métis political organization in Ontario, see Ens and Sawchuk (2016, 419–52).

24 Pulla (2013, 412); and "Métis and Non-Status People in British Columbia," BC Learning Network, viewed July 21, 2016, http://bclearningnetwork.com/LOR/media/fns12/pdf/Module2/2.2%20B6%20Metis%20and%20Non-Status%20People%20in%20British%20Columbia.pdf.

25 "MNC Marks 30th Anniversary in Fiery Display of Métis Nationalism," Métis National Council, March 25, 2013, http://www.metisnation.ca/index.php/news/mnc-marks-30th-anniversary-in-fiery-display-of-metis-nationalism.

26 Interview with George Fleury, June 15, 2017.

CHAPTER 2: PRINCIPLES OF MÉTIS GOVERNANCE

1 Interview with George Fleury, June 15, 2017.

2 Rather than provide direct translations, we use English words that best capture Michif phrases.

3 Adam Gaudry (2014, 79–85) also notes these two dimensions of freedom.

4 "Constitution," Métis Nation British Columbia, revised September 2008, emphasis added, http://www.mnbc.ca/pdfs/constitution_Métis_nation_bc.pdf.

5 "Constitution," Métis Nation-Saskatchewan, amended September 2013, http://www.mn-s.ca/ckfinder/userfiles/files/Constitution-Amended-September-7-8-2013.pdf.

6 As we note in the introduction, much of the most insightful work on Métis political life is found in non-peer reviewed works. The biography of Louis Goulet is one of the most widely known accounts that reflects on the early buffalo hunts. Other narrative accounts of this era were provided by Peter Erasmus (recounted by Henry Thompson in Erasmus [1999]), Ted Trindell (recounted by Morisset and Pelletier [1986]), Antoine Vermette (recounted by Ferland [2006]), and Norbert Welsh (recounted by Weekes [1939]). The accounts of Erasmus, Goulet, Vermette, and Welsh are given scholarly treatment by Rivard (2012). The stories of Louis Goulet and Peter Erasmus are taken up in scholarly discussions by Gaudry (2014) and Drake and Gaudry (2016). The memoirs of Goulet and Trindell are also analyzed by scholars of Canadian literature (e.g., Jannetta [1994]). For other interesting memoirs, see Campbell (1973); Carpenter (1977); and Bird (1991).

7 "Niw_hk_m_kanak ('All My Relations') Métis-First Nations Relations," paper prepared for the National Centre for First Nations Governance by Paul Chartrand, June 2007, http://fngovernance.org/ncfng_research/paul_chartrand.pdf. See also Todd (2016).

8 Interview with Verna DeMontigny, January 22, 2018.

9 Gaudry uses the spelling *kaa-tipeyimishoyaahk*. Our spelling of this concept is consistent with what has been taught to us by Métis elders and language keepers. For a discussion of origins and an explanation of the different forms of spelling in Roman orthography, see Bakker (1997).

10 President's Report, MMF Annual General Assembly, September 26, 2015, Winnipeg.

11 Interview with George Fleury, June 15, 2017.

12 "A History of the Legislative Assembly of Assiniboia/le Conseil du Gouvernement Provisoire," paper prepared by Norma Hall with Clifford P. Hall and Erin Verrier for Indian and Northern Affairs Canada, the Manitoba Métis Federation, and the Province of Manitoba, 2010, 6, https://www.gov.mb.ca/ana/major-initiatives/pubs/laa%20essay%20eng.pdf.

13 Direct ballot box elections for provincial executives, including presidents, is a requirement for membership in the Métis National Council (see

"Consolidated by-laws," Métis Nation Gateway website, Métis National Council, July 23, 2003, http://metisportals.ca/elec/wp-content/uploads/2009/02/mnc-bylaws.pdf).

14 "A History of the Legislative Assembly of Assiniboia/le Conseil du Gouvernement Provisoire," paper prepared by Norma Hall with Clifford P. Hall and Erin Verrier for Indian and Northern Affairs Canada, Manitoba Métis Federation and the Province of Manitoba, 2010, 18, https://www.gov.mb.ca/ana/major-initiatives/pubs/laa%20essay%20eng.pdf.

15 "Oath of Office," Manitoba Métis Federation, 2014. The draft national constitution of the Métis Nation contains a similar oath of office for the national president, vice-president, and ministers.

16 "MN-S Election has a few shockers," *Eagle Feather News*, May 28, 2017, https://www.eaglefeathernews.com/news/index.php?detail=2788.

17 "Thinking about Indigenous Legal Orders," research paper for the National Centre for First Nations Governance, prepared by Val Napoleon, June 2007, http://fngovernance.org/ncfng_research/val_napoleon.pdf.

18 "A History of the Legislative Assembly of Assiniboia/le Conseil du Gouvernement Provisoire," paper prepared by Norma Hall with Clifford P. Hall and Erin Verrier for Indian and Northern Affairs Canada, the Manitoba Métis Federation, and the Province of Manitoba, 2010, https://www.gov.mb.ca/ana/major-initiatives/pubs/laa%20essay%20eng.pdf.

19 "Negotiation and Self-Government," presentation by Jason Madden at the MMF Government Summit, March 12, 2017.

20 When there was a need to apply traditional laws or to sentence transgressions, the Métis would historically strike an ad hoc committee of mutually agreed-upon individuals. See examples in Corrigan (1991a). This practice is still observed in contemporary Métis politics where committees are struck to undertake various roles, from exploring the development of a national constitution to investigating provincial electoral processes.

21 "Métis Political Activist Interviews," Gabriel Dumont Institute, Jim Sinclair and Jim Durocher, interviewed by Ron Laliberte, April 17, 2004, tape 2, http://www.metismuseum.ca/media/document.php/06118.S,%20D,%20and%20L%20(28).pdf.

22 In an attempt to address this and related questions, in 2016 the General Assembly mandated Métis leaders to prepare a document that clearly states their collective goals and outlines the structures and processes through which to achieve them. This document is part of ongoing discussions surrounding the development of a national constitution (see Dubois and Saunders 2017b).

23 "A History of the Legislative Assembly of Assiniboia/le Conseil du Gouvernement Provisoire," paper prepared by Norma Hall with Clifford P. Hall and Erin Verrier for Indian and Northern Affairs Canada, the Manitoba Métis Federation, and the Province of Manitoba, 2010, 5, https://www.gov.mb.ca/ana/major-initiatives/pubs/laa%20essay%20eng.pdf.

24 "Cree, Lakota, Dakota and Saulteaux Warriors Who Fought in the 1885 Resistance," Lawrence J. Barkwell, 2007, Saskatoon, Gabriel Dumont Institute, http://www.metismuseum.ca/resource.php/07206; Interview with Will Goodon, MMF Minister of Housing, April 23, 2015.

CHAPTER 3: MÉTIS GOVERNMENTS

1 "Welcome Remarks," by President Chartier at the Manitoba Métis Federation Government Summit, Winnipeg, March 10, 2017.

2 "Snapshot of the Nation," Métis National Council, 2002, 4. http://www.metisnation.ca/wp-content/uploads/2011/04/ExecSum.pdf.

3 "Métis Section 35 Rights, Recognition and Reconciliation," speech by President Chartier at the Crown-Métis Nation Summit, Ottawa, April 13, 2017, http://www.metisnation.ca/wp-content/uploads/2017/04/Crown-%E2%80%93-Me%CC%81tis-Nation-Summit-April-13-2017-s.35.pdf.

4 "Aboriginal Peoples Highlight Tables, 2016 Census," Statistics Canada, http://www12.statcan.gc.ca/census-recensement/2016/dp-pd/hlt-fst/abo-aut/Table.cfm?Lang=Eng&T=101&S=99&O=A; and "About," Métis Nation British Columbia, http://www.mnbc.ca/about.

5 See Bell (1991); and Teillet (2013).

6 "Strategic Plan," Manitoba Métis Federation, 2013, 18, 47, copy of original document in authors' possession.

7 Closing remarks by President Clara Morin Dal Col at the Métis Nation Governing Assembly, Métis Nation British Columbia, March 28, 2017, Richmond, BC, http://www.mnbc.ca/news-events/posts/governing-our-metis-nation.

8 Interview with Clément Chartier, March 1, 2011.

9 "Strategic Plan," Manitoba Métis Federation, 2013, 24, copy of original document in authors' possession.

10 "Current Government Structure and Local Governance," presentation by Al Benoit at the Manitoba Métis Federation Government Summit, March 10, 2017.

11 While local and regional representatives are expected to attend on the basis of their office, annual assemblies are open to all members of each Métis government.

12 The number of local organizations can vary over time as some existing locals lapse due to inactivity and new locals are established. At the time of writing, the breakdown of locals is as follows: Ontario, 29; Manitoba, 140; Saskatchewan, 130; Alberta, 67; British Columbia, 38.

13 See, for example, "Métis Governance in Saskatchewan for the 21st Century: Views and Visions of the Métis People," report submitted to the Saskatchewan Minister of First Nations and Métis Relations, Saskatchewan, Métis Electoral Consultation Panel, 2005, 14. Many of these concerns were reiterated by local leaders at the MMF Government Summit in Winnipeg, March 10, 2017.

14 The process through which community-level associations are incorporated also varies across provinces. For example, locals in Alberta are incorporated under the Societies Act of Alberta, whereas community associations in Ontario are incorporated through the charters of the MNO and therefore use the MNO's incorporation number. Similarly, each Métis government has its own rules for the creation of community-level organizations, as outlined in its constitution or bylaws. For example, the MMF and the MN-S require a minimum of nine members, the MNA requires ten members, and the MNBC requires twenty-five members before a new local can be established. In order to maintain active status, locals must typically hold a minimum number of public meetings each year, call elections at regular intervals, and be financially accountable to members.

15 MMF, Annual General Assembly, September 24, 2017. The motion was ultimately defeated after a series of regional representatives stood up to speak against it.

16 "Métis Governance in Saskatchewan for the 21st Century: Views and Visions of the Métis People," report submitted to the Saskatchewan Minister of First Nations and Métis Relations, Saskatchewan, Métis Electoral Consultation Panel, 2005, 14.

17 The Métis governments in British Columbia and Saskatchewan also have another body, akin to a "super executive," which contains Provincial Council members along with the heads of the local associations that are responsible for passing legislation, setting policy direction, and making constitutional amendments.

18 "Glen McCallum elected Métis Nation-Saskatchewan President in Huge Turnout at Polls," Métis National Council, http://www.metisnation.ca/index.php/news/glen-mccallum-elected-metis-nation-saskatchewan-president-in-huge-turnout-at-polls. See also "Aboriginal Peoples Highlight Tables, 2016 Census," Statistics Canada website, http://www12.statcan.gc.ca/census-recensement/2016/dp-pd/hlt-fst/abo-aut/Table.cfm?Lang=Eng&T=101&S=99&O=A.

19 With the exception of the MMF and the MNA, which do not have a youth representative, and the MNA, which does not have a women's representative. The MNA is currently exploring the creation of a youth council as mandated by the General Assembly, "Ordinary Resolution #1," Métis Nation of Alberta Annual General Assembly, August 6-9, 2015, http://albertametis.com/wp-content/uploads/2014/05/AGM-2015-Resolutions.pdf.

20 See "Métis Nation of Ontario Youth Council (MNOYC)," Métis Nation of Ontario, viewed July 27, 2016, http://www.metisnation.org/governance/governing-structure/mnoyc-youth/.

21 "Resolution #1 – National Youth Position Paper," minutes of the Métis National Council General Assembly (draft), June 17–18, 2016, 20–21.

22 Interview with Mitchell Case, March 17, 2017.

23 Chapter 5 explores in detail the role of women in Métis governance.

24 "By-Laws of Les Femmes Michif Otipemisiwak," Women of the Métis Nation website, March 2012, http://metiswomen.org/en/wp-content/uploads/2012/03/Les-Femmes-Michif-Otipemisiwak-Bylaws-at-incorporation.pdf.

25 "Consultation Guidebook," Métis Nation British Columbia, February 2009, 5, http://www.mnbc.ca/pdfs/final%20consultation%20guidelines.pdf.

26 The role of elders in general and as a check and balance on executives more specifically has not been without controversy. In Saskatchewan, a senate made up of one elder appointed for life from each of the twelve regions originally had a quasi-judicial role pertaining to dispute resolution. However, controversy over its functions as both an arbiter and a mediator in internal disputes led to reforms that limit its role to ceremonial functions. See "Métis Governance in Saskatchewan for the 21st Century: Views and Visions of the Métis People," report submitted to the Saskatchewan Minister of First Nations and Métis Relations, Saskatchewan, Métis Electoral Consultation Panel, 2005. The Métis Nation of Alberta has also struggled to find the balance between the judicial and ceremonial roles of elders – a subject on the agenda as part of ongoing discussions on governance reform in that province.

27 "Exploring Options for Métis Governance in the 21st Century," Métis Nation Gateway website, Jason Madden, John Graham, and Jake Wilson, Ottawa, Institute on Governance, September 2005, 23, http://www.metisportals.ca/cons/wp-content/uploads/2009/02/metis-governance-in-the-21-century.pdf.

28 At the same time, the political instability of some Métis governments has led to reluctance on the part of some affiliates to establish a formal accountability relationship with them. See "Evaluation of the Gabriel Dumont Institute of Native Studies and Applied Research, Final Report," submitted to Saskatchewan Advanced Education, Employment and Labour and Gabriel Dumont Institute of Native Studies and Applied Research, Ekos Research Associates Inc., May 6, 2008, http://www.ekospolitics.com/articles/eval/GDI-Evaluation-Final-Report-May-2008.pdf.

29 "Governance," Gabriel Dumont Institute, viewed July 24, 2016, https://gdins.org/about/overview/governance/; and "Corporate Information," Métis Capital Housing Corporation website, viewed July 24, 2016, http://www.metiscapital.ca/CorporateInfo.aspx.

30 "Board of Directors," Louis Riel Institute, viewed July 25, 2016, http://www.louisrielinstitute.com/louis-riel-institute-board-of-directors.php.

31 Interview with MNC president Clément Chartier, March 1, 2011.

32 "Keynote Address by President Chartier," Métis Nation, Métis Nation Constitution Workshop in Ottawa, December 11–12, 2011, http://www.metisnation.ca/index.php/news/metis-nation-constitution-workshop-held-in-ottawa.

33 "Message from the Métis Nation of Ontario President," Métis Self-Government, a plainspeak document, Métis Nation of Ontario, 2017, 2.

34 Ibid.

35 "The Métis," Métis Nation, document published for the Decade of the Métis Nation by the Métis National Council, 2011, www.metisnation.ca/wp-content/.../02/The-MEtis-publication.pdf.

36 The Kelowna Accord was a $5.1-billion, five-year agreement between the federal government, provinces, territories, and national Indigenous leaders that sought to improve the education, employment, and living conditions of Indigenous peoples. Initiated by former prime minister Paul Martin, the agreement was abandoned by his successor, Stephen Harper.

37 "Governance and Financial Accountability Accord," Métis Nation, signed April 29, 2013, http://www.metisnation.ca/wp-content/uploads/2013/04/Governance-and-Financial-Accountability-Accordsigned1.pdf.

38 "Speech for the Council of the Federation," by Métis National Council president, Clément Chartier, July 24 2013, http://www.metisnation.ca/wp-content/uploads/2013/07/PDFJuly-24-2013-COF-meeting-notes-FINAL.pdf.

39 "Evaluation of the Federal Interlocutor's Contribution Program and *Powley*: Management of Métis Aboriginal Rights," Indigenous Services Canada, Office of the Federal Interlocutor, February 25, 2008, http://www.aadnc-aandc.gc.ca/DAM/DAM-INTER-HQ/STAGING/texte-text/pwl_1100100011946_eng.pdf.

40 The Manitoba Métis Federation and Manitoba signed a harvesting agreement in 2012; the Métis Nation-Saskatchewan signed an MOU on harvesting with Saskatchewan in 2010; the Métis Nation of Alberta signed the Interim Métis Harvesting Agreement with the province in 2004 and renewed negotiations on a Harvesting Agreement with the province in 2017. The BC government does not currently recognize Métis harvesting rights. For a discussion of Métis harvesting rights in Manitoba, see Saunders (2011).

41 "Métis Nation Relationship Accord," Government of British Columbia, signed May 31, 2005, http://www2.gov.bc.ca/gov/content/governments/aboriginal-people/new-relationship/m-tis-nation-relationship-accord.

42 "Government of Ontario – Métis Nation Framework Agreement," Métis Nation, signed April 17, 2014, http://www.metisnation.org/media/458392/mno_ontario_framework_agreement-2014%20final.pdf.

43 "Manitoba Métis Policy," Government of Manitoba, viewed July 24, 2016, http://www.gov.mb.ca/ana/mbMétispolicy.html.

44 "Canada-Metis Nation Accord," Métis Nation, April 13, 2017, 3, http://www.metisnation.ca/wp-content/uploads/2017/04/Canada-Me%CC%81tis-Nation-AccordEn.pdf.

45 "PM and Métis Nation Enter into Groundbreaking Accord," Métis Nation, Métis National Council, April 13, 2017, http://www.metisnation.ca/wp-content/uploads/2017/04/MNC-Press-Release-April-13-2017.pdf.

46 "Métis Nation of Alberta and Canada Sign Agreement to Advance Métis

Rights and Outstanding Claims in Alberta," Métis Nation of Alberta, January 31, 2017, http://albertametis.com/2017/01/.

47 "Feds Signing Memo with Métis in Ontario to Open 'Nation-to-Nation' Talks," Colin Perkel, *Globe and Mail*, February 3, 2017, http://www.theglobeandmail.com/news/national/feds-signing-memo-with-metis-in-ontario-to-open-nation-to-nation-talks/article33895291/.

48 "A Matter of National and Constitutional Import: Report of the Minister's Special Representative on Reconciliation with Métis: Section 35 Métis Rights and the *Manitoba Métis Federation* Decision," Indigenous and Northern Affairs Canada, June 14, 2016, 34, http://www.aadnc-aandc.gc.ca/eng/1467641790303/1467641835266.

49 Interview with President Margaret Froh, March 18, 2017.

50 "Métis Nation of Alberta Signs Historic Framework Agreement with Provincial Government," Métis Nation of Alberta, February 1, 2017, http://albertametis.com/2017/02/metis-nation-alberta-signs-historic-framework-agreement-provincial-government/.

51 "Overview of Nation-to-Nation Relationship," address by President Chartier at the MNC Special Assembly, March 18, 2017.

52 Interview with former MNO president Gary Lipinski, November 11, 2013, and MNC president Clément Chartier, March 1, 2011.

53 "A Matter of National and Constitutional Import: Report of the Minister's Special Representative on Reconciliation with Métis: Section 35 Métis Rights and the *Manitoba Métis Federation* Decision," Indigenous and Northern Affairs Canada, June 14, 2016, 17, http://www.aadnc-aandc.gc.ca/eng/1467641790303/1467641835266.

CHAPTER 4: (RE)BUILDING A MÉTIS CIVIL SERVICE

1 "Summit Overview," remarks by President David Chartrand at the Manitoba Métis Government Summit, Winnipeg, March 10, 2017.

2 "Founders of the Manitoba Métis Federation," Gabriel Dumont Institute, Lawrence Barkwell, December 2013, http://www.metismuseum.ca/resource.php/14276; "Métis Political Organizations," Lawrence Barkwell, January 2010, http://www.metismuseum.ca/media/db/11913.

3 "President's Report," Manitoba Métis Federation, MMF Annual General Assembly, September 25, 2015, http://www.mmf.mb.ca/docs/aga/President_Report_2015.pdf.

4 "Presentation to the United Nations Special Rapporteur," Métis Nation, Manitoba Métis Federation, Winnipeg, October 12, 2013, http://www.metisnation.ca/wp-content/uploads/2013/10/MMF-UN-SP-FINAL-W-COVER-Brief-to-the-UN-Special-Rapporteur-October-11-2013-.pdf.

5 "Backgrounder: Membership," Manitoba Métis Federation, February 2011, 1–2.

6 At its Annual General Assembly in 2014, the MMF voted unanimously to allow non-residents of Manitoba to also apply for membership based on "a

direct ancestral connection" to the Manitoba Métis community. See "Resolution #2, Minutes of 2014 Annual General Assembly of the Manitoba Métis Federation," Manitoba Métis Federation, November 16, 2014, http://www.mmf.mb.ca/docs/membership/Resolution_2_Manitoba_Metis_Community_and_Membership_Application_2014_AGA.pdf.

7 "2016–2020 Strategic Plan," overview prepared for the Manitoba Métis Government Summit, March 2017, copy of original document in authors' possession.

8 "Backgrounder: Membership," Manitoba Métis Federation, February 2011, copy of original document in authors' possession.

9 Ibid.

10 "Your Government – Departments, Portfolios and Affiliates," Manitoba Métis Federation, viewed July 25, 2016, http://www.mmf.mb.ca/departments_portfolios_and_affiliates.php.

11 "Constitution," Manitoba Métis Federation, modified September 2013, http://www.mmf.mb.ca/docs/constitution_rev2013_3.pdf.

12 "Towards a New Aboriginal Governance Agenda (TANAGA), 2004–2005 series," World Bank website, notes on the First Roundtable Meeting, Ottawa, Institute on Governance, September 21, 2004, 4, http://siteresources.worldbank.org/WBI/Resources/TANAGART1Sept21-04summary.pdf.

13 See Dubois (2013) for a discussion of the Métis Act in Saskatchewan; and "Métis Nation of Ontario Secretariat Act," Government of Ontario, December 2015, https://www.ontario.ca/laws/statute/s15039.

14 "Manitoba Métis Federation Constitution," presentation by Murray Trachtenberg at the Manitoba Métis Federation Government Summit, March 10, 2017.

15 Remarks by Métis Nation of Ontario chair France Picotte at the Commission on Métis Rights and Self-Government meeting in St. Catharines, June 5, 2017.

16 Interview with Gerald Morin, March 21, 2013.

17 As discussed by Gary Lipinski, former president of the Métis Nation of Ontario, in "Revisiting RCAP – Towards Reconciliation: The Future of Indigenous Governance," Institute on Governance, 2015, 10, https://iog.ca/research-publications/publications/revisiting-rcap-towards-reconciliation-the-future-of-indigenous-governance/. See also "The Hecla Retreat: Consolidating Government," Manitoba Métis Federation, 2008, copy of original document in authors' possession.

18 Given the sensitive nature of some of the material, all those interviewed for this chapter requested and received anonymity.

19 The Manitoba Government requires not-for-profits to be governed by a board, see "Non-Profit Organizations Portal," Government of Manitoba, viewed July 13, 2016, http://www.gov.mb.ca/npo/getting-started/governance.html.

20 Interview with a former senior MMF official, April 30, 2015a.

21 Interview with a senior MMF civil servant, June 11, 2016.

22 Interview, May 20, 2015.

23 "The Hecla Retreat: Consolidating Government," Manitoba Métis Federation, 2008, copy of original document in authors' possession; "Report of the Steering and Governance Committee," 2012, Manitoba Métis Federation, copy of original document in authors' possession.

24 Interview, April 30, 2015b.

25 Interview, June 11, 2016.

26 "Manitoba Métis Federation Constitution," presentation by Murray Trachtenberg at the Manitoba Métis Government Summit, March 10, 2017.

27 "Sovereignty, Good Governance and First Nations Human Resources: Capacity Challenges," research paper for the National Centre for First Nations Governance, prepared by Richard Missens, May 2008, http://fngovernance.org/ncfng_research/richard_missens.pdf.

28 According to a report prepared by the Fraser Institute in 2011/12, the Department of Aboriginal Affairs and Northern Development Canada spent approximately $25.6 million on Métis and non-status Indians, an amount representing just 0.3 percent of the department's almost $7.9 billion total spending on Aboriginal matters that year. See "Ever Higher: Government Spending on Canada's Aboriginals since 1947," report prepared for the Fraser Institute, Centre for Aboriginal Policy Studies, by Mark Milke, December 2013, 12, https://www.fraserinstitute.org/sites/default/files/Aboriginal-spending-2013.pdf.

29 Interview with a former senior MMF official, April 30, 2015a.

30 Interview, September 12, 2015.

31 "Province cuts health service funding for Métis," Larry Kusch, *Winnipeg Free Press*, November 29, 2016, http://www.winnipegfreepress.com/local/provincial-govt-cuts-health-service-funding-for-metis-403637666.html.

32 Interview with a former official of the Manitoba government, May 15, 2015.

33 Interview, January 18, 2011.

34 Interview, April 30, 2015a.

35 Interview, April 30, 2015a.

36 Interview with a senior MMF civil servant, April 30, 2015b.

37 "Message from the President," Métis Nation, Métis Nation Newsletter, April 2017, 2. http://www.metisnation.ca/wp-content/uploads/2017/03/Newsletter-April-2017.pdf.

38 Letter from Métis National Council President Clément Chartier to the Right Honourable Justin Trudeau, March 27, 2017 copy of original document in authors' possession.

39 Ibid.

40 Ibid. Subsequent correspondence was sent to President Chartier from various federal ministers clarifying the specific allocations for the Métis in the 2017 Indigenous funding envelopes.

41 "Exploring Options for Métis Governance in the 21st Century," Métis Nation Gateway website, Jason Madden, John Graham, and Jake Wilson, Ottawa,

Institute on Governance, September 2005, 50, http://www.metisportals.ca/cons/wp-content/uploads/2009/02/metis-governance-in-the-21-century.pdf.

42 Interview, May 20, 2015.

43 "State of the Nation – President's Report," Manitoba Métis Federation, 2015, http://www.mmf.mb.ca/docs/aga/President_Report_2015.pdf.

44 "Reclaiming our Inheritance: Our Journey Home," Manitoba Métis Federation Annual General Report, November 2014, 21, http://www.mmf.mb.ca/docs/AGA_2014_OCT28.pdf.

45 "2013-2018 Strategic Plan," Manitoba Métis Federation, 2013, 11.

46 Interview with a former official with the Manitoba government, May 15, 2015.

47 "Sovereignty, Good Governance and First Nations Human Resources: Capacity Challenges," research paper for the National Centre for First Nations Governance, prepared by Richard Missens, May 2008, 5, http://fngovernance.org/ncfng_research/richard_missens.pdf.

48 Interview with a former MMF senior civil servant, May 20, 2015.

49 Interview, May 15, 2015.

50 "Reclaiming our Inheritance: Our Journey Home," Manitoba Métis Federation Annual General Report, November 2014, 21, http://www.mmf.mb.ca/docs/AGA_2014_OCT28.pdf.

51 Personal communication, June 6, 2015.

52 "A Matter of National and Constitutional Import: Report of the Minister's Special Representative on Reconciliation with Métis: Section 35 Métis Rights the *Manitoba Métis Federation* Decision," Indigenous and Northern Affairs Canada, June 14, 2016, 38, http://www.aadnc-aandc.gc.ca/eng/1467641790303/1467641835266.

53 "Memorandum of Understanding on Advancing Reconciliation," Indigenous and Northern Affairs Canada, modified July 15, 2016, https://www.aadnc-aandc.gc.ca/eng/1467055681745/1467055869159.

54 "Framework Agreement for Advancing Reconciliation," Canada and the Manitoba Métis Federation, November, 2016.

55 "President Chartrand presents signed Framework Agreement to Riel during ceremony," Manitoba Métis Federation, November 16, 2016, http://www.mmf.mb.ca/news_details.php?news_id=206.

56 Ibid.

CHAPTER 5: MOTHERS OF THE MÉTIS NATION

1 The title of this chapter comes from a comment made by a female political representative at the Métis National Council Annual Assembly in 2009, where she described the salience of women to the continuation of Métis culture and nationhood in this way.

2 "Le Métis," Manitoba Métis Federation, June 30, 2016, http://www.mmf.mb.ca/docs/LeMetis_2016_06_30.pdf?v=20170607123444.

3 "President's Message," Women of the Métis Nation, viewed July 25, 2016, http://metiswomen.org/en/about-us/message-from-the-president/.

4 Interview, July 31, 2010.
5 Interview, April 22, 2010.
6 With the exception of the Métis Nation of Alberta. A new women's body in Alberta, called the New Dawn Métis Women's Society, held its inaugural meeting in the spring of 2015. The president of this organization, Marilyn Lizee, is on the Board of Directors of Women of the Métis Nation (private correspondence with Melanie Omeniho, president of Women of the Métis Nation, February 2, 2016).
7 "Infinity Women," Manitoba Métis Federation, viewed July 25, 2016, http://www.mmf.mb.ca/departments_portfolios_and_affiliates_details.php?id=20.
8 "Home," Women of the Métis Nation, viewed June 7, 2017, http://metiswomen.org/.
9 Interview with Melanie Omeniho, May 20, 2013.
10 "MN-S Election has a few shockers," *Eagle Feather News*, May 28, 2017, https://www.eaglefeathernews.com/news/index.php?detail=2788.
11 "The Provisional Council of the Métis Nation of Ontario," Métis Nation of Ontario, viewed June 7, 2017, http://www.metisnation.org/governance/governing-structure/pcmno/.
12 Data compiled by authors based on MMF electoral returns.
13 "Métis Political Activists," Gabriel Dumont Institute, interview with Jim Sinclair and Jim Durocher, recorded by Ron Laliberte, April 17, 2004, tape 2, http://www.metismuseum.ca/media/document.php/06114.S,%20D,%20and%20L%20%2824%29.pdf.
14 Interview with Anita Campbell May 17, 2010.
15 Interview, July 31, 2010.
16 Interview, November 16, 2014. For a discussion of how this role extends beyond politics, see Hodgson-Smith and Kermoal (2016).
17 "De Pierre-Esprit Radisson à Louis Riel: Voyageurs et Métis/From Pierre-Esprit Radisson to Louis Riel: Voyageurs and Métis," keynote address by Manitoba Métis Federation president David Chartrand, St. Boniface, Manitoba, November 18, 2010.
18 See Macdougall (2006, 444); Macdougall and St-Onge (2013); and Foster (2006) for a similar discussion of the importance of female kinship in Métis communities in Montana. For a discussion of the role of women in the ethnogenesis of the Métis across borders in the early nineteenth century, see Hogue (2015, 20–28).
19 Interview, March 21, 2013.
20 Senator Cummings was appointed to the Senate of the Métis Nation-Saskatchewan in December 1993, a position she continues to hold. "Métis Political Activist Interviews," Gabriel Dumont Institute, Nora Cummings, Peter Bishop, and Ron Laliberte, February 28, 29, 2004, Interview 38, Tape 3, http://www.metismuseum.ca/browse/index.php?id=787.
21 Interview, March 21, 2013.

22 "Women of the 1885 Resistance," Gabriel Dumont Institute, Lawrence Barkwell, July 23, 2008, http://www.metismuseum.ca/resource.php/09284; and Isabelle (Falcon) Trottier, Gabriel Dumont Institute, June 4, 2014, http://www.metismuseum.ca/resource.php/14797.
23 Interview, April 22, 2010.
24 Interview, July 31, 2010.
25 Interview with Verna DeMontigny, January 22, 2018.
26 Interview, November 22, 2009.
27 Interview, November 16, 2014.
28 Interview, July 31, 2010.
29 Interview, April 22, 2010.

CHAPTER 6: THE ROAD TO MÉTIS SELF-GOVERNMENT

1 "The Prime Minister of Canada and President of the Métis National Council welcome the signing of the Canada-Métis Nation Accord," Office of the Prime Minister, April 13, 2017, https://pm.gc.ca/eng/news/2017/04/13/prime-minister-canada-and-president-metis-national-council-welcome-signing-canada.
2 Cabinet members included the minister for Indigenous and northern affairs; the minister of justice and attorney-general of Canada; the minister of health; the minister of families, children and social development; the minister of employment, workforce development and labour; and the president of the Treasury Board.
3 "PM and Métis Nation Enter into Groundbreaking Accord," Métis Nation, Métis National Council, April 13, 2017, http://www.metisnation.ca/wp-content/uploads/2017/04/MNC-Press-Release-April-13-2017.pdf.
4 "Message from the Métis Nation of Ontario President," Métis Self-Government, a plainspeak document, Métis Nation of Ontario, 2017, p. 1, www.metisnation.org/.../commission-booklets-self-government.
5 "Canada-Métis Nation Accord," Métis Nation, April 13, 2017, http://www.metisnation.ca/wp-content/uploads/2017/04/Canada-Métis-Nation-AccordEn.pdf.
6 Ibid.
7 Ibid.
8 "Trudeau government to recognize Indigenous rights as basis for all government relations with Indigenous Peoples," Métis Nation, Métis National Council, February 15, 2018, http://www.metisnation.ca/index.php/news/trudeau-government-to-recognize-indigenous-rights-as-basis-for-all-government-relations-with-indigenous-peoples.
9 Testimony of Clément Chartier before the House of Commons Standing Committee on Aboriginal Affairs and Northern Development, Parliament of Canada, House of Commons, October 18, 2011, http://www.ourcommons.ca/DocumentViewer/en/41-1/AANO/meeting-6/evidence.
10 "Negotiation and Self-Government," presentation by Jason Madden at the MMF Government Summit, March 12, 2017.

11 *R. v. Powley*, [2003] 2 S.C.R. 207, 2003 SCC 43 at para. 10.

12 Ibid., at para. 49.

13 "Métis Registration Guide," Métis Nation, Métis National Council, April 2011, http://www.metisnation.ca/wp-content/uploads/2011/04/M%C3%A9tis-Registration-Guide.pdf.

14 Cited in *Issues for Canadians,* Nelson (educational publisher) website, p. 159, available online, http://www.nelson.com/albertasocialstudies/productinfo/gr6_9/documents/abss9ch4draft.pdf

15 "President's Message," Manitoba Métis Federation, April 9, 2013, http://www.mmf.mb.ca/docs/presidents_message_2013_04_09.pdf?v=20150626133126.

16 "A Matter of National and Constitutional Import: Report of the Minister's Special Representative on Reconciliation with Métis: Section 35 Métis Rights and the *Manitoba Métis Federation* Decision," Indigenous and Northern Affairs Canada, June 14, 2016, pp. 17–18, http://www.aadnc-aandc.gc.ca/eng/1467641790303/1467641835266.

17 "Building a Strong Middle Class," Government of Canada, March 22, 2017, p. 166, http://www.budget.gc.ca/2017/docs/plan/budget-2017-en.pdf.

18 Clément Chartier, quoted in Mary Agnes Welch, "Métis Bag Hunting Right: Court Dismissed Man's Charge for Taking Duck without Licence," *Winnipeg Free Press*, January 9, 2009.

19 See "Address to the Truth and Reconciliation Commission," by Métis National Council president, Clément Chartier, Northern National Event, Inuvik, NWT, June 28, 2011, http://www.metisnation.ca/index.php/news/trc-event-in-nwt.

20 *Manitoba Métis Federation Inc. v. Canada (Attorney General),* 2013 SCC 14, [2013] 1 S.C.R. 623, at para. 9.

21 *Manitoba Métis Federation Inc. v. Canada (Attorney General),* 2013 SCC 14, [2013] 1 S.C.R. 623, at para. 44. See also on this point, "A Matter of National and Constitutional Import: Report of the Minister's Special Representative on Reconciliation with Métis: Section 35 Métis Rights and the *Manitoba Métis Federation* Decision," Indigenous and Northern Affairs Canada, June 14, 2016, p. 37, http://www.aadnc-aandc.gc.ca/eng/1467641790303/1467641835266.

22 *Daniels v. Canada (Indian Affairs and Northern Development),* 2016 SCC 12 at para. 15. Alberta Métis Settlement legislation stands out as an exception.

23 Ibid., at para. 12.

24 Ibid., at para. 51.

25 "President's Message," Manitoba Métis Federation, April 21, 2014, http://www.mmf.mb.ca/docs/presidents_message_2014_04_21.pdf?v=20150217135018; and "State of the Nation Address," Métis Nation, President Clément Chartier, Métis National Council Annual General Assembly, March 23, 2013, http://www.metisnation.ca/wp-content/uploads/2013/03/state-of-the-nationPDF-final.pdf.

26 "Summit Overview," Presentation by President Chartrand at the MMF Government Summit, March 10, 2017.

27 Interview with John Morrisseau, November 21, 2009.

28 Jason Madden, quoted in "Isaac report provides 'road map' to reconciliation with Métis," Legal Feeds, July 21, 2016, https://www.canadianlawyermag.com/legalfeeds/author/jennifer-brown/isaac-report-provides-road-map-to-reconciliation-with-metis-6997/.

29 "MNC Welcomes Canada's Appointment of Special Representative on Métis Section 35 Rights," Métis Nation, Métis National Council, June 4, 2015, http://www.metisnation.ca/index.php/news/mnc-welcomes-canada%E2%80%99s-appointment-of-special-representative-on-Métis-section-35-rights.

30 "A Matter of National and Constitutional Import: Report of the Minister's Special Representative on Reconciliation with Métis: Section 35 Métis Rights and the *Manitoba Métis Federation* Decision," Indigenous and Northern Affairs Canada, June 14, 2016, 3, http://www.aadnc-aandc.gc.ca/eng/1467641790303/1467641835266.

31 Ibid., 13.

32 Ibid., 3.

33 Ibid., 12.

34 *Alberta (Aboriginal Affairs and Northern Development) v. Cunningham*, 2011 SCC 37, [2011] 2 S.C.R. 670 at para. 66, 70.

35 "A New Direction: Advancing Aboriginal and Treaty Rights," Government of Canada, report of the Ministerial Special Representative on Renewing the Comprehensive Land Claim Policy, Douglas R. Eyford, April 2015, 44, https://www.aadnc-aandc.gc.ca/eng/1426169199009/1426169236218.

36 *Daniels v. Canada (Indian Affairs and Northern Development)*, 2016 SCC 12 at para. 15.

37 "President's Newsletter," Metis Nation, Métis National Council, November, http://www.metisnation.ca/wp-content/uploads/2017/11/Newsletter-November-20171.pdf.

38 Interview, November 3, 2016.

39 Interview, January 22, 2017.

40 "A Matter of National and Constitutional Import: Report of the Minister's Special Representative on Reconciliation with Métis: Section 35 Métis Rights and the *Manitoba Métis Federation* Decision," Indigenous and Northern Affairs Canada, June 14, 2016, 27, http://www.aadnc-aandc.gc.ca/eng/1467641790303/1467641835266.

41 "Métis Nation of Alberta and Canada Sign Agreement to Advance Métis Rights and Outstanding Claims in Alberta," Métis Nation of Alberta, January 31, 2017, http://albertametis.com/2017/01/20612/.

42 "Métis National Council Supports Prime Minister's Nation-to-Nation Approach to First Ministers' Talks with Indigenous Peoples," Métis National Council, February 24, 2016, http://www.metisnation.ca/index.php/news/Métis-national-council-supports-prime-minister%E2%80%99s-nation-to-nation-approach-to-first-ministers%E2%80%99-talks-with-indigenous-peoples.

43 "Memorandum of Understanding on Reconciliation between Canada and Manitoba Métis Federation," Government of Canada, May 27, 2016, http://news.gc.ca/web/article-en.do?nid=1074989; "Canada and Manitoba Métis Federation sign MOU following historic Supreme Court land ruling," Métis Nation, Métis National Council Newsletter, June 2016, http://www.metisnation.ca/wp-content/uploads/2016/06/Newsletter-June-2016.pdf.

44 "Canada-Métis Nation Accord," Métis Nation, April 13, 2017, http://www.metisnation.ca/wp-content/uploads/2017/04/Canada-Métis-Nation-AccordEn.pdf.

45 "A Matter of National and Constitutional Import: Report of the Minister's Special Representative on Reconciliation with Métis: Section 35 Métis Rights and the *Manitoba Métis Federation* Decision," Indigenous and Northern Affairs Canada, June 14, 2016, 25, http://www.aadnc-aandc.gc.ca/eng/1467641790303/1467641835266.

46 "Canada-Métis Nation Accord," Métis Nation, April 13, 2017, http://www.metisnation.ca/wp-content/uploads/2017/04/Canada-Métis-Nation-AccordEn.pdf.

47 As recounted by MNC president Clément Chartier in his State of the Nation Address, Métis Nation, MNC General Assembly, Winnipeg, April 28, 2017, http://www.metisnation.ca/wp-content/uploads/2017/04/state-of-nation-GA-April-2017web-version.pdf.

48 RCAP (1996a, 103). The Centre for First Nations Governance combines many of these principles into the following pillars of effective governance: the people, the land, laws and jurisdiction, institutions, and resources. See "The People, the Land, Laws and Jurisdiction, Institutions, Resources: The Five Pillars of Effective Governance," Centre for First Nations Governance, May 2013, http://www.fngovernance.org/publications. See also, Jodi Bruhn, "In Search of Common Ground: Reconciling Western-Based Governance Principles and First Nations Traditions," Institute on Governance, May 2009, Ottawa, https://iog.ca/research-publications/publications/in-search-of-common-ground-reconciling-western-based-governance-principles-and-first-nations-traditions/.

49 "Current Government Structure and Local Governance," presentation by Al Benoit to the MMF Government Summit, March 10, 2017.

50 Ibid.

51 "A Matter of National and Constitutional Import: Report of the Minister's Special Representative on Reconciliation with Métis: Section 35 Métis Rights and the *Manitoba Métis Federation* Decision," Indigenous and Northern Affairs Canada website, bold in the original, June 14, 2016, 30, 14, http://www.aadnc-aandc.gc.ca/eng/1467641790303/1467641835266.

52 "MNO Commission on Métis Rights," Métis Nation of Ontario, http://www.metisnation.org/governance/governing-structure/mno-commission-on-Métis-rights-and-self-government/.

53 "State of the Nation Address," Métis Nation, President Clément Chartier, Métis National Council Annual General Assembly, March 23, 2013, http://www.metisnation.ca/wp-content/uploads/2013/03/state-of-the-nationPDF-final.pdf.

54 Ibid.

55 See SSCAP (2013). For a critical discussion of the Senate report, see Andersen (2014, 197).

56 See Saunders (2013). The ongoing contested nature of Métis identity is evidenced by the emergence of new groups in Canada claiming to represent the Métis and challenging the authority of the Métis National Council and its Governing Members. One such group, the Métis Federation of Canada, formed in 2013, defines Métis in the following terms: an individual of *Aboriginal ancestry*, connected through kinship or adoption to a "direct" *Métis or Aboriginal ancestor*, who identifies with Métis history and "its appropriate cultural expression in line with the *acknowledgement of diversity*" (emphasis added). See "Membership," Métis Federation of Canada, viewed July 25, 2016, http://www.metisfederationofcanada.ca/eng---application---membership.html.

57 "State of the Nation Address," President Clément Chartier, Métis Nation General Assembly, Winnipeg, April 28, 2017.

58 "President's Newsletter," Métis Nation, Métis National Council, February 2013, http://www.metisnation.ca/wp-content/uploads/2013/02/PDF-Draft-Newsletter-Feb-2013.pdf.

59 "Métis Nation Welcomes Report of Ministerial Special Representative on Canada-Métis Nation Reconciliation," Métis Nation, Métis National Council, July 21, 2016, http://www.metisnation.ca/index.php/news/Métis-nation-welcomes-report-of-ministerial-special-representative-on-canada-Métis-nation-reconciliation.

60 "PM and Métis Nation Enter into Groundbreaking Accord," Métis Nation, Métis National Council, April 13, 2017, http://www.metisnation.ca/wp-content/uploads/2017/04/MNC-Press-Release-April-13-2017.pdf.

61 "President's Message," Manitoba Métis Federation, March 22 2017, http://www.mmf.mb.ca/docs/presidents_message_2017_03_22.pdf?v=20170421131503.

CONCLUSION

1 "State of the Nation Address," President Clément Chartier, Métis National Council Annual General Assembly, June 17, 2016.

2 "Resolution #4 – Governing Members of the Métis National Council and Nation-to-Nation, Government-to-Government Negotiations," Métis National Council Annual General Assembly, June 18, 2016.

3 Interview with George Fleury, June 15, 2017.

4 Interview with John Morrisseau, November 21, 2009.

5 For a list of fallen soldiers during the 1885 Resistance, see "Heroes of the 1885 Resistance. Summary of those killed," Gabriel Dumont Institute, March 3, 2010, http://www.metismuseum.ca/resource.php/11980.

6 *Manitoba Métis Federation Inc. v. Canada (Attorney General)*, 2013 SCC 14, [2013] 1 S.C.R. 623 at para. 140.

7 Interview with George Fleury, June 15, 2017.

References

Adams, Christopher, Gregg Dahl, and Ian Peach, eds. 2013. *Métis in Canada: History, Identity, Law and Politics.* Edmonton: University of Alberta Press.

Adams, Howard. 1975. *Prison of Grass.* Saskatoon: Fifth House.

Adese, Jennifer. 2006. "A Tale of Two Constitutions: Métis Nationhood and Section 35(2)'s Impact on Interpretations of *Daniels*." *Topia: Canadian Journal of Cultural Studies* 36: 7–19.

Alfred, Taiaiake. 2005. *Wasáse: Indigenous Pathways of Action and Freedom.* Peterborough: Broadview Press.

Andersen, Chris. 2008. "From Nation to Population: The Racialization of 'Métis' in the Canadian Census." *Nations and Nationalism* 14 (2): 347–68.

– . 2014. *"Métis" Race, Recognition, and the Struggle for Indigenous Peoplehood.* Vancouver: UBC Press.

Anderson, Grant. 2006. "The Buffalo Hunt." In *Métis Legacy II*, ed. Lawrence Barkwell, Leah Dorion, and Audreen Hourie, 208–12. Saskatoon: Gabriel Dumont Publications.

Anderson, Kim. 2009. "Leading by Action: Female Chiefs and the Political Landscape." In *Restoring the Balance: First Nations, Women, Community and Culture*, ed. Gail Guthrie Valaskakis, Madeline Dion Stout, and Eric Guimond, 99–123. Winnipeg: University of Manitoba Press.

– . 2016. *A Recognition of Being: Reconstructing Native Womanhood.* 2nd ed. Toronto: Women's Press.

Armstrong, Jeannette. 1996. "Invocation: the Real Power of Aboriginal Women." In *Women of the First Nations: Power, Wisdom, and Strength*, ed. Christine Miller and Patricia Chuchryk, ix-xii. Winnipeg: University of Manitoba Press.

Authers, Benjamin. 2014. "'An Insane and Irresponsible Government': Louis Riel and the Representation of Responsibility." In *Riel's Defence: Perspectives on His Speeches*, ed. Hans V. Hansen, 224–46. Montreal and Kingston: McGill-Queen's University Press.

Bakker, Peter. 1997. *A Language of Our Own: The Genesis of Michif, the Mixed Cree-French Language of the Canadian Métis.* New York: Oxford University Press.

Barkwell, Lawrence. 1991. "Early Law and Social Control among the Métis." In *The Struggle for Recognition: Canadian Justice and the Métis Nation*, ed. Samuel W. Corrigan and Lawrence J. Barkwell, 7–38, Winnipeg: Pemmican Publishers.

Barron, Laurie. 1997. *Walking in Indian Moccasins: The Native Policies of Tommy Douglas and the CCF.* Vancouver: UBC Press.

Barsh, Russell Lawrence. 1986. "The Nature and Sprit of North American Political Systems." *American Indian Quarterly* 10 (3): 181–98.

Barter, Virginia (Parker). 2007. "Searching for the Silver Fox: A Fur-Trade Family History." In *The Long Journey of a Forgotten People: Métis Identities and Family Histories*, ed. Ute Lischke and David T. McNab, 247–304. Waterloo: Wilfrid Laurier University Press.

Baskin, Cyndy. 1982. "Women in Iroquois Society." *Canadian Woman Studies* 4 (2): 42–46.

Bastien, Betty. 1996. "Voices through Time." In *Women of the First Nations: Power, Wisdom, and Strength*, ed. Christine Miller and Patricia Chuchryk, 127–29. Winnipeg: University of Manitoba Press.

Begg, Alexander. 1894. *History of the North-West*, Vol. 1. Toronto: Hunter, Rose and Co.

–. 1956. *Alexander Begg's Red River Journal and Other Papers Relative to the Red River Resistance of 1869–1870*. Toronto: Champlain Society.

Belcourt, Tony. 2013. "For the Record … On Métis Identity and Citizenship within the Métis Nation." *aboriginal policy studies* 2 (2): 128–41.

Bell, Catherine. 1994. *Alberta's Métis Settlements Legislation: An Overview of Ownership and Management of Settlement Lands*. Regina: Canadian Plains Research Centre.

–. 1999. "Métis Self-Government: The Alberta Settlements Model." In *Aboriginal Self-Government in Canada*, ed. John Hylton, 329–50. Saskatoon: Purich Publishing.

–. 2015. "*R v. Daniels*: Jurisdiction and Government Obligations to Non-Status Indians." In *Canada: State of the Federation 2013 – Aboriginal Multilevel Governance,* ed. Martin Papillon and André Juneau, 215–33. Montreal and Kingston: McGill-Queen's University Press.

Bell, Catherine, and Clayton Leonard. 2004. "A New Era in Métis Constitutional Rights: The Importance of Powley and Blais." *Alberta Law Review* 41 (4): 1049–83.

Bell, Catherine, and Paul Seaman. 2015. "A New Era for Métis Constitutional Rights? Consultation, Negotiation and Reconciliation." *Manitoba Law Journal* 38 (1): 29–71.

Bird, Madeline. 1991. *Living Kindness: The Dream of My Life: The Memoirs of Métis Elder, Madeline Bird.* Yellowknife, NT: Outcrop.

Blady, Sharon. 1996. "Beadwork as an Expression of Métis Cultural Identity." In *Issues in the North*, vol. 1, ed. Jill Oakes and Rick Riewe, 133–44. Edmonton: University of Alberta Press.

–. 1997. "Les Métisses: Towards a Feminist History of Red River." In *Issues in the North*, vol. 2, ed. Jill Oakes and Rick Riewe, 179–85. Edmonton: University of Alberta Press.

Boldt, Menno, and J. Anthony Long. 1984. "Tribal Traditions and European-Western Political Ideologies: The Dilemma of Canada's Native Indians." *Canadian Journal of Political Science* 17 (3): 537–51.

Borrows, John. 2010. *Drawing out Law: A Spirit's Guide*. Toronto: University of Toronto Press.

Brown, Jennifer. 1980. *Strangers in Blood: Fur Trade Company Families in Indian Country*. Vancouver: UBC Press.

–. 1983. "Women as Centre and Symbol in the Emergence of Métis Communities." *Canadian Journal of Native Studies* 3 (1): 39–46.

–. 2002. "The Métis: Genesis and Rebirth." In *Native People, Native Lands: Canadian Indians, Inuit and Métis*, ed. Bruce Alden Cox, 136–47. Montreal and Kingston: McGill-Queen's University Press.

Bumsted, J.M. 1995. "Crisis at Red River." *Beaver* 75 (3): 23–34.

–. 1996. *The Red River Rebellion*. Winnipeg: Watson and Dwyer.

–. 2001. *Louis Riel v. Canada: The Making of a Rebel*. Winnipeg: Great Plains Publications.

–. 2003. *Trials and Tribulations: The Red River Settlement and the Emergence of Manitoba, 1811–1870*. Winnipeg: Great Plains Publications.

Campbell, Maria. 1973. *Halfbreed*. Toronto: McClelland and Stewart.

–. 2012. "Foreword." In *Contours of a People: Métis Family, Mobility, and History*, ed. Nicole St-Onge, Carolyn Podruchny, and Brenda Macdougall, xiii-xxvi. Norman: University of Oklahoma Press.

Carpenter, Jock. 1977. *Fifty Dollar Bride: Marie Rose Smith, a Chronicle of Métis Life in the 19th Century*. Sidney, BC: Gray's Pub.

Carter, Sarah. 2007. *Aboriginal People and Colonizers of Western Canada to 1900*. Toronto: University of Toronto Press.

Cavanaugh, Catherine. 1997. "'No Place for a Woman': Engendering Western Canadian Settlement." *Western Historical Quarterly* 28 (Winter): 493–518.

Charette, Guillaume. 1980 [1976]. *Vanishing Spaces: Memoirs of Louis Goulet/L'espace de Louis Goulet*. Trans. Ray Ellenwood. Winnipeg: Éditions Bois-Brûlés.

Chartier, Clément. 1988. "In the Best Interest of the Métis Child." Saskatoon: University of Saskatchewan Native Law Centre.

Chartrand, Larry. 2004. "The Definition of Métis Peoples in Section 35(2) of the Constitution Act, 1982." *Saskatchewan Law Review* 67 (1): 209–33.

– . 2008. "'We Rise Again': Métis Traditional Governance and the Claim to Métis Self-Government." In *Aboriginal Self-Government in Canada: Current Trends and Issues*, 3rd ed., ed. Yale Belanger, 145–57. Saskatoon: Purich Publishing.

Chartrand, Paul. 1991. *Manitoba's Métis Settlement Scheme of 1870*. Saskatoon: Native Law Centre, University of Saskatchewan.

– . 2008. "Defining the 'Métis' of Canada: A Principled Approach to Crown-Aboriginal Relations." In *Métis-Crown Relations: Rights, Identity, Jurisdiction and Governance*, ed. Frederica Wilson and Melanie Mallet, 27–70. Toronto: Irwin Law.

– . 2017. "The Constitutional Status and Rights of the Métis People in Canada." *aboriginal policy studies* 6 (2): 120–31.

Chartrand, Paul, and John Giokas. 2002. "Defining 'The Métis People': The Hard Case of Canadian Aboriginal Law." In *Who Are Canada's Aboriginal Peoples? Recognition, Definition, and Jurisdiction*, ed. Paul Chartrand, 268–304. Saskatoon: Purich Publishing.

Childs, John Brown. 1998. "Transcommunality: From the Politics of Conversion to the Ethics of Respect in the Context of Cultural Diversity – Learning from Native American Philosophies with a Focus on the Haudenosaunee." *Social Justice* 25 (4): 143–69.

Chodan, Dan, and Tim Asfar. 2003. *Gabriel Dumont: War Leader of the Métis*. Edmonton: Folklore Publishing.

Combet, Denis. 2006. *Gabriel Dumont, Mémoires/Memoirs*. Saint-Boniface: Éditions du Blé.

Cornell, Stephen. 2007. "Remaking the Tools of Governance: Colonial Legacies, Indigenous Solutions." In *Rebuilding Native Nations*, ed. Miriam Jorgenson, 57–77. Tucson: University of Arizona Press.

– . 2015. "'Wolves Have A Constitution:' Continuities in Indigenous Self-Government." *The International Indigenous Policy Journal* 6 (1): 1–20.

Cornell, Stephen, and Joseph P. Kalt, 1998. "Sovereignty and Nation-Building: The Development Challenge in Indian Country Today." *American Indian Culture and Research Journal* 22 (3): 187–214.

– . 2007. "Two Approaches to the Development of Nations: One Works, the Other Doesn't." In *Rebuilding Native Nations*, ed. Miriam Jorgenson, 3–33. Tucson: University of Arizona Press.

Corntassel, Jeffrey. 2014. "Our Ways Will Continue On: Indigenous Approaches to Sustainability." *The Internationalization of Indigenous Rights, UNDRIP in the Canadian Context*. Special Report. Waterloo: Centre for International Governance Innovation.

Corrigan, Samuel W. 1991a. "Introduction." In *The Struggle for Recognition: Canadian Justice and the Métis Nation*, ed. Samuel W. Corrigan and Lawrence J. Barkwell, iii-viii. Winnipeg: Pemmican Publishers.

– . 1991b. "Some Implications of the Current Métis Case." In *The Struggle for Recognition: Canadian Justice and the Métis Nation*, ed. Samuel W. Corrigan and Lawrence J. Barkwell, 195–206. Winnipeg: Pemmican Publishers.

Daniels, Harry. 1979. *The Forgotten People: Métis and Non-Status Indian Land Claims*. Ottawa: Native Council of Canada.

Devine, Heather. 2001. "Les Desjarlais: The Development and Dispersion of a Proto-Métis Hunting Band, 1785–1870." In *From Rupert's Land to Canada*, ed. Theodore Binnema, Gerhard J. Ens, and R.C. Macleod, 129–58. Edmonton: University of Alberta Press.

–. 2004. *The People Who Own Themselves: Aboriginal Genesis in a Canadian Family, 1660–1900*. Calgary: University of Calgary Press.

Dickason, Olive Patricia. 1985. "From 'One Nation' in the Northeast to 'New Nation' in the Northwest: A Look at the Emergence of the Métis." In *The New Peoples: Being and Becoming Métis in North America*, ed. Jacqueline Peterson and Jennifer S.H. Brown, 19–36. Winnipeg: University of Manitoba Press.

Dobbin, Murray. 1981. *The One-and-a-Half Men: The Story of Jim Brady and Malcolm Norris, Métis Patriots of the 20th Century*. Regina: Gabriel Dumont Institute.

Douaud, Patrick C. 2007. *The Western Métis: Profile of a People*. Regina: University of Regina Press.

Drake, Karen. 2013. "*R. v. Hirsekorn:* Are Métis Rights a Constitutional Myth?" *Canadian Bar Review* 92 (1): 149–73.

Drake, Karen, and Adam Gaudry. 2016. "'The Lands … Belonged to Them, Once by Indian Title, Twice for Having Defended Them …, and Thrice for Having Built and Lived on Them': The Law and Politics of Métis Title." *Osgoode Hall Law Journal* 54 (1): 1–52.

Dubois, Janique. 2013. "From Service Providers to Decision Makers: Building a Métis Government in Saskatchewan." In *Métis in Canada: History, Identity, Law and Politics*, ed. Christopher Adams, Gregg Dahl, and Ian Peach, 433–62. Edmonton: University of Alberta Press.

–. 2015. "Federal-Provincial-Métis Relations: Building Multilevel Governance from the Bottom Up." In *Canada: State of the Federation 2013 – Aboriginal Multilevel Governance*, ed. Martin Papillon and André Juneau, 189–214. Montreal and Kingston: McGill-Queen's University Press.

Dubois, Janique, and Kelly Saunders. 2013. "'Just Do It!' Carving out a Space for the Métis in Canadian Federalism." *Canadian Journal of Political Science* 46 (1): 187–214.

–. 2017a. "Rebuilding Indigenous Nations through Constitutional Development: A Case Study of the Métis in Canada." *Nations and Nationalism* 23 (2): 878–901.

–. 2017b. "Explaining the Resurgence of Métis Rights: Making the Most of 'Windows of Opportunity.'" *Canadian Public Administration/Administration Publique du Canada* 60 (1): 48–67.

–. 2017c. "Unfinished Business: Bringing the Métis into Confederation." In *Surviving Canada: Indigenous Peoples Celebrate 150 Years of Betrayal,* ed. Kiera Ladner and Myra Tait, 294–304. Winnipeg: ARP.

Ens, Gerhard J. 1988. "Dispossession or Adaptation? Migration and Persistence of the Red River Métis, 1835–1890." *Historical Papers* 23 (1): 120–44.

–. 1994. "Prologue to the Red River Resistance: Pre-Liminal Politics and the Triumph of Riel." *Journal of the Canadian Historical Association* 5 (1): 111–23.

–. 1996. *Homeland to Hinterland: The Changing Worlds of the Red River Métis in the Nineteenth Century.* Toronto: University of Toronto Press.

–. 2012. "The Battle of Seven Oaks and the Articulation of a Métis National Tradition, 1811–1849." In *Contours of a People: Métis Family, Mobility, and History,* ed. Nicole St-Onge, Carolyn Podruchny, and Brenda Macdougall, 93–119. Norman: University of Oklahoma Press.

Ens, Gerhard J., and Joe Sawchuk. 2016. *From New Peoples to New Nations: Aspects of Métis History and Identity from the Eighteenth to Twenty-First Centuries.* Toronto: University of Toronto Press.

Erasmus, Peter. 1976. *Buffalo Days and Nights.* Trans. Henry Thompson. Calgary: Glenbow-Alberta Institute.

Ferland, Marcien. 2006. *Au temps de la Prairie: L'histoire des Métis de l'Ouest canadien racontée par Auguste Vermette, neveu de Louis Riel.* 2nd ed. Saint-Boniface: Blé en poche.

Flanagan, Thomas. 1991. *Métis Lands in Manitoba.* Calgary: University of Calgary Press.

–. 2000. *Riel and the Rebellion: 1885 Reconsidered.* 2nd ed. Toronto: University of Toronto Press.

Foster, John E. 1985. "Some Questions and Perspectives on the Problem of Métis Roots." In *The New Peoples: Being and Becoming Métis in North America,* ed. Jacqueline Peterson and Jennifer S.H. Brown, 73–91. Winnipeg: University of Manitoba Press.

–. 1994. "Wintering, the Outsider Adult Male and the Ethnogenesis of the Western Plains Métis." *Prairie Forum* 19 (1): 1–13.

–. 2007. "The Métis: The People and the Term." In *Western Métis: Profile of a People,* ed. Patrick C. Douaud, 21–30. Regina: Canadian Plains Research Centre.

Foster, Martha Harroun. 2006. *We Know Who We Are: Métis Identity in a Montana Community.* Norman: University of Oklahoma Press.

Friesen, Gerald. 1984. *The Canadian Prairies: A History*. Toronto: University of Toronto Press.

Gagné, Natasha, Claudie Larcher, and Sébastien Grammond. 2014. "La communauté comme sujet et objet du droit: Implications pour les Métis du Canada." *Anthropologie et sociétés* 38 (2): 151–74.

Gaudry, Adam J.P. 2014. "*Kaa-tipeyimishoyaahk* – 'We Are Those Who Own Ourselves': A Political History of Métis Self-Determination in the North-West, 1830–1870." PhD diss., University of Victoria.

–. 2016a. "Fantasies of Sovereignty: Deconstructing British and Canadian Claims to Ownership of the Historic North-West." *Native American and Indigenous Studies* 3 (1): 46–74.

–. 2016b. "The New Nation Is Born: Métis-Settler Diplomacy before and after the Battle of Seven Oaks," conference paper presented at the *Native American and Indigenous Studies Association Conference, May 21, Honolulu, Hawaii.*

Gaudry, Adam J.P., and Chris Andersen. 2016. "*Daniels v. Canada:* Racialized Legacies, Settler Self-Indigenization and the Denial of Indigenous Peoplehood." *Topia: Canadian Journal of Cultural Studies* 36: 19–30.

Gaudry, Adam J.P., and Darryl Leroux. 2017. "White Settler Revisionism and Making Métis Everywhere: The Evocation of Métissage in Quebec and Nova Scotia." *Critical Ethnic Studies* 3 (1): 116–42.

Giraud, Marcel. 1984 [1945]. *Le Métis canadien.* Saint-Boniface: Éditions du Blé.

–. 1986. *The Métis in the Canadian West.* Vol. 2. Trans. George Woodcock. Edmonton: University of Alberta Press.

Goulet, George, and Terry Goulet. 2006. *The Métis: Memorable Events and Memorable Personalities.* Calgary: FabJob.

Grammond, Sébastien. 2009. *Identity Captured by Law: Membership in Canada's Indigenous Peoples and Linguistic Minorities.* Montreal and Kingston: McGill-Queen's University Press.

Grammond, Sébastien, Isabelle Lantagne, and Natasha Gagné. 2016. "Non-Status Indigenous Groups in Canadian Courts: Practical and Legal Difficulties in Seeking Recognition." In *From Recognition to Reconciliation: Essays on the Constitutional Entrenchment of Aboriginal and Treaty Rights*, ed. Patrick Macklem and Douglas Sanderson, 259–84. Toronto: University of Toronto Press.

Grammond, Sébastien, and Lynne Groulx. 2012. "Finding Métis Communities." *Canadian Journal of Native Studies* 32 (1): 33–48.

Groarke, Paul. 2014. "Reconstructing the Substantive Argument in Louis Riel's Address to the Jury." In *Riel's Defence: Perspectives on His Speeches*, ed. Hans V.

Hansen, 204–23. Montreal and Kingston: McGill-Queen's University Press.

Haggarty, Liam. 2013. "Sharing and Exchange in Northwest Saskatchewan." In *Métis in Canada: History, Identity, Law and Politics*, ed. Christopher Adams, Gregg Dahl, and Ian Peach, 205–47. Edmonton: University of Alberta Press.

Harrison, Julia. 1985. *Métis: People between Two Worlds*. Vancouver: Douglas and McIntyre.

Hatt, Ken. 1979. "The Land Issue and the Mobilization of the Alberta Métis in the 1930's." In *The Forgotten People: Métis and Non-Status Indian Land Claims*, ed. H. Daniels, 73–87. Ottawa: Native Council of Canada.

–. 1983. "The Northwest Scrip Commissions as Federal Policy: Some Initial Findings." *Canadian Journal of Native Studies* 3 (1): 117–29.

Hodgson-Smith, Kathy L., and Nathalie Kermoal. 2016. "Community-Based Research and Métis Women's Knowledge in Northwestern Saskatchewan." In *Living on the Land: Indigenous Women's Understanding of Place*, ed. Nathalie Kermoal and Isabel Altamirano-Jiménez, 139–76. Edmonton: Athabasca University Press.

Hogue, Michel. 2015. *Métis and the Medicine Line: Creating a Border and Dividing a People*. Regina: University of Regina Press.

Innes, Robert Alexander. 2013. *Elder Brother and the Law of the People*. Winnipeg: University of Manitoba Press.

Iseke-Barnes, Judy. 2009. "Grandmothers of the Métis Nation: A Living History with Dorothy Chartrand." *Native Studies Review* 18 (2): 69–104.

Jannetta, Armando E. 1994. "'Travels through Forbidden Geography': Métis Trappers and Traders Louis Goulet and Ted Trindell." *Review of International English Literature* 25 (2): 59–74.

Kermoal, Nathalie. 2016. "Métis Women's Environmental Knowledge and the Recognition of Métis Rights." In *Living on the Land: Indigenous Women's Understanding of Place*, ed. Nathalie Kermoal and Isabel Altamirano-Jiménez, 107–37. Edmonton: Athabasca University Press.

Kostash, Myrna. 2009. *The Frog Lake Reader*. Edmonton: NeWest Press.

Ladner, Kiera L. 2009. "Gendering Decolonization, Decolonizing Gender." *Australian Indigenous Law Review* 13 (1): 62–77.

LaRocque, Emma. 1996. "The Colonization of a Native Woman Scholar." In *Women of the First Nations: Power, Wisdom and Strength*, ed. Christine Miller and Patricia Chuchryk, 11–18. Winnipeg: University of Manitoba Press.

–. 2007. "Métis and Feminist: Ethical Reflections on Feminism, Human Rights and Decolonization." In *Making Space for Indigenous Feminism*, ed. Joyce Green, 53–71. Halifax: Fernwood Press, 2007.

Lischke, Ute, and David McNab. 2007. *The Long Journey of a Forgotten People: Métis Identities and Family Histories*. Waterloo: Wilfrid Laurier University Press.

Loat, Allison, and Michael MacMillan. 2014. *Tragedy in the Commons*. Toronto: Random House.

Maaka, Roger, and Augie Fleras. 2005. *The Politics of Indigeneity: Challenging the State in Canada and Aotearoa New Zealand.* Dunedin, NZ: University of Otago Press.

Macdougall, Brenda. 2006. "*Wahkootowin*: Family and Cultural Identity in Northwestern Saskatchewan Métis Communities." *Canadian Historical Review* 87 (3): 431–62.

–. 2010. *One of the Family: Métis Culture in Nineteenth-Century Northwestern Saskatchewan.* Vancouver: UBC Press.

–. 2012. "The Myth of Métis Cultural Ambivalence." In *Contours of a People: Métis Family, Mobility, and History*, ed. Nicole St-Onge, Carolyn Podruchny, and Brenda Macdougall, 422–64. Norman: University of Oklahoma Press.

Macdougall, Brenda, and Nicole St-Onge. 2013. "Rooted in Mobility: Métis Buffalo Hunting Brigades." *Manitoba History* 71 (Winter): 21–32.

Madden, Jason. 2008. "The Métis Nation's Self-Government Agenda: Issues and Options for the Future." In *Métis-Crown Relations: Rights, Identity, Jurisdiction, and Governance*, ed. Frederica Wilson and Melanie Mallet, 323–89. Toronto: Irwin Law.

Maracle, Lee. 2006. "Decolonisation of Native Women." In *Daughters of Mother Earth: The Wisdom of Native American Women*, ed. Barbara A. Mann, 29–52. Westport, CT: Praeger.

Martin, Fred V. 1989. "Federal and Provincial Responsibility in the Métis Settlements of Alberta." In *Aboriginal Peoples and Government Responsibility: Exploring Federal and Provincial Roles*, ed. David C. Hawkes, 243–96. Ottawa: Carleton University Press.

Mayer, Lorraine. 2007. *Cries from a Métis Heart.* Winnipeg: Pemmican Publications.

McLean, Donald. 1987. *Fifty Historical Vignettes: Views of the Common People*. Regina: Gabriel Dumont Institute.

Morisset, Jean, and Rose-Marie Pelletier, eds. 1986. *Ted Trindell: Métis Witness to the North*. Vancouver: Tillacum Library.

Morrison, Sheila Jones. 1995. *Rotten to the Core: The Politics of the Manitoba Métis Federation*. Victoria: Gordon Shillingford Publications.

Morton, Arthur S. 1978 [1939]. "The New Nation, The Métis." In *The Other Natives: The-Les Métis*, vol. 1, *1700–1885*, ed. Antoine Lussier and Bruce Sealy, 27–37. Winnipeg: Manitoba Métis Federation Press and Éditions Bois-Brûlés.

Morton, William Lewis. 1937. "The Red River Parish." In *Manitoba Essays Written in Commemoration of the Sixtieth Anniversary of the University of Manitoba by Members of the Teaching Staffs of the University and Its Affiliated Colleges*, ed. R.C. Lodge, 83–105. Toronto: Macmillan.

–. 1967 [1957]. *Manitoba: A History.* 2nd ed. Toronto: University of Toronto Press.

Murphy, Lucy E. 2003. "Public Mothers: Native American and Métis Women as Creole Mediators in the Nineteenth-Century Midwest." *Journal of Women's History* 14 (4): 142–66.

O'Byrne, Nicole. 2013. "'No Other Weapon Except Organization': The Métis Association of Alberta and the 1938 Métis Population Betterment Act." *Journal of the Canadian Historical Association* 24 (2): 311–52.

–. 2014. "'Through the Grace of God I Am the Founder of Manitoba': Louis Riel's Constitutional Thought." In *Riel's Defence: Perspectives on His Speeches*, ed. Hans V. Hansen, 90–105. Montreal and Kingston: McGill-Queen's University Press.

O'Toole, Darren. 2010. "The Red River Resistance of 1869–1870: The Machiavellian Moment of the Métis of Manitoba." PhD diss., University of Ottawa.

–. 2013. "From Entity to Identity to Nation." In *Métis in Canada: History, Identity, Law and Politics*, ed. Christopher Adams, Gregg Dahl, and Ian Peach, 143–203. Edmonton: University of Alberta Press.

Palmater, Pamela D. 2011. "Stretched beyond Human Limits: Death by Poverty in First Nations." *Canadian Review of Social Policy* 65/66: 112–27.

Pannekoek, Frits. 1991. *A Snug Little Flock: The Social Origins of the Riel Resistance of 1869–70.* Winnipeg: Watson and Dwyer.

Payment, Diane. 1996. "'La vie en rose'? Métis Women at Batoche, 1870 to 1920." In *Women of the First Nations: Power, Wisdom and Strength*, ed. Christine Miller and Patricia Chuchryk, 19–37. Winnipeg: University of Manitoba Press.

–. 2009. *The Free People – Li Gens Libres: A History of the Métis Community of Batoche, Saskatchewan.* Calgary: University of Calgary Press.

Pelletier, Emile. 1977. *A Social History of the Manitoba Métis.* Winnipeg: Manitoba Métis Federation Press.

Peterson, Jacqueline. 1978. "Prelude to Red River: A Social Portrait of the Great Lakes Métis." *Ethnohistory* 25 (1): 41–67.

–. 1981. "The People In Between: Indian-White Marriage and the Genesis of a Métis Society and Culture in the Great Lakes Region, 1680–1830." PhD diss., University of Illinois at Chicago.

–. 1985. "Many Roads to Red River: Métis Genesis in the Great Lakes Region, 1680–1815." In *The New Peoples: Being and Becoming Métis in North America*, ed. Jacqueline Peterson and Jennifer S.H. Brown, 37–71. Winnipeg: University of Manitoba Press.

Peterson, Jacqueline, and Jennifer S.H. Brown, eds. 1985. *The New Peoples: Being and Becoming Métis in North America.* Winnipeg: University of Manitoba Press.

Pitsula, James M. 1997. "The Thatcher Government in Saskatchewan and the Revival of Métis Nationalism, 1964–1971." *Great Plains Quarterly* 17: 213–35.

Pocklington, Thomas. 1991. *The Government and Politics of the Alberta Métis Settlements.* Regina: Canadian Plains Research Centre.

Podruchny, Carolyn. 2006. *Making the Voyageur World: Travelers and Traders in the North American Fur Trade.* Toronto: University of Toronto Press.

Pulla, Siomonn P. 2013. "Regional Nationalism or National Mobilization? A Brief Social History of Métis Political Organization in Canada, 1815–2011." In *Métis in Canada: History, Identity, Law and Politics*, ed. Christopher Adams, Gregg Dahl, and Ian Peach, 397–431. Edmonton: University of Alberta Press.

Purich, Donald. 1988. *The Métis.* Toronto: James Lorimer.

Quiring, David. 2004. *CCF Colonialism in Northern Saskatchewan: Battling Parish Priests, Bootleggers and Fur Sharks.* Vancouver: UBC Press.

Racette, Sherry Farrell. 2005. "Sewing for a Living: The Commodification of Métis Women's Artistic Production." In *Contact Zones: Aboriginal and Settler Women in Canada's Colonial Past*, ed. Katie Pickles and Myra Rutherdale, 17–46. Vancouver: UBC Press.

–. 2009. "Looking for Stories and Unbroken Threads: Museum Artifacts as Women's History and Cultural Legacy." In *Restoring the Balance: First Nations Women, Community, and Culture*, ed. Gail Guthrie Valaskakis, Madeline Dion Stout, and Eric Guimond, 283–312. Winnipeg: University of Manitoba Press.

RCAP (Royal Commission on Aboriginal Peoples). 1996a. *Report of the Royal Commission on Aboriginal Peoples. Vol. 2: Restructuring the Relationship.* Ottawa: Public Works and Government Services Canada.

– . 1996b. *Report of the Royal Commission on Aboriginal Peoples.* Vol. 4: *Perspectives and Realities.* Ottawa: Public Works and Government Services Canada.

Reid, Jennifer. 2008. *Louis Riel and the Creation of Modern Canada.* Albuquerque: University of New Mexico Press.

Riel, Louis. 1886. "Riel's Letter to the 'Irish World. An Appeal for Justice.'" In *The Gibbet of Regina. The Truth about Riel*, comp. Napoléon Thompson, 182–87. New York: Thompson and Moreau, Printers and Publishers.

– . 1982. "Last Memoir." In *Hold High Your Heads: History of the Métis Nation in Western Canada,* by Auguste-Henri de Trémaudan, trans. Elizabeth Maguet, 200–10. Winnipeg: Pemmican Publications.

Rivard, Étienne. 2012 "'Le Fond de l'Ouest': Territoriality, Oral Geographies, and the Métis in the Nineteenth-Century Northwest." In *Contours of a People: Métis*

Family, Mobility, and History, ed. Nicole St-Onge, Carolyn Podruchny, and Brenda Macdougall, 143–68. Norman: University of Oklahoma Press.

Ross, Alexander. 1957 [1856]. *The Red River Settlement: Its Rise, Progress, and Present State.* Minneapolis: Ross and Haines.

Saunders, Kelly L. 2011. "The Hunt for Justice: Métis Harvesting Rights and the Pursuit of Self-Government." *Canadian Journal of Native Studies* 31 (1): 161–85.

– . 2013. "No Other Weapon: Métis Political Organization and Governance in Canada." In *Métis in Canada: History, Identity, Law and Politics*, ed. Christopher Adams, Gregg Dahl, and Ian Peach, 339–96. Edmonton: University of Alberta Press.

– . 2014. "Reclaiming Our History: The Legacy of Louis Riel and the Métis Nation in Manitoba." In *De Pierre-Esprit Radisson à Louis Riel: Voyageurs et Métis/From Pierre-Esprit Radisson to Louis Riel: Voyageurs and Métis*, ed. Denis Combet, Luc Côté, and Gilles Lesage, 277-99. Winnipeg: Presses Universitaires de Saint-Boniface.

– . 2015. "Métis Political Identity and the Symbolism of Louis Riel." In *The Politics of Popular Culture: Negotiating Power, Identity, and Place*, ed. Tim Nieguth, 65–82. Montreal and Kingston: McGill-Queen's University Press.

Sawchuk, Joe. 1978. *The Métis of Manitoba: Reformulation of an Ethnic Identity.* Toronto: Peter Martin Associates.

– . 1981. *Métis Land Rights in Alberta: A Political History.* Edmonton: Métis Association of Alberta.

– . 1992. "The Métis, Non-Status Indians and the New Aboriginality: Government Influence on Native Political Alliances and Identity." In *Readings in Aboriginal Studies: Identities and State Structures. Vol. 2: Identities and State Structures,* ed. Joe Sawchuk, 70–86. Brandon: Bearpaw Publishing.

– . 1998. *The Dynamics of Native Politics: The Alberta Métis Experience.* Saskatoon: Purich Publishing.

– . 2000. "Negotiating an Identity: Métis Political Organizations, the Canadian Government, and Competing Concepts of Aboriginality." *American Indian Quarterly* 24 (3): 73–92.

Sealy, Bruce, and Antoine Lussier. 1975. *The Métis: Canada's Forgotten People.* Winnipeg: Manitoba Métis Federation Press.

Shore, Fred. 2001. "The Emergence of the Métis Nation in Manitoba." In *Métis Legacy: A Métis Historiography and Annotated Bibliography*, ed. Lawrence J. Barkwell, Leah Dorion, and Darren R. Préfontaine, 71–78. Winnipeg: Pemmican Publications.

Shore, Fred, and Lawrence Barkwell. 1997. *Past Reflects the Present: The Métis Elders' Conference.* Winnipeg: Manitoba Métis Federation.

Simpson, Audra. 2001. *Indian Women and French Men: Rethinking Cultural Encounter in the Western Great Lakes.* Amherst: University of Massachusetts Press.

–. 2014. *Mohawk Interruptus: Political Life across the Borders of Settler States.* Durham, NC: Duke University Press.

Sprague, Douglas N. 1988. *Canada and the Métis, 1869–1885.* Waterloo: Wilfrid Laurier University Press.

Spry, Irene. 1985. "The Métis and Mixed-Bloods of Rupert's Land before 1870." In *The New Peoples: Being and Becoming Métis in North America*, ed. Jacqueline Peterson and Jennifer S.H. Brown, 95–118. Winnipeg: University of Manitoba Press.

SSCAP (Senate Standing Committee on Aboriginal Peoples). 2013. "'The People Who Own Themselves': Recognition of Métis Identity in Canada." *Report of the Senate Standing Committee on Aboriginal Peoples.* Ottawa.

Stanley, George F.G. 1960 [1936]. *The Birth of Western Canada: A History of Riel Rebellions.* London: Longmans, Green, and Co.

–. 1963. *Louis Riel.* Toronto: The Ryerson Press.

–. 1972. *Manitoba 1870: A Métis Achievement.* Winnipeg: University of Winnipeg Press.

Stanley, George F.G, Raymond J.A. Huel, Gilles Martel, Thomas Flanagan, and Glen Campbell. 1985. *The Collected Writings of Louis Riel/Les écrits complets de Louis Riel.* Vol. 3. Edmonton: University of Alberta Press.

Stark, Jessica. 2013. "Unequal Communities: Exploring the Relationship between Colonialism, Patriarchy and the Marginalization of Aboriginal Women." *Footnotes* 6: 45–54.

St-Onge, Nicole. 2004. *Saint-Laurent, Manitoba: Evolving Métis Identities, 1850–1914.* Regina: Canadian Plains Research Centre.

–. 2008. "Memories of Métis Women of Saint-Eustache, Manitoba, 1910–1980." *Native Studies Review* 17 (2): 45–68.

St-Onge, Nicole, and Carolyn Podruchny. 2012. "Scuttling along a Spider's Web: Mobility and Kinship in Métis Ethnogenesis." In *Contours of a People: Métis Family, Mobility, and History*, ed. Nicole St-Onge, Carolyn Podruchny, and Brenda Macdougall, 59–92. Norman: University of Oklahoma Press.

St-Onge, Nicole, Carolyn Podruchny, and Brenda Macdougall, eds. 2012. *Contours of a People: Métis Family, Mobility, and History.* Norman: University of Oklahoma Press.

Teillet, Jean. 2007. "The Winds of Change: Métis Rights after Powley, Taku and Haida." In *The Long Journey of a Forgotten People: Métis Identities and Family Histories*, ed. Ute Lischke and David McNab, 55–78. Waterloo: Wilfrid Laurier University Press.

–. 2008. "Federal and Provincial Crown Obligations to the Métis." In *Métis-Crown Relations: Rights, Identity, Jurisdiction, and Governance*, ed. Frederica Wilson and Melanie Mallet, 71–93. Toronto: Irwin Law.

–. 2012. "The Métis and Thirty Years of Section 35: How Constitutional Protection for Métis Rights Has Led to the Loss of the Rule of Law." *Supreme Court Law Review* 58: 333–49.

–. 2013. *Métis Law in Canada*. Vancouver: Pape Salter Teillet. Available online at http://www.pstlaw.ca/resources/Metis-Law-in-Canada-2013.pdf.

Todd, Zoe. 2016. "From a Fishy Place: Examining Canadian State Law Applied in the *Daniels* Decision from the Perspective of Métis Legal Orders." *Topia: Canadian Journal of Cultural Studies* 36: 43–57.

Trémaudan, Auguste Henri de. 1982 [1979]. *Hold Your Head High: History of Métis Nation in Western Canada*. Trans. Elizabeth Maguet. Winnipeg: Pemmican Publications.

Troupe, Cheryl. 2009. "Métis Women: Social Structure, Urbanization and Political Activism, 1850–1980." MA thesis, University of Saskatchewan.

Van Kirk, Sylvia. 1980. *Many Tender Ties: Women in Fur-Trade Society, 1670–1870*. Winnipeg: Watson and Dwyer.

–. 2006. "The Role of Native Women in the Fur Trade Society of Western Canada, 1670–1830." In *Rethinking Canada: The Promise of Women's History*, 5th ed., ed. Mona Gleason and Adele Perry, 70–78. Don Mills: Oxford University Press.

Vowel, Chelsea, and Darryl Leroux. 2016. "White Settler Antipathy and the *Daniels* Decision." *Topia: Canadian Journal of Cultural Studies* 36: 30–42.

Voyageur, Cora. 2008. *Firekeepers of the Twenty-First Century: First Nation Women Chiefs*. Montreal and Kingston: McGill-Queens University Press.

Vrooman, Nicholas. 2012. "*The Whole Country Was ... 'One Robe'": The Little Shell Tribe's America*. Helena, MT: Drumlummon Institute.

Weekes, Mary. 1939. *The Last Buffalo Hunter*. New York: Thomas Nelson and Sons.

Weinstein, John. 2007. *Quiet Revolution West: The Rebirth of Métis Nationalism*. Calgary: Fifth House.

White, Bruce M. 2006. "The Woman Who Married a Beaver: Trade Patterns and Gender Roles in the Ojibwa Fur Trade." In *In the Days of Our Grandmothers: A Reader in Aboriginal Women's History in Canada*, ed. Mary-Ellen Kelm and Lorna Townsend, 56–92. Toronto: University of Toronto Press.

Wilson, Frederica, and Melanie Mallet. 2008. *Métis-Crown Relations: Rights, Identity, Jurisdiction and Governance*. Toronto: Irwin Law.

Wolfart, Philip. 2012. "Against Spatialized Ethnicity." In *Contours of a People: Métis Family, Mobility, and History*, ed. Nicole St-Onge, Carolyn Podruchny, and Brenda Macdougall, 120–42. Norman: University of Oklahoma Press.

Wolseley, Field-Marshal Viscount Garnet. 1903. *The Story of a Soldiers Life,* Vol. 2. Westminster: Archibald Constable and Co.

Woodcock, George. 2003 [1975]. *Gabriel Dumont.* Edmonton: Hurtig.

Index

Note: "(i)" after a page number indicates an illustration; "(t)" after a page number indicates a table. Acronyms in the subentries follow the list on page xviii.